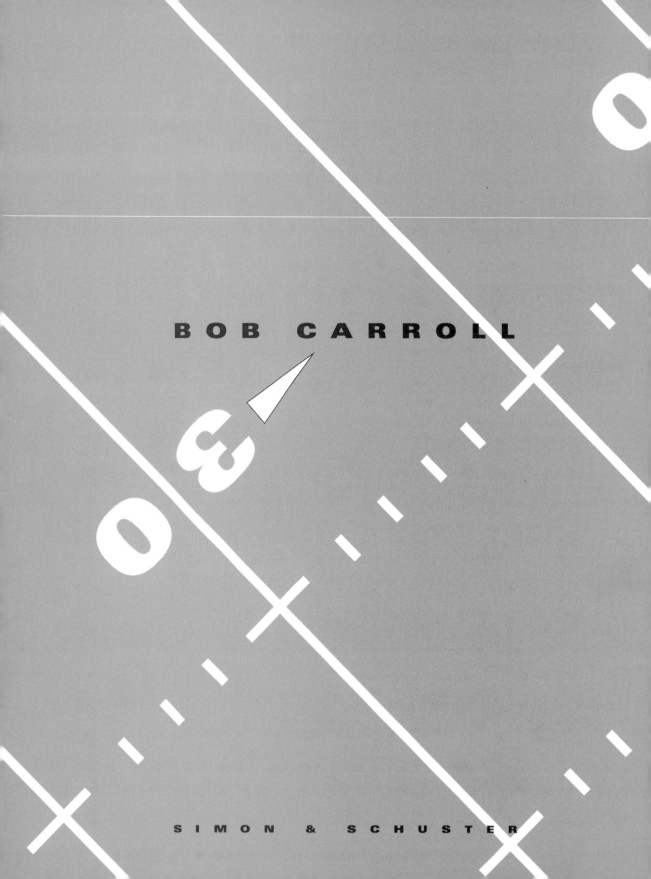

BOB CARROLL

SIMON & SCHUSTER

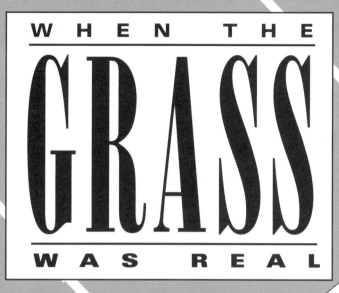

WHEN THE GRASS
WAS REAL

UNITAS,
BROWN,
LOMBARDI,
SAYERS,
BUTKUS,
NAMATH,
AND
ALL THE REST:
THE BEST TEN YEARS
OF PRO FOOTBALL

NEW YORK LONDON TORONTO SYDNEY TOKYO SINGAPORE

SIMON & SCHUSTER
Simon & Schuster Building
Rockefeller Center
1230 Avenue of the Americas
New York, New York 10020

Designed by Songhee Kim
Manufactured in the United States of America

1   3   5   7   9   10   8   6   4   2

Library of Congress Cataloging-in-Publication Data

Carroll, Bob.
When the grass was real : Unitas, Brown, Lombardi, Sayers, Butkus,
Namath, and all the rest : the best ten years of pro football / Bob
Carroll.
p.   cm.
Includes index.
ISBN 0-671-73301-X
1. Football—United States—History—20th century.   2. American
Football League—History.   3. National Football League—History.
I. Title.
GV954.C37   1993
796.332′64′0973—dc20   93-17782
                                                CIP

ISBN: 0-671-73301-X

For the thousands of players who made my Sixties Sundays super, and for Sue, who brightened the other days.

ACKNOWLEDGMENTS

In preparing this history, literally hundreds of sources were consulted, all the way from brief notes at the bottoms of sports pages to full-scale books. There's no way to list them all here, but certain people must be recognized.

First, I'd like to thank the former stars who were kind enough to submit to my interviews. I always go into these things expecting to run up against a hostile or defensive ego somewhere, but greats like Bobby Bell, Willie Davis, Weeb Ewbank, Sid Gillman, Forrest Gregg, Chuck Howley, Sam Huff, Jim Taylor, Bob St. Clair, and Billy Shaw prove the old saw "The bigger they are, the nicer they are."

A number of excellent writers have penned helpful books or articles on various aspects of the period. Among my favorites: Jack Clary, Bob Curran, Stan Grosshandler, Joe Hession, Mickey Herskowitz, John Hogrogian, Beau Riffenburgh, Don Smith, and Shelby Strother. *The Sports Encyclopedia: Pro Football,* by David Neft and Dick Cohen, was invaluable in checking statistics and the spelling of names.

Of course, nothing would have gotten off the ground, much less completed, without the encouragement, advice, and sometime prodding of Jeff Neuman and his assistant Stuart Gottesman at Simon & Schuster.

And finally, all my gratitude to Joe Horrigan and John Thorn, two of the best friends anyone ever had, for doing all the things best friends are supposed to do and then more to get this project completed.

—Bob Carroll

CONTENTS

CABINS ON THE TITANIC

Three days before 1958 ended, a football game was played at Yankee Stadium that changed the future of pro football. The 1958 National Football League Championship Game has often been called "the greatest game ever played." From an artistic standpoint, it wasn't quite that. It was a first-rate affair, all right, but in any given season, you could find games with more spectacular plays or games in which the lead seesawed back and forth more often. Even drawing only from championship games, there have been more thrilling affairs. But the '58 championship between the Baltimore Colts and the New York Giants was different because its national telecast put the NFL in more living rooms than ever before—an estimated 10,820,000 homes across the country. Ironically, New York, the nation's biggest market, was blacked out (and New Yorkers couldn't even read about the game the next morning because of a newspaper strike), but pro football had been established in New York for years. The critical audience was the rest of the country, places without local NFL teams. Pro football had grown in importance during the 1950s, but it still lagged behind baseball and college football in national interest. A few visionaries ached to bring the pro game to their non-NFL cities, but few potential paying customers in those cities shared this enthusiasm. The country—certainly three-quarters of it—needed a good kick in the pants to make it aware of pro football.

As the first nationally televised championship game, it was a showcase, and as a showcase, everything in it became magnified. Good became Great. Fine became Fantastic. The game needed only to be close to be a landmark.

Of course, it was more than close.

At the end of regulation time, the game was tied. For the first time in any regular-season, much less, *championship*, game, the NFL's overtime rule was applied. Before 1974, regular season NFL games tied after 60 minutes went into the record as just that, ties. But in championship games and playoffs where a decision was necessary, the rules mandated an extra period or periods until one side scored. The rule had existed since the 1930s, but there'd never before been an occasion to use it. The Los Angeles Rams had once won an overtime *exhibition* game at Portland in 1955, besting the New York Giants, but that was merely a curiosity. When Steve Myhra's 20-yard field goal tied the '58 championship seven seconds before the fourth quarter gun sounded, NBC-TV announcers Chuck Thompson and Chris Schenkel weren't 100 percent sure what would happen next.

What happened was an example of NFL football at its best. The Colts first stopped the Giants, then moved from their own 20 to the Giants' one in 12 breathtaking plays. At 8:15 of OT, Baltimore's Alan Ameche plunged into the end zone to win the game.

Ironically, NBC nearly missed the winning play. Fans had inadvertently kicked a cable connection apart, plunging TV screens into darkness. Fortunately, a drunk staggered out onto the field and reeled around just long enough to allow the network to get the cable reconnected. Only later was it discovered that the fortuitous drunk was a cold sober NBC vice-president. Television had controlled what happened on an NFL field for the first time.

The next morning, also for the first time in history, the National Football League was the number-one topic at watercoolers from sea to shining sea. Among the *oohs* over Johnny Unitas's passes and the *ahhs* over Sam Huff's tackles came many plaintive wonderings why "our town" didn't have its own pro football team.

––––––––––

Pro football is not a microcosm of life any more than it's a symbol for war or peace or your Aunt Fannie's Pekingese pup. There are poetic types who can find a microcosm of life in a slice of cheese on a china plate, and if that helps them get through the day, more power to them. But pro football is pro football and life is whatever the hell it is.

Still, looking back at the beginning of the sixth decade of the twentieth century, there were clearly similarities in attitude, feeling, momentum, and milieu between life as it was lived and professional football as *it* was lived at that time.

First of all, hope was present in American life, the kind you used to get when your folks and you were driving to Grandma's and you knew her house with all its treasures of cookies and candies was just around the next turn. America was, for most Americans, pretty darn good, but what it wanted to be was almost in sight. Maybe it was the Eisenhower years, nearly a decade when things went pretty smoothly for most of us and convinced us that smooth was the way it should always be. We could all become Ozzie and Harriet.

A significant part of the population got its hope from another source. After nearly a hundred years of being all but invisible to most of white America, black America was entering the public eye. The manifestly unequal doctrine of "separate but equal" was in the dumper, although a few Southern states still needed to be taught to read the writing on the wall (and in the Constitution).

We also had the dedication to keep America perking. Kennedy told us to "ask not" and a lot of us agreed to "ask what." Even those of us who didn't ask (which was most of us, of course) thought asking wasn't such a bad idea. Maybe we were getting just a tad too fat and comfy. How else could you explain Sputnik? But all we really had to do was pull together and in practically no time at all we'd be on the moon, right?

America was young. Okay, the nation was coming up on 200 years old, but, for the first time in God knows, it felt like a colt. The old saw about "the most powerful nation on earth" really was true, and maybe it was time we flexed. We had so much more ahead than behind. Actually, youth wasn't an illusion. There really were more young people around. That spurt of sexual energy that followed World War II was having its inevitable results. Before the decade ended, we'd have more people under 30 than over it. And, thanks to Dr. Spockian principles, they felt like making their presence felt.

Into this volatile mixture of hope, dedication, and youth, professional football emerged as the game of the '60s.

————

It had not been the game of the '50s. The 1950s belonged to baseball. Pro football had grown remarkably in importance during the '50s, however. Championship games and big local games were normally lead stories on the sports page during the Eisenhower era. Sellouts were no longer uncommon. Diligent dial-twisting could often find a fan a televised game on Sunday afternoons in many parts of the nation. A few stars—telegenic Frank Gifford, deadpan John Unitas, handsome Hugh McElhenny, brooding Jim Brown—were regulars on magazine covers. But New York Giants' quarterback Charlie Conerly remained anonymous enough to go on *What's My Line?* as a contestant. It could have been worse; in earlier times, he would have stumped the panel.

One problem was that pro football was too parochial. Through 1959, only 11 cities supported teams in the National Football League, four of them in the East—New York, Philadelphia, Baltimore, and Washington—

Lamar Hunt.

and five in the northeastern Midwest—Pittsburgh, Cleveland, Detroit, Green Bay (the last holdover from the days when the game was played mainly in small towns), and Chicago, which had two teams. The West Coast had a pair of teams, in Los Angeles and San Francisco. Between the streets of San Francisco and Chicago's Loop, pro football wasn't very important at all. There were no teams in the South, the Southwest, the far Midwest, the Rockies, or the Northwest.

Occasionally someone called for expansion. Nothing was done.

The desultory TV coverage made it difficult for any fan without a team in his backyard to even follow—much less care about—the championship races. Pro football feared television. If fans could watch for free, it was reasoned, they wouldn't buy tickets. Each of the 12 teams negotiated its own television deal with a local station, usually agreeing to show only Sunday road games.

The National Football League's approach to expansion, television, and its own marketing was, in a word, *conservative* throughout the 1950s. And from the perspective of those pioneer owners like George Halas, Art Rooney, George Preston Marshall, Wellington Mara, and the others who had seen the game through its rag days, that approach was wonderfully successful. Average game attendance had ballooned from 25,356 in 1950 to 43,617 in 1959. Few in the NFL felt like rocking what appeared to be a very seaworthy boat.

"You know in the cartoons when the light bulb comes on over your head?" Lamar Hunt explains. "I can see very vividly that that was one of the few times that I had a light bulb go on over my head. I thought, 'Well, why not?'"

When Hunt's great idea struck him—the idea that would change pro football forever—it's unlikely anyone else sitting on the airplane returning from Florida that day in 1958 noticed any change in his demeanor, if they noticed him at all. Even if he had jumped up and hollered "Eureka!"— he'd probably have gotten only a few quizzical looks from his fellow passengers. Hunt doesn't have the kind of presence that makes folks sit up and take notice. Six feet tall, 175 pounds, soft-spoken, round-faced, decked out in heavy horn-rims and wavy dark hair, he could have come straight from central casting to read for the part of a young Texas CPA.

In fact, of course, he was the youngest son of fabled H. L. Hunt, the god-awful rich oil tycoon and contributor to right-wing causes. But even knowing that, you'd never pick him out of a crowd as a leader of men.

Otis Taylor played for Hunt's team for 11 seasons: "Lamar's Lamar. He's not going to change too much. And you're not going to find out too much

14

about him if you know him for 50 years. He's just Lamar. He's going to dress the same. He's going to act the same. With that same smile. He's a nice man. That's all you can say."

Until his light bulb went on, it had been a discouraging day for Hunt. He'd just been turned down in his bid to buy the snake-bit Chicago Cardinals professional football team. If he couldn't buy the Cardinals, a team that had been a losing proposition both on the field and at the turnstiles for just about all of its 38 years in the National Football League, what chance did he have of ever fulfilling the dream he'd nurtured ever since his days as a third- team end for SMU—the dream of having his own pro football team? There were, after all, only 12 teams in the whole NFL in 1958. And only 11 cities. NFL Commissioner Bert Bell had told him earlier that the likelihood of any league expansion in the foreseeable future was nil. The only way for Hunt to join the exclusive club of NFL owners was to purchase one of the existing franchises.

The Cardinals of Chicago, where the Bears got most of the fans and headlines, were by far the sickest franchise in the league. The vultures had been making lazily anticipatory circles over Comiskey Park for years. Hunt had learned he was only one of several men trying to purchase the team so it could be moved out of Chicago and re-established in a new city. Walter and Violet Wolfner, the Cardinals owners, had flirted with K. S. "Bud" Adams in Houston and a group from Minneapolis. Hunt wanted the Cardinals in Dallas.

That's what triggered the light bulb. "If all these people are interested in buying the Cardinals and moving them to their respective cities," Hunt reasoned, "why not talk to those people about"—CLICK!—"a new league."

And that was the birth—or at least the conception—of the American Football League.

Well, why not indeed? All Hunt had to do was find seven other millionaires willing to buy cabins on the Titanic.

———

As the 1960s approached, the relatively short history of pro football had a lesson for brave new entrepreneurs who dared consider starting up a football organization to oppose the entrenched National Football League. The lesson was simple: DON'T. In nearly 40 years, ever since the humble birth of the NFL in a Canton, Ohio, auto showroom on September 17, 1920, no one had been able to figure out how to do it again. Not that there weren't plenty of foolhardy attempts. Most of them died quietly after a meeting of prospective investors and a macho announcement of plans that never came to be. Counting only those attempts at leagues that actually put games on football fields, newcomers were oh-for-four against the NFL.

Way back in 1926 when the NFL was barely out of diapers, a nine-team American Football League was formed by Harold "Red" Grange, the most adulated and exciting football personality of the time. Alas, by December, the most visible "red" was in league ledgers. The football public never took to the Grange league.

Ten years later, in 1936, a second American Football League squared off against the NFL, made up mostly of NFL castoffs and rejects. This AFL had trouble convincing anyone it was really a major league, and most newspapers—even in cities where league teams resided—confined their coverage to brief notes at the bottom of the sports page. Attendance flickered and went out. The NFL ignored the new AFL on the assumption it would soon go away. When it did just that after 1937, hardly anyone knew it was gone.

In 1940, a third American Football League rushed to fill the supposed void. Again castoffs and unknowns dominated the rosters of the new league's six teams, fans refused to fill acres of empty seats at the games, and newspapers generally refused to think of the league as major. When World War II broke out, AFL owners decided that the best thing they could do for the war effort was to declare their league KIA.

Yet hope springs eternal in the heart of the football entrepreneur. The war was barely cold when still another league tried for the fan's dollar. Recognizing that "American Football League" had proved a three-strike jinx, the new crew settled on All-America Football Conference as a title. Because that was much too long for headlines (and no one was ever sure whether it was "All-America" or "All-American"), newspapers usually referred to the new league as the AAFC.

In one way, the time was propitious for starting a new football league.

The AAFC signed up a coterie of disaffected NFL players, and didn't have to depend on retreads for marquee names. Between 1942 and 1945, numerous exciting footballers had performed prodigious feats on college gridirons and then gone off to war without signing NFL contracts. Many had shown their mettle performing with service teams. As the war ended, AAFC owners began signing men in uniform for postwar football.

At first, the NFL tried ignoring the upstarts, the tactic that had worked so nicely with the three AFLs. NFL commissioner Elmer Layden, one of Notre Dame's famed "Four Horsemen," sneered, "Let 'em get a football first." But when it became obvious that the AAFC had enough footballs and a number of good football players, the NFL could see it was in for a legitimate challenge.

Layden was replaced as commissioner by Bert Bell, who'd been terrifi-cally unsuccessful as owner of the Philadelphia Eagles and later part-owner of the Pittsburgh Steelers. Bell's only real claim to pro football fame up to then was that in 1936 he'd convinced the other NFL team owners to accept the idea of drafting college players, thus giving the weaker and poorer clubs (such as Bell's Eagles) a crack at some of the better college seniors. But actually, Bell was an inspired choice for commissioner. He combined the oratorical persuasiveness of an Aesopian fox, the common sense of the proverbial horse, and the cussed stubborness of a Missouri mule. For the forthcoming war with the AAFC, he was the NFL's Churchill.

From 1946 through 1949, the NFL and AAFC fought for dominance. Skirmishing took place over who could sign which famous college senior, but the major battles were in New York, Chicago, and Los Angeles, where teams from each league played in direct competition. For the first couple of years, the AAFC's Yankees held their own against the NFL's Giants in New York, but a Brooklyn Dodgers team never caught on and folded after three seasons. The Chicago Rockets were an embarrassment to the AAFC, ugly losers while the Bears won the NFL championship in 1946 and the Cardinals won it in 1947. The Los Angeles Dons' $1,700,000 loss set a new standard for red ink in pro football.

The knock on the AAFC was that it lacked competitiveness. Whereas the NFL had three different teams finish on top in 1946, 1947, and 1948, the AAFC was all Cleveland. The Browns, who'd moved in along Lake Erie as soon as the Rams moved to Los Angeles, won the first AAFC champi-onship in 1946, the second with more ease in '47, and went through the entire '48 season undefeated. The AAFC was Cleveland and the other guys. If Cleveland wasn't visiting, fans had little reason to see a game.

Despite the Rockets, Dodgers, and a really bad experience trying to put a team in Miami in 1946, the AAFC's attendance was competitive with the NFL's through the first three years of its existence. Some bean counters had the new league ahead, thanks to fair attendances in San Francisco, Buffalo, and Baltimore (replacing Miami), and a real bonanza in Cleve-land, where the Browns were packing them in. However, what with the "huge" salaries (almost every team had several players earning more than $10,000 a year), just about everybody was losing his shirt. The AAFC blinked first. When they tried to talk the NFL into a peace settlement in 1948, their war was as good as lost. The rebuffed AAFC limped through 1949 as an awkward seven-team league and then surrendered.

Technically, it was called a merger. In 1950, the Browns and San Fran-cisco 49ers were taken into the NFL as full-fledged franchises. The Balti-

more Colts were also added as a thirteenth team, but they never had a chance and were dropped after one year (only to be reborn in 1953 in the franchise slot that had once been Ted Collins's Boston Yanks). The players from the Chicago Rockets (renamed the Hornets in 1949), Buffalo Bills, LA Dons, and New York Yankees were divvied up among the NFL teams, and the AAFC was history.

Since 1951, the NFL had held steady at 12 teams. One of them deserves a footnote because its sad history cast a dark shadow over Lamar Hunt's plans to set down one of his new league's teams in Dallas. After the '51 season, Ted Collins, best known as singer Kate Smith's manager, turned his star-crossed New York Yanks franchise back to the league. With much fanfare, the NFL awarded its new 12th franchise to Dallas. The Dallas Texans had a new franchise, a new city, and unfortunately, the same old Ted Collins players. The team was, in the words of one of their running backs, "a disgrace." Halfway through their inaugural season, the Texans gave it up and finished the year as a road team playing out of Hershey, Pennsylvania. The next year, Baltimore replaced the Hershey Texans.

Actually, history had several lessons for Lamar Hunt:

1. Never start a new pro football league.
2. If you do, never put the words "American" or "America" in its name.
3. Regardless, never open a team in Dallas.
4. And, if you do, don't call them the Texans.

When soothsayers prognosticated the new AFL's chances for success, they resurrected the memories of the failed AAFC and the disgraceful Texans for guidelines.

———————

Hunt telephoned K. S. "Bud" Adams, the Houston oilman, and suggested they talk. The two had never met, but Hunt knew Adams had been offered 49 percent of the Chicago Cardinals' stock by the Wolfners. Adams wasn't the kind who'd settle for less than 51 percent of anything. The son of the former president of Phillips Petroleum, Adams had carved his own fortune out of Texas oil and then diversified into other businesses. At 36, he was about ten years older than Hunt and in many ways his opposite. Heavyset and swarthy, Adams radiated Texas confidence. Next to him, Hunt seemed to speak only in whispers.

Hunt flew down to see Adams in Houston in January of 1959. For three hours they talked of everything but football. Then, on the way to the airport, Hunt asked: "If I could get people in four other cities to sponsor teams in another professional football league, would you come in?"

"Yes."

According to Hunt: "A major part of my plan was to include a Houston-Dallas rivalry. I felt that the Rams-49ers rivalry was the best in the NFL, and I wanted to help build the league around another rivalry like that. Houston and Dallas had a natural rivalry anyway, and pro football teams would just make that flourish. So I went to Bud Adams first because he was the key. If he hadn't been interested, I wouldn't have gone on and we never would have proceeded."

———————

In early 1959, Hunt began contacting others who'd sought either an NFL expansion team or who wanted to buy an existing franchise like the Cardinals. Bob Howsam had made the Denver Bears into one of the most successful minor league baseball teams in the country. Unlike Hunt and Adams, he'd had hands-on experience in running a sports franchise, and he was enthusiastic about making Denver a major league city in both baseball and football.

The Minneapolis group was headed by H. P. Skoglund, a local businessman, and Max Winter, former general manager of the Minneapolis Lakers basketball team. When they came aboard, Hunt's league was up to four. But the four cities represented—Dallas, Houston, Denver and Minneapolis—were all marginal major league sites. To succeed, Hunt's league would have to play in some of the nation's major markets. He turned to New York.

There he met with William A. Shea, a highly successful attorney and a man closely connected with a proposed third major baseball league, the Continental League, that was being enthusiastically trumpeted as the next important pro sports organization. New York's Shea Stadium is named after him. Although Shea wasn't interested in diluting his resources and energies by taking on a pro football team, he had a suggestion—how about Harry Wismer?

Wismer, the high-profile broadcasting voice of the Washington Redskins, jumped at the chance to come in on the ground floor of a new league. When the names of the league's owners were eventually announced, Wismer's was the only one that meant anything to the average fan. As such, he was seen by many, particularly those who knew him only through his broadcasts, as a source of stability in the new league. Time would show just how misguided that assessment was.

With five teams in hand, Hunt went owner-shopping on the West Coast. Barron Hilton, the youngest son of hotel magnate Conrad Hilton, was interested but not ready to commit. He asked for time to investigate the situation.

Things were bubbling along. Hunt decided it was time to contact the NFL. The last thing he wanted was a repeat of the ugly and costly NFL–AAFC war. In June, he met for 90 minutes with Washington Redskins' owner George Preston Marshall, head of the NFL's expansion committee. Marshall was noncommittal, which in itself was a hopeful sign. The crusty owner was known as a bad enemy to acquire.

Next, Hunt turned to Bert Bell. He reasoned that things would go more smoothly if the NFL commissioner was also named commissioner of the new league. Opting for an intermediary, Hunt asked his friend Davey O'Brien to make the overtures. O'Brien, a Heisman Trophy–winning quarterback at TCU in 1938, had played for Bell's Philadelphia Eagles in 1939–40. Talks were to be general; O'Brien was not to reveal to Bell the names of the new league's backers. Predictably, Bell declined becoming commissioner of a drawing-board league, but he did ask if he might mention its existence before a Congressional hearing at the end of July. The NFL was catching antitrust flack, particularly about its refusal to expand. Over the next few weeks, in the course of several telephone calls, Bell queried Hunt about the backers, finally getting him to reveal the cities and people involved.

On July 29, Bell dropped the new-league bombshell into his Congressional testimony. He said the NFL was all for it and would try to nurture it. Hunt, having flown up from Dallas, was sitting quietly in the back of the hearing room with Harry Wismer. "I actually heard him announce this new league, which didn't have a name at the time. It got fantastic coverage. I remember the headlines read, 'Bert Bell Announces New Grid League.' From the beginning, that set a very positive tone."

The canny Bell had seen brave new proposals come and go. In the summer of 1959, any new league was far in the future—if ever. A cynic might suggest that he was simply using Hunt's dream to get a few meddling legislators off his back. How could there be grounds for antitrust action if this whole new league was springing up?

After the hearing, Hunt, O'Brien, and Bell held a friendly talk at Bell's farm near Atlantic City. Hunt was left with the impression that Bell would support the new league and help it avoid any of the nasty incidents that had always accompanied the formation of an upstart league impinging on the domain of an older organization. What Bell really thought isn't known.

In his statements to the legislators and press, Bell hadn't revealed the proposed new league's backers, and his announcement brought the expected press speculation. When Hunt and Adams held a press conference in Houston a few days later, the revelation that these two young oilmen were the main movers and shakers was greeted by the press with something less than unabashed enthusiasm. Affecting the fourth estate's appreciation was the fact that the formation of a third baseball major league—the Continental League—had been announced in the same week. The Continentals had the backing of venerable Branch Rickey, baseball's leading mountain-mover. This new football bunch was going to be launched by two guys named Hunt and Adams. It didn't take many smarts to figure which of the two proposed leagues was likely to prosper.

————————

A day or so later, Barron Hilton told Hunt he was coming aboard. With six teams lined up, Hunt called for the league's first organization meeting to be held in Chicago on August 14. They met in the South Imperial Suite of the Conrad Hilton hotel. Hunt (Dallas), Adams (Houston), Bob Howsam (Denver), Harry Wismer (New York), and Max Winter (Minneapolis) all attended. Hilton sent representatives. Also present was Willard Rhodes of Seattle, the president of Pacific Northwest Sports, Inc., who was interested in placing a team in San Francisco. Hunt chaired the meeting, and Gregory R. Dillon, a lawyer for Hilton, served as temporary secretary.

Although they discussed a constitution and bylaws, TV contracts, and a player draft, nothing was carved in stone. Hunt later told newsmen that the tentative name for the new league was the American Football League and it planned to begin play in 1960 with at least six teams.

The name became official at the next meeting, held eight days later at the Statler-Hilton in Dallas. Here, the men finally got down to talking

"The Foolish Club": AFL franchise owners (*sitting* L–R) K.S. "Bud" Adams, Jr., Commissioner Joe Foss, (*standing* L–R) Billy Sullivan, Cal Kunz, Ralph Wilson, Lamar Hunt, Harry Wismer, Wayne Valley, and Barron Hilton.

money. Each team was asked to put up a $100,000 performance bond as well as toss $25,000 into the league treasury. In view of later events, the figures seem absurdly small, but there was some hesitation. After all, this was real money, not speculation.

An eight-team league was deemed preferable to six, both for scheduling and credibility. Representatives of a number of cities had made inquiries as to the possibility of a franchise. These ranged from Miami, Buffalo, San Diego, and New Orleans all the way down to Lincoln, Nebraska.

Another subject of discussion was finding a suitable commissioner. The nearly universal respect accorded Bert Bell made it important to select someone of top caliber. By a September meeting in Beverly Hills, the candidates were down to Fritz Crisler, the athletic director and former football coach at the University of Michigan, Elmer Layden, the old Notre Dame Horseman and a former NFL commissioner, and Joe Foss, the Medal of Honor winner and former two-term governor of South Dakota.

On October 11, Bert Bell died in Philadelphia. The 65-year-old commissioner suffered a fatal heart attack during the final two minutes of the Philadelphia Eagles-Pittsburgh Steelers game at Franklin Field. Ironically, Bell had founded the Eagles in 1933 and owned them through 1940. Then, until he became commissioner in 1946, he'd been co-owner of the Steelers with his friend Art Rooney.

Bell's death was a blow to the American Football League. Hunt had believed that with Bell at the helm of the NFL, an all-out war between the leagues could be avoided. Without Bell, the chance for peaceful coexistence dimmed. And already the NFL had begun divide-and-conquer tactics.

George Preston Marshall had said that the NFL would expand "over my dead body," but more than expansion (and the prospect of adding weak franchises just when most league teams were finally beginning to make money), the NFL feared facing competitors in New York and Los Angeles. If they had to swallow new franchises in Houston and Dallas to keep LA and New York pristine, so be it. Representatives of the NFL approached Barron Hilton. If the new league was taken off the drawing board, Hunt and Adams would be given new franchises and he'd be allowed to buy into an existing franchise. Hilton turned them down. When Adams and Hunt were offered NFL franchises—exactly what they'd originally sought—they also stood firm. In another scenario, Clint Murchison, who was seeking an NFL franchise for Dallas, offered Hunt 50 percent of the stock, but again Hunt passed.

Despite the NFL's tactics, Hunt was still talking peaceful coexistence.

He told newsmen he did not expect a war with the older circuit, but "we won't be run over or stepped on." The AFL had no plans to raid players from the NFL or from either of Canada's two professional leagues, Hunt said. "We will honor all players under contract to other leagues, even those only under option to clubs in another league. I have talked with the commissioner of the Canadian Football Leagues and we have verbally agreed to honor each other's contracts." However, he added, the AFL did intend to compete with the other leagues in the college draft and for free agents.

Meanwhile, the American Football League moved up to eight teams. Ralph C. Wilson, Jr., a trucking and insurance millionaire out of Detroit, had held some stock in the Lions. He approached Hunt about the possibility of establishing an AFL team in Miami, where he maintained a winter home. That seemed a good possibility until Wilson met with the president of the University of Miami and was told point blank that the university opposed any professional inroads into its comfy football program. With Miami closed, Wilson lost interest. A suggestion that Buffalo might be ripe didn't excite him; he had no personal ties to that city. But once he went there to look over the situation, he was favorably impressed. Buffalo had been one of the old AAFC's stronger franchises and had drawn well. War Memorial Stadium was a workable ballpark. "If you will support me," Wilson told *Buffalo Evening News* managing editor Paul Neville, "I'll give the city a team for three years."

The eighth team was Boston, led by Billy Sullivan, a longtime friend of former Notre Dame coach Frank Leahy, who was serving as football advisor to Barron Hilton. Before World War II, Sullivan had been sports publicity director for Boston College, where Leahy coached prior to ascending to Notre Dame. One Sunday, Hunt told Sullivan he could have a team if he could put up $25,000 by the next day. "I had $8,000 to my name," Sullivan said later, "not all of it in cash." Nevertheless, when Monday rolled around, he had the dough. Billy didn't have the millions of a Hunt or Adams, but he knew the ins and outs of Boston's labyrinthine politics and had a reputation for getting things done.

––––––––

On November 23, 1959, the American Football League held its first player draft. The order of selection was determined by drawing lots, with Dallas winning the first pick—SMU quarterback Don Meredith. Other first round selections were Louisiana State halfback Billy Cannon by Houston, Penn State quarterback Richie Lucas by Buffalo, Notre Dame quarterback George Izo by New York, Syracuse halfback Gerhard Schwedes by Boston, Trinity center Roger LeClerc by Denver, Notre

Dame end Monte Stickles by Los Angeles, and Wisconsin quarterback Dale Hackbart by Minneapolis.

There was immediate sniping by the NFL that the AFL's draft had been made straight off the All-America lists. To some extent, the criticism was justified. For example, Schwedes had been a terrific all-around college back at Syracuse, but he lacked the specialized skills to succeed in pro football. When the NFL draft was announced a week later, he wasn't taken until the fourth round, and though he eventually signed with Boston, his career was short and unproductive.

Hunt readily admitted that his league was looking for "name" players rather than "the Harlon Hills at Florence State Teachers Colleges." (Hill had been an unknown who became a receiving star with the Bears in the mid-1950s.) The AFL needed immediately recognizable stars to lure the customers.

In retrospect, that first draft was not a bonanza for the AFL. The NFL's draft had already been held in secret so that the AFL could not use its lists as a guide. Meredith, the first choice of Hunt's Dallas team, had been taken by Clint Murchison's Dallas team even though the Dallas Cowboys would not become official NFLers until another month had passed. Dandy Don signed with the Cowboys. Others lost to the NFL were Izo, LeClerc, Stickles, and Hackbart. Schwedes and Lucas signed with the AFL but failed as pros.

And that left Billy Cannon. The Heisman Trophy winner was the biggest name available. Only he wasn't available to Bud Adams. "I could just smell something was up because I couldn't get him on the telephone, couldn't find him, or anything. So I called Alvin Roy, who ran a health club in Baton Rouge, where Cannon lifted weights. I knew Alvin had to know where Billy was. He said he hadn't seen Billy, so I said, 'Look, if you see him, will you just tell him one thing. I think he has signed with the Rams already, but that doesn't make any difference to me. You just tell him that I'll pay him double whatever they paid him.' It wasn't but fifteen minutes later that [Cannon] called me back. He *had* signed with the Rams, but I didn't figure they'd blow the whistle on it, because he still had the Sugar Bowl to play. So we signed him under the goal posts after the Sugar Bowl.

"After that, the Rams took the case to court. And we did win the case. Not on the signing date. The judge said a contract's a contract, and he signed with the Rams first, so he *should* go to the Rams. But he said that he wasn't going to let Cannon go to the Rams but would let him remain with Houston because the Oilers were never able to talk to him. He felt he would be denying Cannon the salary he would have been getting out of the Oilers because he had never been allowed to hear the other side of the story."

Heisman Trophy winner, Billy Cannon, the AFL's first marquee player.

Federal Judge William J. Lindberg handed down his Cannon verdict in June 1960. By then, several events had helped draw the battle lines between the two leagues, but it didn't help that Lindberg strongly criticized the Rams' general manager for the way he treated Cannon, the "exceptionally naive . . . provincial lad untutored and unwise in the ways of the business world." The Rams' GM came off sounding like a big-city sharpy with a strong streak of con man. Of course by June, the Rams had a new GM, their former man, having succeeded Bert Bell, now was referred to as NFL Commissioner Pete Rozelle.

Losing Cannon (and Mississippi fullback Charley Flowers) by lawsuit enraged the NFL. But the whole AFL draft was a blow. For years, NFL

25

teams had been drafting to fill gaps, shore up weaknesses, and replace retirees. If, for example, your team desperately needed a defensive tackle, you would look over the crop of college seniors and rank the available defensive tackles in order of desirability. If another team drafted your top choice tackle before you could, then you simply took the next highest rated man. But once the AFL entered the picture, you had no guarantee of getting *any* defensive tackle.

Some teams were hurt worse than others. For example, Green Bay didn't lose a single player of consequence to the AFL in the 1960 draft, but Baltimore draftees who went on to become All-AFL stars included offensive tackle Ron Mix, defensive end Don Floyd, and linebacker Larry Grantham. It can be argued that the NFL's Western Division championship over the next few seasons may have turned on the absence of those three star players from the Baltimore roster.

———

Shortly after the draft, the AFL gained a commissioner and lost a city. War hero Joe Foss was a unanimous choice for the commissioner's chair. No doubt the 26 Japanese planes he'd shot down in four months during World War II were the first things that came to mind in considering Foss. That made him a bigger ace than Rickenbacker in WW I and earned him the Congressional Medal of Honor, but he had other pluses. He'd entered the

War hero Joe Foss, the AFL's commissioner.

Marine Corps as a private and risen to the rank of major by VJ Day, then gone back to Korea as a colonel. That he had followed that as a two-term governor without getting his state put on the endangered species list indicated some executive ability. That the state was South Dakota was all the better because he wasn't likely to have any political enemies in places that were also likely to have pro football teams. But his biggest plus was his own persona. At 45, Joe (not Joseph F.) came across as an honest, open, hard-working, four-square guy—a "man's man" who could be trusted to do the right thing. It was just the image the AFL needed.

What it didn't need was the defection that became official in late January 1960. The H. P. Skoglund–Max Winter Minneapolis group withdrew and asked for their money back, citing "stadium problems." That Winter's group would pull in its oars had been predicted, even headlined, for months. By doing so, it was said, they would receive an NFL franchise in 1961. But leaving the AFL for the NFL wasn't a simple declining of a bird in a bush league to become a bird in the NFL's flock. The stadium problem was legitimate. Most influential Minnesotans—the people whose support was crucial to success—favored installing an NFL team. Without their help, Skoglund-Winter were unlikely to find a satisfactory place to play, much less fill any grandstands.

To replace Minneapolis, the AFL awarded its eighth franchise to Oakland with some misgivings. Atlanta had made a bid, but Barron Hilton wanted another West Coast team to pair with his Los Angeles franchise. No matter where the new franchise was located, it was doomed to be the runt of the litter. Oakland inherited the Minneapolis draft list but it was only a might-have-been list. Skoglund-Winter had made virtually no stabs at signing anyone on it. With February coming up, almost all the players on the list worth signing were safely in the NFL camp. As an emergency plan, the league held a one-time draft to fill Oakland's roster. Each of the other seven franchises "froze" 11 players, but made the others available to Oakland, which could pick five from each list, cutting even further into the AFL's already weak talent pool.

Oakland didn't come in with their eyes closed; they knew their situation was shaky and recognized the emergency draft was slightly bonkers. As a matter of fact, it was Wayne Valley, one of the Oakland leaders, who took a name originally applied to his Oakland group and tagged the assembled AFL owners "The Foolish Club."

BOB ST. CLAIR: "I LOOKED LIKE I WAS GULLIVER"

At six-nine, tackle Bob St. Clair was the tallest player in the NFL during his 11-season (1953–63) career with San Francisco. That was one distinction that set him apart from the other, mostly anonymous offensive linemen in the league. Another was his consistently superior blocking. Bob opened holes for such 49er runners as Hugh McElhenny, Joe Perry, and John Henry Johnson and kept pass rushers away from quarterbacks Y. A. Tittle and John Brodie so well he earned five trips to the Pro Bowl and enshrinement in the Pro Football Hall of Fame in 1990.

Nevertheless, whenever St. Clair's name comes up, it's not his unusual height, unusual durability, or unusual skill that is mentioned first. It's his diet. St. Clair ate—and enjoyed—raw meat.

"Everybody always asks about the raw meat. I had a Yaqui Indian grandmother from Mexico, and when I was little, she fed me blood gravy and bits of raw meat. So I developed a taste for it.

"Then when I was a sophomore in high school, I was five-nine and 150 pounds. I went out for football and they sent me home. I spent the next year eating health foods, honey, wheat germ, raw eggs, and of course, raw meat. When I went out for football as a junior, I was six-four and 210.

"Sometimes it's a problem. I order my meat raw in a restaurant and the waiter says, 'You mean rare?' and I say, 'No. Raw.' Pretty soon, people come out of the kitchen to look.

"At training camp, teammates used to turn away. I figured that was *their* problem. Bruno Banducci, a terrific offensive guard for the 49ers, gave me the nickname 'The Geek.' It came from that old movie where Tyrone Power would eat live chickens in a carnival sideshow. I don't eat chickens like that. The feathers, you know. But I like them rare.

"I'll leave the sideshows to Tyrone Power, but I nearly got into the movies. This was back when I was still playing. Johnny Weissmuller had just retired, and they were looking for a Tarzan. Walt Daley, a sportswriter out here, thought of the idea and acted as my agent. He called down to Paramount Studios and asked them if they were still looking for a Tarzan. He tells them about my playing and some of my habits—the raw meat, etc.—so they ask me to come down for an interview.

"I went down and actually went through an audition. I read lines, went out on the back lot and climbed a rope hand-over-hand, swung from platform to platform, dove into a water tank and they took some water shots of me with a knife in my mouth. Walt Daley was very optimistic. He thought we were really going to do this.

"The only thing was, they had me running into a bamboo-walled village and confronting these savages. Well, all these guys were about five-feet-seven. I'm six-nine. I looked like I was Gulliver! I didn't know if they were going to throw ropes over me or what. The movie people were going to build a trench for me to run around in so that I would look small with all these short guys. Kind of the opposite of those ramps they used to have Alan Ladd walk on so he'd look taller.

"Eventually, a pro football player did get to play Tarzan—Mike Henry who was a linebacker with the Steelers and Rams—but that was later. I think Ron Ely was the Tarzan they chose at the time I was trying for it. I didn't like Cheetah anyway. Terrible breath!

"When you're my size, you're a target. Once, after a Green Bay game, three pretty good-size fans came after me as I was getting into my car in the parking lot. I thought just getting out of the car would stop the nonsense, that I'd scare them. But that wasn't enough. One guy whacked me and the fight began. Two of them wound up in the hospital. I don't know what happened to the third guy. But there were no charges.

"Whether it was the diet or not, I've always been able to withstand pain. I broke my back in the Bears game as a rookie. I had two bones broken in the transverse process in the lower back. They usually put you in traction for that. I wore a sort of plastic jacket and played the next game against Pittsburgh. Then in 1957, I broke my shoulder in a game and went on and played eight more minutes before going to the sideline.

"Another thing I'm proud of is that in 1960 I was elected mayor of Daly City, as well as captain of the 49ers. When both your fellow citizens and your teammates show that kind of faith in you, it's something. The captaincy changed over a period of time. In the 1950s they were elected. Then they started appointing them because if the quarterback needed a quick time-out, the referee couldn't be looking for me because I'd be off someplace with my face in the mud. But when there were elections, the guys were always naming me.

"I was in my eighth year in the NFL when the American Football League was formed. We looked at it as a minor league. The Oakland Raiders were practicing over at Youell Field, and we looked at them as just a sandlot team. They were nothing. I have a very close friend, Don Manoukian, who was a guard in that league. He's a super guy and everything but he's about five-nine, weighs about 225 pounds, and he was about the best guard they had. Don't get me wrong, he was a hell of a football player—but for his *size!*

"See the problem was in those days, we only had about 33 players on a team—I think 35 by that time. And there wasn't room for good football players who actually could have made the team, but who weren't in the right place at the right time. We played everything. In my first three years, back in the '50s, I played both offense and defense—hardly left the field. And all the special teams—that was an automatic. So there really wasn't any room for a guy who could only do one thing. There was no room for specialists. No way.

"We knew that a second league could make a difference in salaries and such, but we didn't think the AFL would be around long enough to make any difference. We didn't think it would last. In those days, we kind of just chuckled."

————

The 49ers had been willing to send Y. A. Tittle to the Giants because Coach Red Hickey had a whole new offense mapped out for them—the shotgun. Alternating quarterbacks John Brodie, Billy Kilmer, or Bobby "Muddy" Waters stood seven-to-nine yards behind a spread line, took a direct pass from center, and then either ran or passed. It was so simple that the rest of the league was caught flat-footed. San Francisco zipped off to a 4-1 record, scoring at least 35 points in each win. But just when it looked like the shotgun was the wave of the future, the Bears unloaded it, stopping the 49ers cold, 31–0. Once Chicago showed how to solve the shotgun, the rest of the league followed suit. The 49ers went back to a normal T and their normal, disappointing season. Every once in a while their fans heaved a sigh over Tittle, who was ripping it up in New York.

————

"I guess what a lot of fans remember about the 49ers in those days is the shotgun.

"I think we all had certain apprehensions about the shotgun offense. Doubts. But we tried it out a few times and all of a sudden it totally befuddled the other team. The first time we used it was against Baltimore in 1960, a very good team. They didn't know what the hell to do. I remember [Colts' defensive tackle] Artie Donovan and those guys looking around and looking back and forth and saying 'What the hell is going on here!' By that time we had snapped the ball. We were off and running.

"We started using it in 1960. Then at the beginning of '61, Tittle was traded to New York and that was the reason they gave. Tittle didn't fit into that kind of an offense. Tittle was your conventional drop back passer, and a damned good one obviously. But not for Red Hickey's idea of revolutionizing football. We had Billy Kilmer, Muddy Waters, and Brodie. Those were the shotgun quarterbacks. And Brodie had trouble in that type of position as well. He'd played a T at Stanford. But certainly Billy Kilmer, who in college at UCLA was a tailback, did everything—run, pass, kick—he fit right in. So did Muddy Waters. So this was the wave of the future. It didn't last long.

"The explanation of what stopped the shotgun is always given that the Bears moved Bill George over center and crashed him through, but that's oversimplified. See, when you move your guards a yard away from your center, then the tackles two yards out from them the way we did, you have gaping holes. That's the idea, of course. The hole is already there for the runner. But what the Bears did was overload a side with defenders. We had no blockers available to pick up the extra men. And that was it. They would come up with these different stunts where they'd put two men from guard to center, and Bill George would stunt up the middle. Well, it was like he was on a fast track. No one in between him and the quarterback getting the ball. A field day! And we just weren't able to adjust to that kind of a defense.

"We didn't drop the shotgun immediately after that game. We tried to make a few adjustments, but the defenses were on to it. You just couldn't use the shotgun as we did with the split line. They have shotguns today. But it's not the same thing.

"I played with and against some of the greatest players ever. One was Dick Stanfel, who played with the Detroit Lions and Washington Redskins. He was a little ahead of me in school, but we played together one year at the University of San Francisco. I consider him one of the best blocking guards the league has ever seen.

"Gino Marchetti, the Colts' defensive end, was also out of USF. He was in a class by himself.

"The 49ers had some terrific players too. Jimmy Johnson was one of the best defensive backs in the history of the game. He played about fifteen years, and you could ask anybody who played against him and they'll say he covered them like a glove. Teams would stay away from his area. In a crucial time of the game they would *never* throw in his area. Great ability to cover and he was a hitter too!

"Linebacker Dave Wilcox is another guy who, hopefully, the Hall of

Fame will be looking at some time. Take a look at his record and longevity.

"John Brodie was better than any other passer we had during my time with the 49ers. But he wasn't built like Y. A. Tittle or Billy Kilmer. He was a true, stay-in-the-pocket, throw-strikes type of quarterback. He wasn't a scrambler who wanted to get out in the heavy traffic. That wasn't what his job was supposed to be, and he took a great deal of criticism for covering up and taking sacks rather than throw the ball and get totally wiped out. Physically he wasn't that kind of a player. But he had a great record and a helluva career.

"If you don't have the offensive line up there blocking for you and the defense is coming through like a sieve, the poor quarterback is going to take the heat.

"We were handicapped by the way we had to block. We couldn't use our hands the way they do now. I watch linemen block now with their arms spread out, and it's hard for me to believe that anyone could have got by me with my wingspread if I could have done that. I would have loved to have played under those conditions.

"We had to be innovative. I would fire out on a pass play just to try to fool them. And I would leg-whip like crazy. Leg whipping was legal in those days. Ask some of those guys I played against about leg whips. They thought they got by me and then—*whacko!* Down they would go. My heel would be hitting them right in the groin or in the chest. I used to put shin guards on backwards so I wouldn't hurt my calves.

"The Packers dominated the NFL in the 1960s. But we never felt we were certain to lose. There really isn't that much difference between a championship team and another good team. You know that if you play your game you can beat them. And anything can happen in a football game because the ball is oblong instead of round. I can remember in those years we beat Green Bay in '61 at the end of the year. We had our great players, and it all came down to who was healthy at the end of the year. If all your players were healthy, you had a pretty good chance."

3   IN-VINCE-ABLE!

The new coach stood in front of his players for the first time. "This is a football, gentlemen," he said, holding a ball aloft. "Before we're through with it, we're going to run it down everybody's throats."

Nobody laughed. Damn good thing!

A continuing myth is that Vince Lombardi came to Green Bay in 1959 and Svengalied a bunch of no-talent rinky-dinks into all-stars. The part about arriving in 1959 is true enough; the rest ain't. It wasn't from lack of football talent that the Packers had been bottom-feeding in the NFL West for more than a decade. The Pack's problem was leadership. There was too much of it.

Green Bay is unique in the NFL in that it has something like 1,800 owners. The popular saying is that the town owns the team, but the actual owners are the stockholders of Green Bay Packers, Inc., a nonprofit-sharing company. The majority of stockholders have a single share and no one may have more than 200. True, most of them live in Green Bay, but some are scattered all over the country and one even lives in Scotland. During the 1950s, a board of 13 businessmen ran the Packers, with the coach and general manager answerable to them. All of these people were successful in one walk of life or another, and each was sure he knew just what to do to make the local football team a winner. So the Pack took the field each fall like a batch of badgers in a bag—bulging here, pushing there, striking somewhere else, but always staying in the bag.

This lack of cohesion at the top carried down to the players. Any player who was anybody had some of the diffused power structure in his corner. The name of the game was to play well enough to keep getting a paycheck. By the mid-'50s Coach Liz Blackbourn completely lost control and was replaced in 1958 by the worst possible choice, Ray "Scooter" McLean, an ex-Chicago Bear and Packer assistant who was one of those nice guys that

Vince Lombardi.

Leo Durocher had in mind. The Packer players ran all over Scooter but not NFL gridirons and finished 1-10-1, the worst record in Green Bay history.

Everybody around the NFL, including the Packers' 13 directors, knew what was wrong and how to fix it—put the right man in charge, then shut up and let him do his job. They began asking around, looking for the right man. Bert Bell, Cleveland coach Paul Brown, and Rams' coach Sid Gillman all came up with the same name: Vince Lombardi.

Lombardi wasn't as widely known around NFL lockerrooms as, say, analgesic balm, but he'd earned a solid reputation as a New York assistant coach. The New York situation was special. Head Coach Jim Lee Howell put Assistant Coach Tom Landry in charge of his defense, Assistant Coach Lombardi in charge of his offense, and then retired to the head coach's room to read his newspaper, secure in the knowledge that he had a pair of genius elves cobbling his shoes. Perhaps Howell was the greatest genius of all for knowing when *not* to give it his awl. The Giants won the NFL title in 1956 and almost won it in 1958. Everyone knew it was only a matter of time before Landry and Lombardi had their own teams to play with. The only question was which ship would be launched first. On February 4, 1959, the Packers appointed Lombardi head coach and general manager.

"Let's get one thing straight," Lombardi told the directors. "I'm in charge."

In retrospect, it's likely that any strong-willed, competent coach could have improved the Green Bay situation. Sick of losing, the board of directors and the citizens of Green Bay were finally willing to let one mind rule. It didn't necessarily matter which direction the Packers went in. Going in any *one* direction was help enough. With the same talent and the authority to make and stand by one's decisions, another coach might have made Green Bay a winner. But there was probably no other coach more perfectly geared to take the Packers as far or as fast as Lombardi.

Surprisingly, for a team at the bottom of the standings, the Packers had a decent reservoir of talent. The NFL draft isn't the quickest way to rebuild a team, but after years of losing, the Packers had assembled some fine football players even before Lombardi arrived.

Dave "Hawg" Hanner, a rugged 250-pound defensive tackle who stayed on the line for 13 seasons, was drafted out of Arkansas in 1952. So was defensive back Bobby Dillon of Texas, who became a regular all-NFL selection even when the Packers were at their worst. In 1953, the Packers drafted Bill Forester, an SMU tackle who became an all-NFL linebacker, and Syracuse's Jim Ringo, a Hall of Fame offensive center. In 1954, the Pack drafted free-spirit receiver Max McGee out of Tulane. In 1955, they added Tom Bettis, a solid linebacker from Purdue. Back Jack Losch, the first draft pick in 1956, never helped, but the second choice, offensive tackle Forrest Gregg of SMU, became an all-pro and Hall of Famer. Fifth choice, tackle Bob Skoronski of Indiana, wasn't in Gregg's class, but he was a reliable performer through the 1960s. Baylor's Hank Gremminger, the seventh choice, became a useful defensive back, and way down as the 17th choice was Alabama quarterback Bart Starr. Golden Boy Paul Hornung arrived from Notre Dame in 1957, along with big end Ron Kramer from Michigan. Defensive back John Symank was drafted out of Florida in the 23rd round.

In one of the best drafts any team ever had, the Packers picked up two Hall of Famers, LSU fullback Jim Taylor and Illinois linebacker Ray Nitschke, and two near–Hall of Famers, Michigan State linebacker Dan Currie and Idaho guard Jerry Kramer, in 1958. Finally, in 1959, nearly two months before Lombardi was hired, the Pack drafted out of Colorado quarterback Boyd Dowler, whom Lombardi would turn into a top wide receiver. Through trades, Green Bay had acquired such useful pros as offensive tackle Norm Masters, defensive back Jess Whittenton, and receiver Gary Knafelc.

This is not to say that Lombardi didn't play a large part in developing these athletes into superior football players. Or that they would have won titles without him. Michelangelo could carve the *Pieta*; most of us couldn't get a decent doorstop out of the same chunk of marble.

––––––––

Speaking of stone, Vince Lombardi earned his football spurs in the mid-1930s as a 170-pound guard on the Fordham U. line that became cele-

Ray Nitschke.

brated as "The Seven Blocks of Granite." The block at center, All-America Alex Wojciechowicz, went on to an outstanding pro career with Detroit and Philadelphia, good enough to be elected to the Pro Football Hall of Fame several years before Lombardi. Too small a block to think seriously about playing pro ball, Lombardi went into teaching and coaching at St. Cecilia High School in Englewood, New Jersey, from 1939 through 1946. His football teams won six straight state championships. He was an assistant football coach at his alma mater, Fordham, in 1947–48 and then at Army under Earl "Red" Blaik from 1949–53. Lombardi always credited Blaik with teaching him organization and commitment and with helping him to control his often volatile temper.

New York Giants owner Wellington Mara had been one of Lombardi's classmates at Fordham. In 1954, the Giants were undergoing their first head coaching change since 1931: crusty, defensive-minded Steve Owen out; organization man Jim Lee Howell in. Mara hired Lombardi as one of Howell's assistants. Five years, one league championship, and one near miss later, Lombardi moved to Green Bay with a five-year contract as coach and general manager. And, most important, answerable only to the Packers' president—and then only on budget matters.

When a team goes 1-10-1, the natural assumption is that it harbors few athletes able to do much more than tie their shoes, but Lombardi knew better. The only really bad area was the defensive line, where "Hawg" Hanner was the lone standout. Lombardi knew just where to go to find a couple of good linemen. For five years with the Giants, he'd plotted his offense against New York's chief rival, the Cleveland Browns. As events were to show, he knew more about some of the Browns' defenders than did the Cleveland coaches.

First, he bundled up receiver Billy Howton, the biggest star on the Packers' roster, and offered him to the Browns in a deal they couldn't refuse. Howton had been All-NFL a couple of times, but his best days were behind him. Worse, he'd grown used to having things his own way at Green Bay. When he was shipped off, Lombardi was telling the other Packers that from now on things would be done *his* way. In exchange for Howton, the Packers got a free-spirited defensive end named Bill Quinlan and a useful running back named Lew Carpenter. Quinlan was the key for the Packers. Never an all-pro because he lacked the speed to be a great pass-rusher and with a "what-the-hell" attitude that endeared him to neither Paul Brown in Cleveland nor Lombardi in Green Bay, he nevertheless knew how to close down an opponent's running attack in a less-than-gentle fashion.

Lombardi's biggest coup was prying tackle Henry Jordan out of the Browns. The former Virginia tackle had languished for two years on the Cleveland bench. He was fast and combative but, at 240 pounds, was considered too small for regular duty. Lombardi had his run-stoppers in Hanner and Quinlan; he needed Jordan's speed to harry rival passers. The cost for this man, who became one of the best defensive tackles in Green Bay history, was a paltry draft choice.

Two other Lombardi pick-ups were offensive guard "Fuzzy" Thurston, who'd spent a couple of NFL seasons being cut from other teams, and safety Emlen Tunnell, who'd been great for a decade in New York but was expected to retire.

Lombardi is given credit for turning Paul Hornung's career around. At least, he knew what to do with him. Shuffled between quarterback and fullback for two seasons by previous Green Bay coaches, the former Notre Dame Heisman Trophy winner had been a bust. No wonder. Hornung had neither a fullback's power nor an NFL-caliber passing arm. Most of his quarterbacking consisted of roll-out runs. Lombardi put him firmly into

Henry Jordan.

the left halfback spot and Hornung became a star. In reality, the move was obvious. Lombardi's offense required a versatile left halfback, one who could run, catch passes, block, and occasionally throw a pass. At New York, he'd had Frank Gifford. It didn't take much of Lombardi's abundant gray matter to see the only back on the Green Bay roster with the range of required skills was Hornung. Had Hornung continued to flounder, Lombardi would have been forced to trade for a left halfback.

In tandem with Hornung, Lombardi put fullback Jim Taylor. The former LSU Tiger weighed about the same as Hornung, 215, but he hit like a Mack truck. The hard-charging Taylor had sat on the bench for ten games in 1958 but had produced when given a chance in the Packers' final two contests. Lombardi watched all the game films and decided Taylor could do the job.

Lombardi's main work wasn't reshaping the Packers' roster; it was reshaping their thinking. From the moment he arrived, he talked victory: "Gentlemen, I've never been associated with a losing team. I do not intend to start now." He focused the squad on winning and set about convincing them it was possible. Of all his talents, Lombardi's chief ability was as a motivator. He was a Knute Rockne of the 1960s. Henry Jordan's famous line, "He treated us all the same—like dogs," was funny but inaccurate. Lombardi had the true psychologist's gift of seeing which player responded to a pat on the back and which to a kick in the ass and then dealing out appropriate pats and kicks.

Guard Jerry Kramer took some kicking, tackle Bob Skoronski needed praise, and receiver Gary Knafelc responded well to terror.

Sonny Jurgensen was Lombardi's quarterback with the Redskins in 1969. "I played for nine different coaches, but the one year with Lombardi was the high point of my career. I worked harder that year and had more fun than any other year."

Jurgensen marveled at Lombardi's ability to inspire confidence. "He could diagram a play on the blackboard and say, 'Now there's no way the defense can stop that.' And you'd believe him. Then he'd leave the room and tell an assistant to draw the same play up in left formation. The assistant would draw it up, and you'd say, 'There's no way that play can work.'

"It was just his ability as a motivator. He was a teacher. He knew how to motivate individually. He'd ask of some, demand of others."

The Packers opened the 1959 season at home with a shocking 9–6 win over the Chicago Bears. The players carried Lombardi off the field. After all, they'd just matched their victory total of the year before. They continued to surprise with two more home wins over Detroit and San Francisco. The Lions were weak, but the 49ers were title contenders. The 49ers traditionally ran hot and cold, but they were hot at the start of the 1959 season. In fact, the 21–20 defeat would be San Francisco's only defeat in its first seven games. Lombardi was hailed as a miracle worker.

Reality returned in week four. In their fourth straight home game, the Packers were embarrassed by the Los Angeles Rams, 45–6.

Bart Starr was not yet the quarterback he would become. His arm was weak by NFL standards, and Lombardi felt he lacked leadership. Veteran signal caller Lamar McHan had been brought in during training camp and handed the number-one job. The week after the Rams debacle, McHan suffered a shoulder injury at Baltimore. Starr wasn't able to turn things around and the Packers suffered another loss.

In week six, Lombardi made his return to New York, but it was less than triumphant. McHan was kayoed early, but instead of Starr, Lombardi brought in Joe Francis, a single-wing tailback in college who was trying to learn how to play T-quarterback with the pros. New York won easily, 20–6.

The losses continued through two more games. Same old Packers! Part of the problem was that Taylor was lost for four games with nobody to replace him. And after the three opening wins, opponents began taking the Packers seriously.

However, the fifth loss—to the champion Colts—had some bright spots. Starr replaced McHan and played decently, if not outstandingly, and the final 28–24 score was a moral victory, not that Lombardi was in the market for moral victories.

This was a critical moment for the Packers. They'd opened the season on the high of Lombardi's enthusiasm, but after five straight losses, some of them had to be questioning their coach's methods and their own abilities. It was a great opportunity for the season to go into the dumper.

But here Lombardi caught a break—the final four opponents were all reeling under their own ineptitude. Washington was just a bad team. Detroit was old and slow. Los Angeles, in the midst of an eight-game losing streak, was discovering that the 11-for-1 deal they'd made for runner Ollie Matson had left them too thin in the line. San Francisco, after a 6-1 start, could win only one more game because of a shaky defense. The Packers took their last four to finish 7-5 and make Lombardi Coach of the Year.

Hornung won the NFL scoring championship with 94 points. His 7-for-17 field goal record left something to be desired, but he led the team in rushing with 681 yards. Boyd Dowler caught a team-high 32 passes to earn NFL Rookie of the Year honors. Starr played well in the last four victories. Overall, the team that had scored a mere 193 points in 1958 upped that to 248 under Lombardi. More important, the porous defense allowed 246 points compared to a whopping 382 in 1958.

––––––––

Tom Landry finally got *his* team in 1960 when the Dallas Cowboys were admitted to the NFL as an expansion team. Saddled with expansion-type players (i.e., we don't want him you can have him), Landry managed only one tie in 12 games. The first of his 250 regular season wins wouldn't come until 1961.

The NFL's second experiment in Dallas (remember that awful '52 team?) went head-to-head against Lamar Hunt's AFL Texans. No, the American Football League had nothing to do with expansion to Dallas, NFL spokesmen said with straight faces. Why would anybody think that?

Another new NFL city was St. Louis. At long last the Cardinals gave up on Chicago about a half dozen years after Chicago gave up on them. The Wolfners were still in charge, minus ten percent of their stock, which was sold to beer baron Joseph Griesedieck. "This is great for St. Louis," said a truck driver. "Every football fan in the area will go nuts over the Cardinals—if they win!"

The NFL was also looking for a new commissioner. The leading candidates to succeed Bert Bell were Austin Gunsel, the former FBI man who'd become acting commissioner on Bell's death, and Marshall Leahy, a West Coast lawyer who'd often represented the league. But Gunsel wasn't a favorite among the owners, and Leahy insisted he'd move league headquarters from Philadelphia to San Francisco, a shift that didn't please most of the eastern owners. Somebody suggested Cleveland Coach Paul Brown as a compromise candidate, but Brown turned that idea down himself. The owners went round and round before settling on someone nobody had even considered going in—33-year-old Pete Rozelle. Pete Who? The former PR man turned LA Rams GM, was the compromise choice on solid ground—nobody disliked him. On the other hand, the *Los Angeles Herald Examiner* gave him less than a vote of confidence: "The enlisting of Pete Rozelle as czar of the National Football League has to be the zaniest act of the century."

––––––––

Going into the 1960 season, the smart money said Green Bay might have an improved team, but it was not likely to win as many games. They wouldn't be able to blindside anyone this time around. As often is the case, the smart money wasn't so smart after all.

After eight games, Baltimore's defending champions stood at 6-2 under Coach Weeb Ewbank despite a fractured vertebra in quarterback Johnny Unitas's back. The NFL's way of ranking didn't put him at the top, but

P.R. whiz-kid Pete Rozelle became the NFL's commissioner after Bert Bell's death.

Unitas was the league's best passer, broken vertebra or no. The crewcut quarterback led in attempts, completions, yards, and touchdowns. More important, he led the world in coolly holding the football under a rush until the last possible split second, allowing his receivers to break loose of coverage. Many around the league insisted he held it even longer than was necessary, just to show his disdain for blitzers. Johnny U. had two of the best receivers in the world in Raymond Berry and Lenny Moore. Between them they caught 19 touchdown passes, and Berry led the league with 1,298 yards. But when fullback Alan Ameche suffered a career-ending Achilles tendon tear, the Colts lost their running game. Left with a one-dimensional attack—even with Unitas as the dimension—Baltimore dropped its last four games and slipped to 6-6. The Chicago Bears also suffered a late collapse.

Although the Packers' offense would become the most imitated in the NFL over the next few seasons, it was the defense that set the team above all others. As good as the Lions were defensively year after year, the Pack was nearly always better. In two of the five championship years, Lombardi's troops led the league in points scored, but in three seasons they gave up the fewest points.

Raymond Berry.

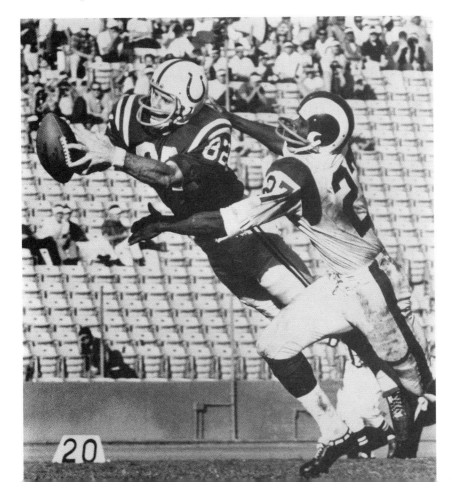

New roster additions in 1960 were Tom Moore, drafted from Vanderbilt, and free agent Willie Wood, a USC quarterback who made the team as a defensive back. Moore never made it big in the NFL, but he became a reliable sub for Hornung. Wood eventually became one of football's great safeties, although he spent most of 1960 returning kicks. For his most important off-season acquisition, Lombardi went back to Cleveland and talked them out of defensive lineman Willie Davis, who the Browns' coaches considered too small. Sound familiar? Lombardi plugged the cat-quick Davis in at right defensive end where he became an all-pro pass rusher.

On Thanksgiving Day, the Lions upset the Packers at Detroit, 23–10, to set the Green Bay record at 5-4-0. The road seemed open to the division title for defending champion Baltimore. But that Sunday, San Francisco bushwhacked the Colts at Baltimore, 30–22, to leave the Packers only a game behind.

One week later, while Baltimore continued to crash—20–15 to Detroit—the Packers moved into a tie for first with a 41–13 thrashing of Chicago. A rugged 13–0, Green Bay victory at San Francisco on Saturday, December 10, followed by the Colts' third straight loss the next day put the Packers in front, and they wrapped it up in the season finale at Los Angeles with their third road win in a row, 35–21. In two seasons, Lombardi had taken the team from the joke of the league to a division championship.

Paul Hornung had the season of his life, setting a new league scoring record with 176 points. Eighty-six of those came on 41 extra points and 15 field goals, but he also scored 15 touchdowns—13 by rushing. Jim Taylor rushed for 1,101 yards to finish second behind perennial leader Jim Brown of Cleveland.

By 1960, after only four years in the NFL—and four straight rushing championships—Jim Brown was generally recognized as the greatest runner in pro football history, a status he is still widely accorded nearly 30 years after his retirement. In a league filled with powerful runners, blazing fast runners, and incredibly elusive runners, Brown came closest to perfection. Built along the lines of a comic book superhero—a huge chest that suggested he was smuggling in a cash register under his number 32, legs so muscled they seemed designed to support a railroad bridge, and a flat 32-inch waist—he could explode his 232 pounds into a pile of heavier linemen and move them back yards, nip through a crack so tiny a Band-Aid would hide it, or burst around end like a runaway freight train. When defensive coaches laid their plans for every other team in the league, they started with the opponent's quarterback. With Cleveland, they always began with Jim Brown.

Combined with his tremendous talent was Brown's stoic durability. It was often said that he was never hurt, but that wasn't really the case. It was true that he never missed a game during his nine seasons in the NFL, but anyone who exposed his body to the angry aggressions of NFL defenders 30 or 40 times a game as Brown did was going to be hurt. Jim simply didn't let it stop him. He wouldn't even allow opponents the satisfaction of knowing they had really dinged him. When he was downed, he'd lie there for a few extra seconds, then climb laboriously to his feet and move slowly back to the huddle. He looked like he was half dead, but since he did that after every play, opponents had to figure it was *always* a fake.

During his first couple of years in the league, most fans thought of Brown as a running machine. He had a certain brooding presence, but his fiercely independent personality lay hidden for the most part by carefully bland PR. Only when his autobiography, *Off of My Chest*, was published did fans learn that Jim Brown was an outspoken black man with definite ideas on improving the Browns, the NFL, and the United States. If that cost him the adulation of some white fans who preferred their black athletes strong and silent, well, to hell with them.

Jim Brown.

45

Cleveland had the world's number-one running back in Brown and, apparently, the league's best passer in Milt Plum, whose 60.0 percent completion percentage, 9.19 average per pass, 21 touchdown passes, and low interception rate put him at the top of the stats. However, Plum acheived those numbers by throwing mostly into the flats where Brown or speedy halfback Bobby Mitchell could turn a ten-yard flip into a long gain. Moreover, because of the presence of Brown and Mitchell, every opponent had to play run first in defensing Cleveland, giving Plum an advantage whenever a pass was called. But when opponents stopped Brown and Mitchell (admittedly a tall order), Plum was seldom able to bring the Browns back with his flips. This happened just often enough to cost Cleveland three games by a total of ten points, and *that* was enough to let the Eagles slip in ahead of them for the Eastern championship.

In the championship game, the Packers ran into one of those "teams of destiny" that seem preordained to win no matter the odds. The Philadelphia Eagles, no one's preseason favorite, had successfully negotiated the Eastern Division for silver-haired coach Lawrence "Buck" Shaw on the inspirational play of veteran quarterback Norm Van Brocklin and veteran center Chuck Bednarik.

Shaw, like Lombardi, had been an undersized college lineman on a celebrated team—a 178-pound tackle for Knute Rockne's 1919–21 Notre Dame powerhouses. Also like Lombardi, he eschewed playing pro football to go directly into coaching after graduation. By the late 1930s, he was raising bowl teams at Santa Clara. When World War II ended, he signed up with the All-America Football Conference as coach of the San Francisco 49ers. There he produced winners in eight of nine years but never a championship. In 1954, after yet another close finish, he was fired.

In the meantime, the Philadelphia Eagles, the NFL's premier team of the late 1940s had crashed and burned. When they looked around for a new coach in 1958, they found Shaw at the brand new Air Force Academy organizing its athletic program. Reasoning that he'd never had a season as bad as those the Eagles were becoming used to, they lured him back into pro coaching. He promised to give them two seasons just to turn things around.

Shaw had one advantage over his Eagles predecessors: the same season he arrived, the Birds got Norm Van Brocklin. One of the great passers in pro history, the Dutchman had been frustrated in Los Angeles through the 1950s as the Rams constantly experimented to find someone even better. First, he shared the job with Bob Waterfield and then with Billy Wade. Finally, he'd managed to get himself traded to Philadelphia, arriving in 1958 to find himself at last in charge—but of a losing team. At the time, he considered retiring but relented when he received what he thought was a firm promise that he'd become Eagles coach when Buck Shaw gave up the reins.

The coach and the quarterback formed the NFL's odd couple. Shaw, always the gentleman, had been heard, when really miffed, to comment, "Shucks!" Van Brocklin, with a much earthier vocabulary, was so intense he practically crackled. Together Shaw and Van Brocklin compelled the team to respectability in 1959. Shaw was so pleased that he decided to forego his announced retirement for one more season to see what 1960 would bring. And to the astonishment of everybody but Shaw and Van Brocklin, it brought a winner.

One of the season's major stories was Chuck Bednarik. With an armored brow and exquisitely broken beak, Bednarik was the consummate old pro in his 12th NFL season. Around the league, they called him "Concrete Charlie." He'd started his pro career as a regularly selected all-NFL linebacker but in the mid-1950s shifted to offensive center. Early in the 1960 season, when injuries denuded the Eagles' linebacking corps, Bednarik

Chuck Bednarik.

stepped in at middle linebacker, while continuing to hold down his regular job at center. It had been years since the NFL had seen a two-way player on a regular basis, yet here was this 35-year-old doing it game after game and in all-pro style! It was all very heartwarming, especially for middle-aged fans.

For some fans, the Philadelphia center-cum-linebacker went from Lovable Ol' Chuck to That Bastard Bednarik in one memorable hit. In a game the Eagles had to win at New York, he caught media darling Frank Gifford napping and blindsided him so determinedly he turned Frank's nap into a week-long siesta in the hospital and seemingly ended his career. Dirty play, screamed New Yorkers! "I hit Frank head on," Bednarik explained. "It was one of the hardest tackles I ever made but it was a clean shot."

Photos bore out Bednarik's story, but proof was beside the point to Giants' fans who watched Bednarik dance with joy over the unconscious Gifford. Of course, the fact that Gifford had fumbled to give the Eagles the ball with two minutes left and a seven point lead gave Chuck good reason to chuckle and he had no idea at the time how badly he'd hurt Gifford.

The Eagles had one of the league's weaker rushing attacks and a so-so offensive line, but Van Brocklin made up for it by averaging two touchdown passes a game. Fleet Tommy McDonald, close to being the smallest player in pro football, caught 13 TD passes. Bobby Walston and Pete Retzlaff were also ace receivers. Philadelphia's defensive line was suspect, too, but a good defensive backfield led by Tom Brookshier and Don Burroughs helped. It was a team of hoary veterans having one last hurrah and it wasn't to be stopped.

In the title game, before 67,325 at Franklin Field, the Packers took a 13–10 lead late in the final quarter only to see the Eagles bounce back. Rookie Ted Dean returned a kickoff to the Green Bay 39 and then scored for a game-winning touchdown from five yards out seven plays later. The game ended appropriately enough with Bednarik tackling Jim Taylor at the Philadelphia nine and then sitting on him until time ran out.

It was the only playoff game Lombardi would ever lose.

———

When Buck Shaw retired on top after the 1960 championship game, Van Brocklin also retired as a player, fully expecting to be named Eagles head coach. He was outraged when Philadelphia handed the top job to Nick Skorich, and Van had the kind of temper that would have made Mount St. Helens proud. Shortly thereafter, he was hired as the first coach of the NFL's expansion team in Minnesota, where he would spend the next six years tearing his hair out over the scrambling tactics of his quarterback Fran Tarkenton.

With Van Brocklin on the Minnesota sideline in 1961, the NFL East became the domain of another veteran quarterback, Y. A. (for Yelberton Abraham) Tittle. "Yat," as he was acronymed, had begun tossing pro passes back in 1948 with the old Baltimore club of the AAFC. Throughout the 1950s he'd earned admiration but no championships with his passing and ball-handling for the ever-disappointing San Francisco 49ers. They called him "Colonel Slick" in deference to his crafty, seamless way with a football (though some said it applied to the traction on his head during a rainstorm; Tittle was bald as a coot from the time he came into the league). In 1961, at age 34, San Francisco was happy to send him off to New York where the Giants figured he was just the youngster to replace their 37-year-old incumbent, Charlie Conerly.

Surprisingly, the Giants were right.

But replacing an entrenched quarterback can get ugly. New Giants' coach Allie Sherman played it smart. He let Conerly go all the way in the season-opening loss to St. Louis and halfway through a lackluster performance at Pittsburgh before inserting Tittle. By then Conerly was ready to admit that maybe the time had come to take a backup role—one that he filled ably the rest of the season on Tittle's rare off-days. By handling his

quarterbacks with tact, Sherman may have lost his opening game, but he won the season.

The Giants still had most of the defense that had won fame and most of their games in the previous decade. It was growing a bit long in the tooth, but made up for any creakiness with smarts. Jim Brown recalls: "The Giants were sophisticated assassins. . . . They were football intellectuals, the smartest team in the league. Also the most calculating. Other teams would have one or two thugs who'd randomly jump you, hit you in the head. New York did *nothing* helter-skelter. The Giants would determine, as a unit, who they were going to get, then go out and get him."

But for all their calculating defense, Sherman's Giants won on firepower. With Tittle throwing to newly acquired receivers Del Shofner and Joe Walton, the New Yorkers chased still-tough Philadelphia through eight weeks. On November 12, they caught them with a 38–21 victory at Yankee Stadium. In week 13 of the expanded NFL season, the Giants eased into first place by virtue of a 28–14 win at Philadelphia, then cinched the eastern title with a 7–7 tie against Cleveland in the final regular-season game. The Eagles, under Coach Nick Skorich, finished 10–4. Sonny Jurgensen, who'd seen very limited duty as Van Brocklin's sub, emerged as a terrific passer with 3,723 yards gained and 32 TD passes. Thirteen of his touchdown tosses went to swift Tommy McDonald. With Pete Retzlaff and Bobby Walston catching what McDonald missed, Philadelphia had the league's most explosive offense, despite a poor running game. The championship was lost in the eighth game, a 16–14 win over the Bears, when Tom Brookshier broke his leg. Minus his inspirational play in the secondary, the Eagles dropped two to the Giants and one to the Browns.

While the Eagles and Giants fought it out in the East, Lombardi's Packers had no such dogfight in the West. With all the pieces in place, Green Bay sewed up its second straight division crown with two weeks to go. Huge Ron Kramer, who'd been in Lombardi's doghouse all of 1960, won the tight end job from Gary Knafelc and improved the running game with his monstrous blocking. Willie Wood became a regular at safety. Hornung, Dowler, and Nitschke were called into the army over the Berlin Crisis resulting from the erection of the Wall. They missed practice time but were generally available on weekends. The team didn't miss a beat. Starr established himself at quarterback, and Jim Taylor again rushed for over a thousand yards. Scoring machine Paul Hornung chipped in 146 points. The championship game, held December 31 in subfreezing weather at Green Bay, shaped up as an all-star game going in—nine Packers and six Giants had been named all-NFL by at least one of the wire services—but it turned into a Packer rout. Hornung, on leave from the army, scored the

first Green Bay touchdown on a six-yard sweep in the second quarter and went on to register 19 points—a new individual record for a championship game—by adding four conversions and three field goals. He rushed for 89 yards in the 37–0 win that gave Green Bay its first NFL championship since 1944, when they'd also beaten the Giants.

Jim Taylor leading Paul Hornung on a sweep to the left.

After the Packers' 1961 championship game victory, Lombardi observed: "There has never been a better team than this one was today." He could have said that after nearly every game in 1962. Green Bay had the best of everything.

Starr led the NFL in passing, completing 62 percent of his tosses. Taylor led in rushing, breaking Jim Brown's streak, with 1,474 yards. Hornung was injured much of the season, but the slack was taken up by second-year man Tom Moore and rookie Elijah Pitts. The scoring crown even stayed in Green Bay, as Taylor scored 114 points on 19 touchdowns. Although the Packers were a "running team," Dowler and Max McGee each caught 49 passes, and Ron Kramer caught 37 for seven touchdowns. Jim Ringo, Jerry Kramer, Fuzzy Thurston, Forrest Gregg, and Bob Skoronski formed the best blocking wall in football. On defense, Willie Davis and Henry Jordan continued their spectacular play along the line, with Hawg Hanner and Billy Quinlan providing steady support. The linebacking crew of Bill Forester, Dan Currie, and Ray Nitschke was the envy of all. Veteran Emlen Tunnell finally retired for good, but he wasn't missed as Willie Wood and Herb Adderley starred in the defensive secondary. Wood's nine interceptions led the league; Adderley had seven. Jess Whittenton, Hank Gremminger, and John Symank were consistent. No fewer than 14 of the 22 starters were named to at least one "all" team at season's end.

Only the Lions provided a challenge. Detroit lived by its defense, which featured tackles Alex Karras and Roger Brown, linebacker Joe Schmidt, and an outstanding secondary. The Packers barely survived a 9–7 defensive battle with the Lions in week four. By the annual Thanksgiving Day game at Detroit, the Lions stood 7-3 while the Packers were still undefeated. Brown and Karras played perhaps the best games of their careers, sacking Bart Starr for 110 yards in losses to lead a 26–14 Detroit upset. Played before a national TV audience, the game was christened "The Thanksgiving Day Massacre" and is still remembered fondly by Lions fans, but all that it really accomplished was to keep Green Bay from a perfect season. The Pack won its last three games handily to leave the 11-3 Lions in the dust.

In the NFL East, the Giants also had smooth sailing, as Y. A. Tittle set a new NFL record with 33 touchdown passes. Twelve went to Del Shofner and nine to Joe Walton, but seven went to Frank Gifford, making a fine comeback after laying out a year to recover from Chuck Bednarik's boom-lowering in 1960.

One landmark in 1962—the Washington Redskins finally allowed a black player to wear their burgundy and gold, the last NFL team to integrate. The lily white skins of the Redskins, the team representing the nation's capital, had been an ongoing embarrassment to the league. The assertion of crusty George Preston Marshall that "We'll start signing Negroes when the Harlem Globetrotters start signing whites" made sense only if you watched your football through two eyeholes cut in a sheet. The situation was intolerable. Pressure from fans, newspapers, the league, and the government finally forced Marshall to yield. In the 1962 draft, the Redskins took three black players: Ernie Davis, Syracuse's All-America halfback in the first round, halfback Joe Hernandez of Arizona in the second, and fullback Ron Hatcher of Michigan State in the eighth.

Hatcher would play for the 'Skins in 1962 and Hernandez in '64, but Davis was the big news. A few days after the draft, Marshall announced he'd traded the rights for the potential superstar to Cleveland for Bobby Mitchell, a black halfback who'd spent four years with the Browns. Mitchell had enjoyed some spectacular games with the Browns, but at 188 pounds he wasn't the big blocker Paul Brown wanted to pair with Jim Brown in his backfield. It was assumed that the 215-pound Davis would give Cleveland a Green Bay–like "big back" offense.

As it turned out, Davis would never play for the Browns, but Mitchell, switched to wide receiver, became a Hall of Fame player in Washington. In his first year with the Redskins he led the NFL in receptions (72) and yardage (1,384), while scoring 11 touchdowns. His performance only underlined the stupidity of Marshall's previous all-white policy.

The Packers came to Yankee Stadium for the championship game and brought their Green Bay weather with them. The temperature shivered at 20 degrees at game time, with an icy 35-mile-per-hour wind refrigerating the House That Ruth Built. The wind disrupted Tittle's passes—he completed only 18 of 41—and played nicely into the hands of Green Bay's power-running attack. Taylor made 31 smashes into the line, and though he averaged less than three yards a pop, it was enough to control the football. His second quarter, seven-yard touchdown and three field goals by Jerry Kramer, standing in for Hornung whose injuries limited him to running, gave the Pack a 16–7 win and their second consecutive NFL title.

Bobby Mitchell, the first black player to suit up for the Washington Redskins.

WILLIE DAVIS: "I LIVE EVERY DAY ... REPLAYING THAT IN MY MIND"

That Willie Davis was a flat-out success during his 12 years in pro football is inarguable: five seasons All-NFL, five times selected to the Pro Bowl, six championship games (including five on the winning side), two Super Bowls, and election to the Pro Football Hall of Fame in 1981. Along with speed, agility, and a six-three, 245-pound physique, he added intelligence, durability, and determination to make one terrifying defensive end. After two seasons with Cleveland (1958–59), he was traded to Green Bay just in time to enjoy and contribute immeasurably to the Packers' string of championships.

Although less headline-making, his subsequent success in business as a West Coast beverage distributor has shown that he still retains those same inner qualities that helped make him an all-pro. A former NAACP Man of the Year, he was considered one of the leading candidates for NFL Commissioner when Pete Rozelle stepped down.

"Probably the unique thing in my life is that I played for three great coaches: Eddie Robinson, in college, and Paul Brown, and Vince Lombardi in the NFL. One thing all three had in common is that they were good people. They had the players' interests at heart as well as wanting to win. And each played a role in my life at a time when that role was very important.

"In fact, I can say I played for four great coaches. My high school coach is a legend in Texarkana [Arkansas] today—Nathan 'Tricky' Jones. He was probably as successful as any high school coach around. He was a science teacher who managed to intimidate us all the way to the classroom. He intimidated us on the practice field and he intimidated us in class. He made about half of us take his classes. No question that he was in charge. But he was really kind of the perfect high school coach for what I needed. My mom and dad were separated when I was eight years old, and I was really looking for a father figure. I think I found it in coaches, and it started in high school.

"And, of course, Eddie Robinson at Grambling was the perfect guy to go to from Tricky Jones. We had this slogan, 'Grambling, where everybody is somebody.' And that's a rather interesting statement to make. It's one of the problems at the major universities—they become so huge that there's a problem identifying everybody. Grambling was small enough that you could get personal attention, and you *got* personal attention. And that was rather good for me.

"Everybody who ever played for Eddie, if he didn't graduate on time, Eddie provided an opportunity for that person to come back and complete his degree. To Eddie, that degree, if not equal, was real close to winning football games in terms of importance. Whether Eddie was coming through the dormitory checking on your work habits or getting athletes out to class, this thing was extremely important to him. He was always someone you could go to to discuss a personal problem and come away with the feeling that you'd been with someone who showed sensitivity and understanding. And that was important.

"The other thing that was uniquely identified with Eddie—and a major reason why Grambling, as small as it is, has sent so many players to the pros—was Eddie had a total commitment to making sure that his players knew what was the latest technique, trend, or training mechanism. When I walked into the Cleveland Browns' training camp in 1958, I had the distinction of being the youngest guy in camp and probably the one from the smallest institution. I've often thought of that. For about five minutes it was overwhelming. All at once I'm competing with players I had read about every Sunday or Monday for years, and for a minute you almost want to treat them as stars. Yet you had to put on your pants 'one leg at a time' and go out and compete. Not only are these your peers but on this day they're not any better. And you're going to try to be a little better than they are. So coming out of Eddie's program, you had this feeling that you were well prepared.

"I found Paul Brown someone who was almost the essence of today's game—in the sense of how you systematically play the game and make it a science. It was not a major adjustment for me. I think from terminology to technique, I was able to adapt real well to the pro football scene even though the division that I'd been involved in would have been considered way down the road from where most of the guys had matriculated from.

"The Browns were a top team. They'd just come out of the championship the year before.

"In Paul Brown, what can I say? A bit caustic in his handling of you in the sense that he could look you in the face with the most cutting kind of expression and say, 'We can show you, we can teach you, but we can't do it for you.' This thing is open but it's very rational. You get it done or goodbye. That clearly made you realize you'd better take responsibility if you wanted to be around there very long. It made you grow up real quick as to whether you would accept the challenge to play up to a level or retrogress back to a feeling of 'well, I'm not good enough.'

"And I guess I had decided way back in high school when I started out that I was going to ride something to some glory in life. I flat out wanted success very badly. And not just in financial terms. I wanted success in the sense that I could say I achieved something. It's a good feeling. Whatever that competition is, you can look back and say, 'Hey, maybe we didn't all start out at the same place, but right now we're at this point in time and I'm going to show I can get it done.'

"Paul—great teacher, great organizer, great system. I think I was experiencing a level of progression at each stop. And boy, stopping at Cleveland coming out of college really was progress! Paul Brown probably was copied in the 1960s and 1970s and even today more than any other coach in the game. And for good reasons. This guy had the game down to a science.

"You'd line up in practice and he'd stop play and have a player move in by a half-yard or a foot. I had never been exposed to playing the game in that much of a technical format. Move in a foot? Are you serious? It was an exact science: You line up here, you cut this way, you flare this way. To me it was refreshing. It was a learning process.

"What was interesting—and it probably hurt me early in my career— was that I was one of those guys who it was hard to determine where to play me. I had speed and quickness to play on defense. When we came into training camp that year, they had me play mostly on defense. But then we took those Sunday exams that Paul used to give. In the Cleveland Browns' training camp, about the second Sunday they'd give everybody a test. This was something that was feared as much in the Cleveland training camp as anything. Whether you played offense or whether you played defense, you had to write down the assignments for 22 players. The offense and the defense. Well, here I am as a rookie and I guess I had the second highest score on that Sunday test. The veterans started calling me 'Univac.' Chuck Noll, who was practically a coach on the field, was one of the guys. But what happened was that because I did so well on the test, they switched me to offense as a kind of backup. They were keeping 33 players, and I was kept as third defensive end and as a third offensive tackle behind Lou Groza and Mike McCormack.

57

"This was a trivia question and I think it's still true—the last Browns player to play a full game on both offense and defense was yours truly. I had beaten Paul Wiggin out at defensive end in my rookie year. Then Mike McCormack was injured, so I played the entire game against Washington at defensive end and at offensive tackle.

"That whole sense of having been well and fundamentally trained in football enabled me to do that. Obviously, I'd picked up the system well enough to play both ways. And this occurred pretty early in the season— maybe the third or fourth game. I look back at that today, and it kind of scares me. But it was clearly something that I credit to coming to Cleveland, understanding football, and having such a great coach. And Paul Brown probably had the best staff around at this time. So the Cleveland experience for me was one where everything worked well.

"When I went to Green Bay and I met Lombardi, all at once I met someone who took all of the football fundamentals, all of the training, all of the things that I had been exposed to up to that time, good people, good training, good coaching, and added one other element—motivation! Motivation in that it was almost a personal reason you had to play this game with a certain kind of identity and a certain kind of pride to make sure it represented all the things that were important to you.

"As a motivator, Coach Lombardi could put that finishing touch on things about playing a game for a reason, a purpose, and make it reach all the way up to your manhood. If you had it coming, he could get on you in a rough way on the sideline.

"The Packers were not physically bigger or faster. We were not anything but guys who were willing to work hard enough to get themselves ready to play. And, with Lombardi in charge, maybe sometimes it was not an option.

"So to me, Lombardi added that human emotion that just made you walk out on a football field and say, 'Hey, on this day, I'm going to prove to the world that I can play this game with a certain desire and a certain determination.' You get 11 of us doing that on offense and 11 doing it on defense and we're going to be a tough team to beat. To me, that was Lombardi—the emotional build-up that he created was unlike any other coach. Nobody ever sent me on the field more emotionally charged than Vince Lombardi. That was his strong suit. He could look you in the face and transmit that sense of something that made you flat out say, 'I'm going to will this. It's going to be done!'

"By then you've collected all this along the way. And there was one other thing with Vince. Not only had Lombardi introduced me to that whole sense of winning on the football field, but I was ready to say, 'This thing is sweet. I'm going to take this with me for the rest of my life.' That was one of the things Vince used to say, 'Don't kid yourself. If you can't win here, you're not going to win in the other things you do either. Conversely, if you win here, you're not going to stop winning when you leave here.'

"I live every day with some reality of replaying that in my mind. You don't win all the time, but you manage to win more than you lose. That's how you survive in this crazy business world; you try to make more right than wrong decisions over time. They say successful business decisions today are somewhere in the 55 to 60 percent range. You make some mistakes out there, but when you're programmed to win, that commitment is there. You always try to prepare yourself to go out next time and win it. Setbacks can literally knock you to your knees sometimes, but your great belief is that you can win over a period of time. That's what makes you get up the next day and come out. Yesterday was a disastrous day, but today, I'm going to rise again."

NEW KIDS ON THE BLOCK

At a few minutes after 8 P.M., on Friday, September 9, 1960—a 77-degree, muggy night—Tony Discenzo did something at Boston University Field that a lot of people never thought would be done. He kicked a football and thus launched the American Football League's first official game. Discenzo, a 245-pound Boston Patriots' tackle out of Michigan State, would play only one season in the AFL, but with that boot he secured his place in trivia history.

There had been exhibitions going on for nearly six weeks—the first, a 28–7 Boston win over Buffalo on July 30 before 16,000 fans—so the first official game was only a surprise in relation to the many predictions of the previous spring that the AFL would never get off the ground. By midsummer, with eight teams in training camp, most doomsayers were willing to admit that the new league would, against all odds, play its first season—or at least part of it.

The crowd of 21,597 at BU Field for that first game was paltry by NFL standards, but encouraging for a league materializing out of dreams and promises. They were treated to a night of firsts. Discenzo booted the first kickoff into the end zone, where Denver's Bob McNamara began the first return, then executed the first reverse to Al Carmichael, who took the ball to the 17. Moments later, Carmichael made the first run from scrimmage, good for five yards. Dave Rolle of Denver accomplished the first first down rushing on a pitchout from quarterback Frank Tripucka, but after a couple of more runs failed, George Herring made the first AFL punt.

The players on the field typified AFL rosters in that brave new year: rookies like McNamara, Discenzo, and Rolle, NFL castoffs like Carmichael, and Canadian Football League imports like Tripucka. Quite a few had been out of football for years. One of those was Boston's Gino Cappelletti, who scored the first AFL points before the quarter ended on a 34-yard field

goal. Cappelletti had been recommended to Boston coach Lou Saban by McNamara, his old college roommate at the University of Minnesota. Ironically, McNamara, a college star in the mid-1950s, was dealt to Denver before the end of training camp and lasted only two seasons in the AFL, while Cappelletti, who'd played briefly in Canada after not even being drafted by the NFL, went on to become the AFL's all-time scoring leader.

Gino Cappelletti.

"At the time, I didn't have the luxury of thinking I had made history by scoring the first AFL points ever," Cappelletti explained. "We didn't have much time for history. We were concerned about surviving. I knew that if I messed up that first kick, I might not get a chance to try another one. In the beginning, you never really knew if you had made the team. I had been out of college since 1956. Then I played ball in Ontario for two years. When Bob McNamara mentioned me to Lou Saban, I was working at my brother's bar in Minneapolis, wondering if I'd ever get a chance to play pro football."

In that first game, Cappelletti played defensive back—"You couldn't be just a kicker then, because the teams carried only 33 players"—but he was slow afoot and Denver took advantage of that. Shortly afterward, he was switched to wide receiver where his soft hands enabled him to catch anything he could reach. By the time he retired 11 seasons later, he had made 292 catches good for 42 touchdowns.

The first AFL touchdown came on the first play of the second quarter when two old pros combined for Denver. Tripucka fired a short pass to Carmichael in the right flat. Al reversed the field and zipped 59 yards down the left sideline to score.

Carmichael, a scatback out of the University of Southern California, spent six seasons with the Green Bay Packers in the pre-Lombardi years, specializing in kick returns. On one occasion he brought a kickoff back 106 yards for a touchdown against the Chicago Bears. "I saw the AFL as a chance to play more pro football," he said. "I didn't think of it as a step backward to play in the new league. It never mattered to me who was hitting me when I was playing. You felt it just as hard in the AFL as you did in the NFL."

Tripucka had been a standout quarterback at Notre Dame in 1948. After four so-so years in the NFL, he headed for Canada where he became a star. At 33-years-old, he was ready to forego the aches and bruises, so "when they asked me to come to Denver, I thought I would be only a coach. I thought I was through with playing." With that understanding, he signed with the Broncos for $15,000—$20,000 less than he was making in Canada.

Also pressed into surprise service for Denver in that first AFL game was Gene Mingo, the team's placekicker. "I didn't expect to be returning punts that night," he remembers, "but someone had gotten hurt and so the coach asked me to go in and return kicks." In the third quarter, he brought a Boston punt back 76 yards for a touchdown. "I was so tired I couldn't get the full leg strength I needed for the extra point, and I hit it weak and it went off." It wasn't needed. The Broncos held on to win 13–10.

———

Harry Wismer's association with the American Football League as owner of the New York Titans would be, in the long run, unfortunate. Before he left, he became both a drag and an embarrassment. Yet something he did at the beginning paved the way to ultimate success for the league. When doomsayers equated the AFL with the old AAFC, they ignored one crucial new factor—television. As chairman of the new league's television committee, Harry succeeded in pushing through a plan to sell the TV rights as a whole instead of letting each team arrange its own deal. The teams then shared the money equally. Obviously, this was a godsend to teams like Oakland and Denver, whose TV rights would have gone for peanuts if sold separately. Just as obviously, the team most hurt by Wismer's plan was Wismer's. No matter what kind of product the Titans put on the field, the TV rights to it in New York City could bring more into the till than those of any other league team.

On June 9, ABC announced it was granting the AFL a five-year contract. $1,785,000 would be paid for the first year, and yearly increases would make the average worth $2,125,000 per season over the length of the contract. Split eight ways, the TV money would keep some of the Foolish Club from losing their shirts. Only their cuffs and collars.

"That's something the AFL was always proud of," Billy Sullivan said, "that we had national TV every Sunday, even when our teams weren't drawing well and people didn't know who we were. And the man most responsible for getting us that national TV contract was Harry Wismer. Without Harry getting us that, there's really no way the AFL could have stayed in business those first few years. He may have had his weaknesses— and he was not a well-liked person—but he did that one thing for the AFL which can never be overlooked."

There was a definite ad-lib quality to the AFL's first year.

For instance, the league had terrible problems in finding places to play. Until 1973, the Buffalo Bills used WPA-built War Memorial Stadium— called "The Rockpile" for its granitelike playing surface—which fans and players hated. Tucked away in the heart of a ghetto, The Pile wasn't the safest place to be. Indeed, a Bills' vice-president was mugged after one game. The stadium had no public parking, and those who drove to the game left their cars in driveways or yards where one paid the owner "$2 to park and $5 to watch your car." Despite the setting, Buffalo was consistently among the AFL leaders in attendance. Reportedly, the Bills' losses in the AFL's first season were the smallest in the league—$175,000. When War Memorial was expanded to seat 45,000 (from 36,000) in 1965, the average attendance went up to 43,811.

That was small consolation for the players who had to put up with the shoddy dressing rooms. "If two showerheads worked and you got warm water, you considered yourself fortunate," Bills defensive end Ron Mc-Dole, who joined the team in 1963, said. "It was the worst!"

"War Memorial Stadium was one of the worst stadiums in the world," says quarterback Len Dawson. "I don't know which war had been fought there, but it must have been an old one. I used to get nauseous there. When you went out of the locker room, you stopped in front of an old coffee-and-hot-dog stand to wait for player introductions, and I'll bet the coffee grounds had been there since the Civil War. The smell made me sick. And the quarterback was always introduced last."

The Bisons, Buffalo's minor league baseball team, tore up the field well into the fall. The city tried special winter grass seeds only to discover they provided a gourmet feast for every pigeon within flying distance. "So one day, the city sent a bunch of guys out with guns to shoot the pigeons,"

McDole remembered. "We're there practicing and these guys are running around like lunatics shooting pigeons.

"Finally our coach, Lou Saban, gets this idea that we should put poison in the seeds to kill the pigeons. Next day we're at practice and we spend half the time picking dead pigeons off the field. It was a helluva sight."

As bad as War Memorial was, at least the Bills had no major competition for the fan's buck during most of the football season. The 1960 Chargers performed in Los Angeles Memorial Coliseum, which seated 100,000 for the Rams but was cavernously empty whenever the Chargers were in town. Why go out to see the new guys when the Rams were on the tube?

A similar situation applied to Dallas, where the Texans shared the Cotton Bowl with the NFL Cowboys and both looked at mostly empty seats. The Texans outdrew the Cowboys slightly in their first year, but reportedly Clint Murchison's Cowboys lost "only" $700,000 to Lamar Hunt's $1,000,000 on the Texans. This led old H. L. Hunt to remark that at that rate the "boy only has 123 years to go," which is even funnier if you didn't hear it first in *Citizen Kane*. Lamar Hunt could afford the bill, but his league couldn't afford to lose face in all three of its head-to-head battles with the NFL.

In 1960, the Patriots played on Boston University's field, which had previously been the unsatisfactory home of baseball's old Boston Braves. Even getting that took some doing. The Patriots were first turned down by Fenway Park, Harvard, Boston College *and* BU. Finally, Boston mayor John Collins persuaded Boston University president Harold Case to relent and allow the Pats in. With Boston U. playing on Saturdays and most New England football fans watching the Giants on Sunday TV, the Patriots played their home games on Friday nights.

In Denver, Mile High Stadium (then known as Bears Stadium) was still a minor league baseball park. In Houston, the Oilers, who'd hoped to play in Rice University Stadium were forced instead into Jeppesen Stadium, a high school field. The league lost a lot of face when it played its championship game there. "Once we chased the seagulls off the field," Raider center Jim Otto recalls, "the rain and humidity made the stench pretty bad." The Raiders couldn't even play in Oakland in 1960 and had to settle for decrepit Kezar Stadium across the bay in San Francisco.

The Titans had perhaps the worst deal. While they waited around for Shea Stadium to be built—expected in 1962, delivered in 1964—they were stuck in the drafty, dirty, dreary Polo Grounds, a monstrosity the baseball Giants had abandoned in 1957 to head west. (Jim Otto: "When they turned on the lights, the drunks woke up.") No one in his right mind wanted to be in the Polo Grounds, especially for a night game, when it was positively scary. New York football fans proved to be mostly in their right minds, although Harry Wismer regularly announced attendances in excess of 20,000. These became known as "Wismer attendances," crowds in which two-thirds of the people came, in the words of sportswriter Dick Young, "disguised as empty seats."

———————

As much as by inadequate ballparks, the AFL was hurt by the decidedly minor league aura that shrouded some of the teams. Patriots kicker-receiver Gino Cappelletti remembers hanging bedsheets to watch game films. "One trip, the plane stopped in Buffalo where we picked up the Bills. We dropped off in Denver, and they went to the West Coast. Ralph Wilson and Billy Sullivan had some kind of deal."

But Cappelletti kept things in perspective. "When I played in Canada, they were wrapping guys' ankles with black friction tape. What did we know from luxury?"

The travel accommodations in the early AFL weren't always first class. "We used to play New England [Boston]," Jim Otto remembers. "We'd fly to some place in Rhode Island, get on a bus for five hours, play the game, get back on the bus, and fly out because that was the cheapest way. One time we took a train from New York to Boston and everybody got off at the wrong stations. So from New York to Boston, we had football players all over the Eastern seaboard."

The worst from the git-go was Denver, where Bob Howsam was decidedly underfinanced. Realizing his team would have to live or die on a shoestring, Howsam brought in Dean Griffing, one of the all-time masters at running a team on the cheap, as general manager. For years, Griffing had been an executive in the Canadian Football League, where a penny saved was the only penny earned. The one incident always mentioned in connection with his time as the Broncos' GM is the day he followed an extra point into the stands and attempted to wrestle the football away from a fan. When Griffing was handed the Denver job, he went with what he knew and hired former CFL coach Frank Filchock for the Broncos. Then he discovered that Saskatchewan coach and quarterback Frank Tripucka didn't want to live in Canada the year round. Griffing made Tripucka an offer, and Frank, thinking he was coming aboard as an assistant coach, resigned his job with the Rough Riders. Since his contract with Saskatchewan was for coach-Tripucka only, there was no problem with player-Tripucka leaving the CFL.

Tripucka expected to play very little if at all. From past experience, Tripucka knew Filchock was the kind of coach who'd often give his team afternoon practice off so he could go fishing. With NFL veteran Tom

Frank Tripucka in
training camp at the
Colorado School
of Mines.

Dublinski and touted rookie George Herring in camp to play quarterback,
Frank assumed his main duty would be to help Filchock with the offense.
As it turned out, he played almost every offensive down of the Broncos'
first three seasons.

With a coach and quarterback in place, Griffing turned to other aspects
of his general managership. The results have provided Bronco survivors
horror stories for years.

For a training camp, Griffing used the Colorado School of Mines, a
perfectly nice school with several fine dormitories and one miserable
barracks-type barn, the fourth floor of which was one large, unair-

conditioned furnace with squeaky cots and only bare pipes to hang clothes on. Guess which dorm Griffing got a deal on for his team?

The camp was open to anyone who showed up and said he wanted to be a Bronco. When Goose Gonsoulin, who played seven years as a Bronco safety, arrived, "There were about 120 players going through camp. That was cut down to 90. But the team kept picking up National Football League cuts all the time. We would get ten new faces and cut 30 old ones every week for a while." Eventually more than 200 human beings, only a few actually football players, passed through the camp, and many weren't there long enough to sample the sleeping arrangements or even the meals.

The regular cuisine was suitable only for residence in a vomitorium. The staple was some sort of hash, antecedents dubious. Players found it had a habit of returning for a farewell appearance shortly after practices began. Steak was served one night a week—Friday. Several players swore that evening was chosen so the Catholics in the crowd would bypass the meat and save the team's grocery bill.

For uniforms, Griffing made another deal, this with the sponsors of a long-forgotten all-star game. The yellow jerseys were, or at least had once been, sort of a mustard that someone euphemistically called "gold." The trousers were brown, some but not all, a shiny brown. No doubt yellow and brown have been attractively combined in some uniforms somewhere, but the washed-out Denver togs looked like dead dandelions on a compost heap. Presiding over this was a helmet logo exhibiting an unconsciously appropriate, ratty-looking bronco rider. The *pièce de résistance* of this un-attractive ensemble was the socks, which were striped vertically! Of all the minor-league symbols of the AFL, those Bronco socks take first prize hands down.

The Denver Broncos and their vertically striped socks.

From the start, the new league was acutely aware of its television persona. Commissioner Joe Foss announced the cameras would be allowed to show anything that happened on the field. This was in direct contrast to the staid NFL's policy of having the cameras look elsewhere whenever a fight broke out among the players.

Even more attuned to TV tune-ins was the decision to have the players' names sewn on the backs of their uniforms above the numbers. After all, fans in their living rooms weren't likely to have programs to turn to if they wanted to know who 57 was. The new league had few name players when it began, and the sooner the public became familiar with who was who, the better.

Another preseason decision brought a bit more suspense to the games. The AFL opted to utilize the college rule that allowed a team to kick the extra point for one point or run or pass it in for two—an "extra points." In the league's first year, the two-point option was tried 16 times with 10 successes. Its greatest benefit was in cutting down the number of ties that plagued pro football each year. Ties satisfied the fans on neither side. In 1960, the NFL had five ties in 78 games; the AFL had only one in 56.

The new league divided itself into two divisions, with the Boston Patriots, Buffalo Bills, New York Titans, and Houston Oilers in the Eastern Division, and the Dallas Texans, Denver Broncos, Los Angeles Chargers, and Oakland Raiders in the Western. A 14-game schedule meant each team would play all the others home-and-home. NFL teams had been playing 12 games a season since 1950, so AFL fans would have two more chances to attend, or stay away from, games.

But the AFL's major appeal to both TV viewers and fans in the stands was in its brash, wide-open offenses. The impression was that the new league was putting the ball in the air more and scoring more often. And that impression was correct.

The New York Titans had an early season four-game stretch in which they lost 24–28, won 28–24 and 37–35, and then lost 21–27. Their final game of 1960 was a 43–50 shootout with Los Angeles. In the final stats, the Titans scored the most points in the league, 382, but they also gave up the most, 399. New York fans couldn't anticipate victory, but they were almost sure to see points scored. The same was only slightly less true all over the league. In its first season, the AFL averaged 66.1 passes and 48.3 points per game—14 more passes and five more points per tilt than the NFL.

To some extent this gung-ho, offensive onslaught was intentional. AFLers knew they couldn't wean fans away from the NFL with defense. But for the most part, the fireworks were the natural and unavoidable effect of putting teams together from scratch. It takes years to build a good defense. Eleven players need time to learn to work as a unit. An offense of sorts, however, can be created out of one strong-armed quarterback and a speedy receiver or two.

––––––––

Veteran quarterbacks were at a premium. Denver had Tripucka. Oakland had Babe Parilli, a veteran from Green Bay and Cleveland, although rookie Tom Flores, the future NFL coach, played about as often. Lamar Hunt's Dallas Texans were led by erratic "Cotton" Davidson, who'd seen action with the Baltimore Colts. Jackie Kemp, the future politico, had been cut by the Pittsburgh Steelers in 1957, but he won all-AFL honors for the Chargers in the league's first year by throwing for 3,018 yards and 20 touchdowns.

The Boston Patriots brought "Butch" Songin out of retirement. The 36-year-old local had starred at Boston College a decade earlier, In Buffalo, Tommy O'Connell, who'd once led the NFL in passing with Cleveland, also came out of retirement for one last hurrah but he had little left. After a sad season, he joined the coaching staff.

Al Dorow, ex-Washington quarterback, threw 26 touchdown passes for the 7-7 Titans to lead the league in that department. Most of the Titans' offense consisted of Dorow running for his life, hoping he could spot a receiver. In the season's final stats, Dorow was listed as the team rushing attempt leader with 124, very few of which were called that way in the huddle.

Houston landed the plum among quarterback retreads. George Blanda had put in ten seasons with the Chicago Bears and at times been their number-one quarterback, but in the late 1950s, he was being used strictly as a placekicker. Frustrated, he retired after the 1958 season. When the Oilers offered him the chance to play quarterback again, he jumped at it. In one swoop, Houston had itself a crafty veteran passer and the best placekicker in the league.

Although the glamour quarterback positions were filled with overage cast-offs, the league developed a few stars of its own in its first year.

Lionel Taylor, an NFL reject as a defensive back because he was too slow, joined the Broncos before their third game and was such a wonder at catching the football that Coach Filchock put him in at end. It was probably Filchock's greatest contribution to the Broncos and the AFL. In the league's first season, Taylor hauled in 92 passes, more than any NFL player had ever done in one year. The next season, he broke 100. Though he never got any faster, Lionel in his prime had a knack for getting open and an amazing ability to catch any airborne football.

Few of Oakland's players would last more than a year or two in the AFL,

Lionel Taylor.

but Jim Otto was chosen All-AFL center every year of the AFL's existence. Jim, a 205-pound center and linebacker at the University of Miami, was considered too small for the NFL. The stillborn Minneapolis AFL franchise took him without much expectation and then withdrew from the league. By the time Oakland replaced them, what few draft picks that hadn't gone to the NFL were scattered among the other seven AFL teams. "I actually signed with Houston and was an Oiler for about a week in March 1960," Otto recalls. Otto and a few of the original picks were recovered by the Raiders; most were lost. "We got what Pat shot at," says Otto.

The undersized center used the doubts of others about his ability as a source of inspiration. On the day he signed his pro contract, one respected Florida sportswriter announced, "A University of Miami athlete just committed suicide," and went on to add, "I predict that he will not last more than two days in professional football." To everyone's surprise except Jim's, the too-small center built himself up to a robust 255 pounds and played 16 seasons.

"Once you have a desire to be recognized," Jim says, "it's amazing what you can do."

Otto was more easily recognized than most centers because he wore the unusual number of double zero. During his rookie year, he wore his Miami number, 50. But after he was named all-league, someone suggested to the equipment manager that he be given the number zero as a pun on the word "aught." That was extended to double zero, or more properly, "aught-oh."

Abner Haynes, a quick but smallish halfback with the Texans, was the league's first homegrown star. Haynes turned down a better money offer

Jim Otto.

from the NFL Steelers to sign with the Texans ("My friends thought I was crazy.") so he could stay close to home. After making a name for himself at Lincoln High in Dallas, Haynes became the first black to attend nearby North Texas State College, where he led his team to its first Missouri Valley Conference title.

Haynes won the AFL's first MVP Award by rushing for 875 yards and catching 55 passes for another 576. He tied the Chargers' Paul Lowe for the league lead with nine rushing TDs. He matched his on-the-field derring-do with a pleasant off-the-field demeanor that could be humorously self-effacing: "I played defense a lot in high school. Maybe that's why I never grew up [he was actually five-eleven]—I got my head knocked down so much."

He was the most popular athlete in Dallas. In a seven-hour session at the State Fair, he signed an estimated 2,300 autographs. After a Texans' game at the Cotton Bowl, the PA announcer intoned: "Good afternoon, ladies and gentlemen. Thank you for coming, and please remember to drive carefully. The life you save may be Abner Haynes'."

The Chargers had a top back in Paul Lowe, a burner who by his own count telephoned the Rams 93 times seeking a job before joining the Chargers. Lowe lacked the hands to be an outstanding pass catcher, but he raced for 855 rushing yards and scored nine touchdowns on the ground.

Future Hall-of-Famer Ron Mix cleared the way for Lowe on sweeps and was hailed as the league's top offensive tackle. Mix, unusually bright and unusually lethal, gained the nickname "The Intellectual Assassin."

Don Maynard had started his pro career as a halfback with the New York Giants in 1958, after twice being All-Border Conference at Texas Western. At six-one and 180, he looked too fragile to last. Mostly he returned punts, although he was listed as backup to star Frank Gifford. From the first, he ran afoul of Allie Sherman, at that time the Giants' backfield coach. "It was only a matter of time until Allie and I had a parting of the ways," Maynard explained. "It came down to his not liking my running style. He told me—he didn't ask or suggest, he told me—to shorten my steps. I told him I could cover more ground with one step than anybody he had out there could with three. The next day I was cut."

He played a season in the Canadian Football League, then hurried back to the United States to become the first player signed by the Titans. His speed and unpredictable moves made him one of the top long-distance threats in the league. His 1,265 yards were second highest among AFL receivers in the league's first year.

Eventually, Otto, Mix, and Maynard (as well as George Blanda) would be enshrined in the Pro Football Hall of Fame.

72

The Dallas Texans had the league's best personnel over all, but hot and cold quarterbacking torpedoed them.

The Chargers had the league's most sophisticated attack, thanks to coach Sid Gillman. A one-time star end at Ohio State, Gillman had coached the Los Angeles Rams to a division title in 1955, and then saw his team slide into the doldrums through an excess of egos, a nasty ownership fight, and some questionable deals promulgated by the front office. When he was fired by the Rams after the 1959 season, the Chargers were happy to get him and so was the AFL. He gave the new league its only authenticity in the coaching ranks. The AFL's other coaches had come from college jobs (Boston's Lou Saban, Oakland's Eddie Erdelatz, Dallas's Hank Stram, and New York's Sammy Baugh) from being NFL assistants (Houston's Lou Rymkus and Buffalo's Buster Ramsey) or from Canada (Denver's Frank Filchock). Only Gillman had been a head coach, much less a *successful* head coach, in the NFL.

Gillman was an old-fashioned coach in that, like Paul Brown and Vince Lombardi, he was *the boss*. Chargers owner Barron Hilton wanted it that way almost as much as Gillman. "Barron Hilton was a great owner and a perfect gentleman," Gillman said in looking back. "He never meddled. I was my own general manager, so I was in charge of the whole football operation. I think that's the way it should be. It's the coach's funeral. He's the guy who dies, he's the guy they bury, so he's the guy who should run the show."

Gillman could tyrannize his players. One remembered, "Those who prayed before games didn't ask for victory or immunity from injury. Instead, they prayed, 'Please God, don't let me be the first to screw up.'"

But, if he was old-fashioned in his insistence on complete control, his game plans were years ahead of other coaches. Standard wisdom said a team had to run the ball to win. Such successful NFL offenses as Cleveland's and Green Bay's followed the "run first" principle. To Gillman, that was bassackwards. "The big play comes from the pass. The runners get you the first downs and give you ball control, but if you want to score, you have to pass. Our concept was to use the entire field, 100 yards long and 53 and 1/3 yards wide. This stretched the defense and made it harder to cover the five receivers we sent out on every play. All of the receivers' routes were compatible, so the quarterback had a choice based on what he saw downfield."

The Chargers started slowly, losing three of their first five games, but then roared to eight wins in their last nine. Coach Gillman concentrated on putting points on the scoreboard. His defense was only ordinary, al-

though NFL-retread tackle Volney Peters was strong. With Dallas up and down, the Chargers won the Western Division with a 10-4 mark.

Houston, with Blanda, Billy Cannon, and a pair of ace receivers in Bill Groman and Charley Hennigan, had no problem winning the Eastern Division. Under Coach Lou Rymkus, a hard-as-nails ex-Cleveland Browns tackle, the Oilers won ten of 14 games to easily outdistance the 7-7 Titans in second place.

The first American Football League Championship was settled at Houston on New Year's Day 1961. The Oilers and Chargers had both spent the season lighting up scoreboards, so the mostly defensive first half was a surprise. Forty-one year old Ben Agajanian, who'd been kicking in pro football since *before* the All-America Conference, accounted for nine points for the Chargers on three field goals of 38, 22, and 27 yards. Blanda, nine years younger than Agajanian, put Houston in front 10-9 by throwing a 17-yard TD pass to his fullback Dave Smith and kicking the extra point and later an 18-yard field goal.

In the second half, both sides opened up a bit. Blanda hit Bill Groman for a seven-yard touchdown to move the score to 17–9 Houston, but the Chargers closed the gap to a point on Paul Lowe's two-yard run. In the fourth quarter, Blanda tossed a short pass to Billy Cannon flying out of the backfield, and Billy took it all the way for an 88-yard touch. With an eight-point lead, the Oilers would have been safe in the NFL. But Los Angeles was still in striking distance because the AFL had its "college-style" two-point conversion. Twice the Chargers drove into Houston territory only to lose the ball on downs, the last time with less than a minute left.

A pre-geriatric George Blanda led the Houston Oilers to back-to-back championships in the AFL's first two seasons, before ending the decade with the Oakland Raiders.

When the final gun sounded, the AFL had actually completed its first season.

Postmortems within the AFL were generally upbeat, at least those that reached publication. Assistant commissioner Milt Woodward typified the party line: "We might have died last year, but we got great acceptance. We might yet lose a franchise along the way, as has happened to the NFL many times, but we're definitely in business to stay. We've got too many other cities waiting in line to join up."

Most neutrals judged the new league's success by how it stacked up against the old league. Joe Kuharich had once been the Redskins' coach but by the 1960s he presided over a less-than-successful reign at his alma mater Notre Dame. He predicted, "It will take them three years to organize and field solid teams of 22 to 33 men that can play effectively as a unit. If the AFL can stand its ground for that long and battle for top names, it should survive profitably. The market is there."

Woodward more or less echoed Kuharich's three-years-to-parity evaluation when he said, "We'd like to think we could take on their champion in another two or three years."

One man who'd seen both leagues plus the Canadian from the inside was Frank Tripucka. His comparison: "The difference is in size. We have one 270-pound tackle at Denver, and we think it would be just great to have another. But in the NFL they're all big. Club for club, we simply cannot cope with that kind of depth and size. For the same reason, the Canadian clubs couldn't meet us on an equal basis. But I'll say this. Match our all-league team against the NFL's and let the offensive and defensive units play without substitutes—then we'd do all right. It's mostly a matter of depth and experience. We'll catch up eventually."

Aside from survival (which, of course, was the most important thing) and signing Billy Cannon and a few other "name" stars, the AFL was decidedly the "other" league in its first few seasons. One possible way toward equalization was through the courts. The upstarts filed a $10 million suit against the National Football League, charging the older league with monopoly and conspiracy in the areas of expansion, player signings, and television contracts. A key exhibit for the AFL was Dallas, where they contended the NFL Cowboys had been installed only to block Hunt's Texans. If successful in proving their point, the AFL asked treble damages.

The suit dragged on for two and a half years. Finally, on May 21, 1962, after a two-month trial, Judge Roszel Thomsen of the U.S. District Court in Baltimore ruled against the AFL.

Equality would have to come on the field, not through the courts.

————————

The American Football League, much to the surprise of many, completed its inaugural season and came back for more. But it wasn't all beer and skittles. The league had averaged only 16,000 in attendance per game. Those kind of figures hadn't been good enough for the NFL since the 1930s.

The AFL's 1961 draft brought in no big names of the Billy Cannon variety as the teams concentrated on linemen. Buffalo signed virtually a whole offensive line in Ken Rice, Billy Shaw, Stew Barber, and Al Bemiller. Rice, the first pick, would play most of his career in Oakland, but the other three would be regulars when the Bills won a championship in 1964. The Chargers shored up their defense with huge end Earl Faison and even more huge tackle Ernie Ladd. They also added a versatile running back in Washington State's Keith Lincoln and a useful defensive back in Claude Gibson. The Texans successfully drafted four players who would win all-AFL honors: linebacker E. J. Holub, defensive end Jerry Mays, offensive tackle Jim Tyrer, and tight end Fred Arbanas. Boston did okay with offensive lineman Charlie Long and defensive end Larry Eisenhauer.

But Houston, Denver, New York, and Oakland were unable to sign a single draft choice who proved of any consequence in the 1961 season. The Oilers, however, came up with a player coup when Chicago Bears receiver Willard Dewveall joined Houston as a free agent after playing out his option. That made him the first former NFL player to join the AFL who was not in some way a castoff. A former SMU Mustang, Dewveall wanted to play in Texas, but the clincher may have been his off-season vocation in the insurance biz. A year before coming to Houston he wrote a tidy little million-dollar policy for Mrs. K. S. "Bud" Adams.

————————

Only one franchise move took place for the AFL's second season. After absorbing $900,000 in losses with a 10-4 championship team, Barron Hilton bid a not-so-fond farewell to Los Angeles and moved his Chargers to San Diego, where he was given Balboa Stadium rent free. As far as Hilton was concerned, the NFL Rams hadn't forced him out of LA, NFL television had. On the day the Chargers clinched the Western Division title with an exciting 41–33 victory over the Broncos, only 9,928 fans showed up. Several million other Los Angelinos, including more than 3,000 Charger season-ticket holders, stayed home to watch the Colts and 49ers play on the tube.

Meanwhile, Bob Howsam sold the Broncos to a group headed by Calvin Kunz.

The 1961 Western Division race was no race at all. Dallas continued to flounder with erratic quarterbacking. Denver had a quarterback and not much else. The only thing that kept them out of last place was that Oakland was even worse. The Raiders lost their first two games 55–0 to Houston and 44–0 to San Diego. Coach Eddie Erdelatz was fired. Under new coach Marty Feldman, the team scored 35 points against Dallas but gave up 42. While all this was unfolding, San Diego raced off the mark with 11 straight wins.

The Eastern Division was a donnybrook, with Buffalo the only noncontender. The Titans led early in the season, but their cream-puff defense and the distractions wrought by Harry Wismer proved too much. Wismer criticized Coach Sammy Baugh to the press more than once, apparently in the hope that Baugh would walk out on his air-tight, three-year contract and save Wismer a few dollars. (The story is that Wismer named the team after he saw the old New York Giants sign outside the Polo Grounds and realized he could save money by shifting letters and buying only a "T".) Certainly Baugh, who brought his team of mostly misfits in at 7-7 for the second straight year, deserved better.

In 1962, Wismer got nasty. He hired ex-Chicago Bear all-pro center Clyde "Bulldog" Turner as head coach and demoted Baugh, who still had a year to run on his contract, to "kicking coach." Baugh dug in his Texas heels and refused to be bulldogged into quitting just to save Harry a few bucks. He faithfully came to practices, even though he had nothing to do. At last Wismer had to pay him off.

Boston stood at 2-3 five games into the '61 season when Coach Lou Saban was fired. Under Mike Holovak, the Patriots caught fire and roared through the rest of the season with only one loss. One was enough, however. In Houston, the Oilers staggered from the blocks even more badly than Boston, going 1-3-1. The blame, right or wrong, fell on Coach Lou Rymkus and his boot camp regimen. "If you smiled [in practice]," said one Oiler, "it was like you committed a crime. If a guy laughed, Lou would stop practice and lecture us on being hard-nosed." When Rymkus was replaced by kinder, gentler Wally Lemm, the Oilers went undefeated through their final nine games. More important than Lemm's personality was his decision to turn the quarterback job back over to George Blanda, whom Rymkus had benched in favor of young Jackie Lee. Blanda responded by throwing for 36 touchdowns, a new pro record. Charley Hennigan led all AFL receivers with 1,746 yards, another new pro record, and Bill Groman tied Don Hutson's NFL record with 17 TD pass receptions. The Blanda air attack, coupled with AFL rushing leader Billy Cannon, took the Oilers to 513 points, still one more pro record.

The championship game, held at Balboa Stadium, figured to be an

Charley Hennigan gathers in a reception despite pressure from a Broncos defender.

offensive shoot-out. Instead, the 29,556 who attended saw a defensive struggle. Blanda's 35-yard TD pass to Cannon and his 42-yard field goal were the Oilers' only points, but the high-powered Chargers could muster only a single field goal in reply.

———————

Houston, Boston, and Buffalo showed slight increases in attendance in 1961. San Diego nearly doubled the turnouts the Chargers had gotten in Los Angeles. It was enough to get the league average up to 17,904 per game—small potatoes next to the NFL's 40,675. TV ratings were up, too, but still lagging behind the NFL's. After two years, the older league was winning in the stands, on TV, and in signing college stars.

In order to improve the latter, AFL owners quietly held a secret draft in November—so quiet that they didn't mention it to Commissioner Joe Foss. Each club took six name players from the year's top college seniors. When Foss learned about the end run, he ruled the secret draft invalid in favor of the official draft scheduled for December. Harry Wismer, who'd tabbed Syracuse All-America Ernie Davis for his Titans, exploded, calling for Foss to be fined, fired, drawn and quartered. Foss for his part publicly mused about having Wismer replaced as franchise owner in New York. A showdown seemed inevitable, but it didn't come. In January, the owners tore up Foss's old contract and gave him a new one for five years. That spring, Foss was best man at Wismer's wedding!

———

The good AFL news in 1962 was that attendance went up to 20,487 per game; the bad news was that it was still less than half what the NFL was getting.

In Denver, where the sad-sack 1961 Broncos had barely averaged 10,000, a surprising early season surge that got the 1962 team to 7-2 before they lost their last five lifted attendance to an average of 25,059. New coach Jack Faulkner, a former Sid Gillman assistant, instituted such revolutionary ideas for the Broncos as actual game plans. Happily, he canned the yuck-yellow and brown team colors in favor of orange, blue, and white. The hated vertically striped socks were burned at a public bonfire. Faulkner received coach-of-the-year honors, but his offense still consisted entirely of Frank Tripucka-to-Lionel Taylor.

———

Houston began its defense of its 1961 championship with its third coach in three years. Wally Lemm parlayed his ten straight '61 wins into being named head coach of the NFL's St. Louis Cardinals. To replace him, the Oilers brought in Frank "Pop" Ivy, who just happened to have spent the previous four years as Cardinals coach. George Blanda was sidelined by a thyroid operation during much of training camp, and when he came back, his passes had lost some of their zing. He threw an incredible 42 interceptions during the season. To further complicate matters, Billy Cannon was only so-so because of a bad back and a bad case of the anti-Ivy's.

Through it all, Houston kept winning. They still had all those receivers, and sawed-off fullback Charley Tolar rushed for over a thousand yards. The Oilers' 11-3 record was actually the best of their three years and good enough to hold off the Boston Patriots, whose championship pretensions were derailed when quarterback Babe Parilli suffered a broken collar bone against the Oilers in the season's tenth game.

Buffalo, under Lou Saban, eked out a winning season, 7-6-1, thanks to a tight defense and a new fullback—246-pound Carlton "Cookie" Gilchrist, a free spirit imported from Canada where he'd set a passel of records. Cookie never went to college, but it wasn't for any lacking in smarts. He just wanted to get on with his football career and went north to become a star while still in his teens. With eight years of Canadian football behind him, Gilchrist wasn't your typical rookie, but then he wasn't your typical fullback either. He had the size and power to smash any line to tinders, but once he got in the open he could outrun most defensive backs. In short, he was the AFL's answer to the NFL's Jim Brown. He broke

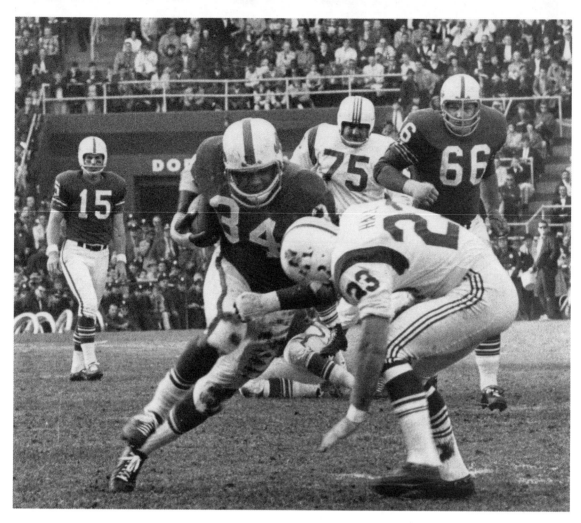

Carlton "Cookie" Gilchrist, the AFL's Jim Brown.

in by leading the league in rushing with 1,096 yards on 214 carries. He scored rushing touchdowns in seven straight games and led with 13 for the season.

Out west, San Diego collapsed to 4-10 under an unbelievable run of injuries. The biggest loss was quarterback Jack Kemp, who went out with a broken finger early in the season. The loss became permanent when Kemp was picked up on waivers for a paltry $100 by the Buffalo Bills. He'd been placed on the injured deferred list but through a mix-up wasn't removed soon enough. He became fair game for the Bills, who had desperately needed a quarterback since their beginning. Gillman was ready to spit nails, but his blunt manner hadn't made any friends among the league's other coaches, and they were happy to see someone one-up Sid. After losing the AFL's first two championship games, Kemp had acquired something of a can't-win-the-big-ones reputation, but without him, the

Chargers didn't come close to getting into the big one. Rookie QB John Hadl wasn't ready to handle Gillman's intricate offense.

With the Chargers struggling, attendance fell off in San Diego. Barron Hilton gave some thought to selling out or moving the franchise but finally announced: "I've decided it's just as easy to lose $300,000 in San Diego as anywhere else. After all, it's not fashionable to make money these days."

Even with healthy players, the Chargers would have had trouble heading off the Dallas Texans. For two years, the Texans had been credited with having the most talent in the league—except at quarterback. In '62, they got one.

Len Dawson had been a hot property back in 1957. The Cleveland Browns wanted to draft the Purdue quarterback, but the Pittsburgh Steelers beat them to it, and Cleveland had to settle for Jim Brown instead. After much fanfare, Dawson found a place on the Steelers' bench and stayed there for three years. The Browns finally got hold of him in 1960. They dusted off a spot on *their* bench and proceeded to let him watch Browns' games for free for two seasons. Before the '62 season, Dawson asked for his release. By then, the Browns had pegged him as just another overrated college star who flopped with the pros.

But Texans' coach Hank Stram had been an assistant at Purdue when Dawson was terrific. He believed the magic was still there. The Texans signed Dawson and exiled their former quarterback, Cotton Davidson, to Oakland. Dawson didn't have the howitzer arm of, say, Y. A. Tittle, but he was deadly accurate—the same kind of smart thrower as Bart Starr of the Packers. Under Dawson, the Texans whipped through the first half of the season. In their tenth game they brushed off upstart Denver 24–3 to move their record to 8–2 and the Western Division race was over.

Dawson led the AFL in passing, his first of four titles, and was named league player of the year. All-AFL halfback Abner Haynes ran for 1,019 yards and scored 19 touchdowns. AFL Rookie of the Year Curtis McClinton rushed for 604 yards. Other all-league or near-all-league performers were receiver Chris Burford, tight end Fred Arbanas, tackle Jim Tyrer, defensive linemen Jerry Mays and Mel Branch, linebackers E. J. Holub and Sherrill Headrick, and defensive backs Bobby Hunt, Bobby Ply, Dave Grayson, and Johnny Robinson.

For Stram, there was double vindication—both for his faith in Dawson and for himself as a head coach. Until taking over the Texans in 1960, he'd always been an assistant. Although widely admired as an innovator, some fans questioned his ability to run the whole show, especially when the obviously talented Texans disappointed in their first two seasons.

"We called him 'The Mentor,' " remembers Otis Taylor, who first played for Stram at Kansas City in 1965. "He laid down the rules, but in a friendly way. Things were going to be done in his way.

"Sometimes we tried to play tricks on him. I know I tried like hell. Like sometimes I'd get a little angry when he'd keep us late at practice. I'd tell Len [Dawson] to throw me a sideline pass so I could crush him. But he was always a little ahead of us—moving around.

"Sometimes during practice you'd wonder if the man had a heart. Then you'd be coming in and he'd have the clubhouse man pick up some barbecue—Kansas City's a great barbecue town—and two or three kegs of beer. Three or four hundred dollars' worth. And he'd say, 'Hey, guys, it's on me.' You wanted to kill him one minute, and then you'd say, well, the guy's all right.

"He was a player's coach."

––––––––

The AFL Championship Game, held two days before Christmas at Houston, was one of the most unusual—make that strangest—ever. It went into overtime, and just like the Colts–Giants extended game of 1958 boosted the NFL's stock, the Dallas-Houston overtime game called attention to the AFL. Not only did it set a new length record, but more important, it kept television viewers across the country watching well into the evening.

It began as a rout. The first half was all Dallas. Tommy Brooker kicked a 16-yard first-quarter field goal to put the Texans in front. In the second quarter, Abner Haynes scored touchdowns on a 28-yard pass from Dawson and on a two-yard run. Holding a 17–0 lead at the half, Dallas seemed to have the game well in hand. But Blanda brought his Oilers back in the second half. He fired a 15-yard scoring pass to Willard Dewveall early in the third quarter. Four minutes into the fourth and supposed final quarter, Blanda tightened the game with a 31-yard field goal. Then, with about five minutes to go, Charley Tolar plunged over from the one and Blanda's extra point tied the score at 17 all. That's the way it stood when the gun sounded, with each team having won a half.

Dallas coach Hank Stram decided to kick off in overtime to keep the wind at his back. But Texans' captain Abner Haynes became confused on the coin toss and mistakenly shouted, "We'll kick to the clock!" Houston had both the ball and the wind.

It didn't do them any good. Dallas put on the clamps and the overtime period stretched on, breaking the old Colts-Giants record. Shortly before the end of the "fifth" quarter, Bill Hull of the Texans intercepted a Blanda pass at midfield. It was Blanda's fifth interception of the day and 47th of the season, and it proved fatal. With fullback Jack Spikes making the key plays, Dallas moved down the field into the "sixth" quarter to place the

Abner Haynes, the
most popular Dallas
Texan.

ball at the Houston 19. Brooker came in, and at 17:54 of overtime booted
a 25-yard field goal to make the Texans champs.

———————

Lamar Hunt's league was on the brink of breaking through, but his team
was failing at the Dallas box office. With a championship team, and one
that played exciting football to boot, the Texans still barely outdrew the
5-8-1 NFL Cowboys. Hunt didn't like to think what would happen if the
Cowboys ever started winning. Like so many cinematic Texans and Cowboys, he'd discovered: "This town ain't big enough for both of us."

83

Neither team could live on a continuation of the three-year attendance figures:

	TEXANS			COWBOYS		
Year	Record	Attendance	Average	Record	Attendance	Average
1960	8-6-0	171,500	24,500	0-11-1	128,500	21,417
1961	6-8-0	123,000	17,571	4-9-1	172,000	24,571
1962	11-3-0	155,409	22,201	5-8-1	152,446	21,778

On May 14, 1963, Hunt surrendered Dallas to the Cowboys and announced that he was moving his Texans to Kansas City. KC mayor H. Roe Bartle sold him with a promise to enlarge Municipal Stadium, a $1 rent for the first two years, and a guarantee of tripling season ticket sales. Hunt also liked the idea that there wouldn't be another pro football team within 250 miles of his. Of course, Kansas City *Texans* was out. The new name, Hunt said, would be Chiefs. By some strange coincidence, "Chief" just happened to be Bartle's nickname.

For those interested in trivia, the Texans weren't the first champions to pull up stakes. The NFL Canton Bulldogs were shifted to Cleveland in 1924 after winning the title, and more recently, the Cleveland Rams won the 1945 championship and then headed west for 1946.

The Chiefs' first public appearance in Kansas City was disconcerting. They expected a big turnout for an August preseason affair with the Chargers, but only 5,721 showed up. Before the game, Lamar Hunt had his players autograph 45 footballs with instructions to punt or pass them into the stands during warm-ups. When the players saw the sparse turnout, they asked if Mr. Hunt would prefer to have the football's hand-delivered. To add insult to injury, when the Chiefs entered their locker room, they found that the Kansas City American League baseball team, with whom they shared facilities, had nailed boards over the lockers.

Among the excuses given for the poor turnout was that fans stayed home to watch Kansas City's baseball game televised from Cleveland. Eventually, Hunt's Chiefs had the last laugh. Attendance at their games improved, and a few years later, the Athletics baseball team moved to Oakland.

If Hunt lost a little face in the shift from Dallas, at least he stopped losing money. Despite a 15,000 season-ticket sale, the team's attendance for seven home games was about 5,000 below what they'd got in Dallas in '62, but buoyed by a better deal on the stadium, the Chiefs made a small profit in their first season in Kansas City.

———

By the end of 1962, everyone in the AFL knew that Harry Wismer had been a mistake. The man could antagonize anyone within screeching distance and was presiding over a disaster in New York.

Most fans thought of Harry Wismer as a radio sportscaster. That's how they first heard him. He broadcast a ton of bowl games and games of the Detroit Lions, Washington Redskins, and Notre Dame. The Notre Dame games were done as voice over on day-old tapes, and that gave Harry a chance to look like a football genius. He'd announce that "it looks like a passing situation" and sure enough the Irish would throw on the next down. Or he'd tip the listeners that so-and-so was in the Irish backfield just before so-and-so ran the ball. If you didn't know Harry had gone over the tape beforehand, you'd figure he really knew his stuff.

Harry Wismer.

Harry's style over a microphone as well as in real life was top-of-his-lungs all the way. Sportswriter Jimmy Cannon had it right when he said Harry announced "a football game like a holdup victim hollering for a cop." It was Harry who relined a football field during one hectic broadcast by screaming into a microphone—you must have heard of it—"he's up to the 40, the 45, the 50, the 55 . . ."

The truth was Harry did sports broadcasts only incidentally. His real avocation was selling. And his product was Harry Wismer. If Harry could take ball carriers to unprecedented yard lines, he took himself a lot farther than anyone would have predicted back on that day in the 1930s when, as a hustling undergraduate, he spent a Saturday afternoon spotting for Bill Stern and Graham McNamee while they broadcast a Michigan State game. Stern and McNamee were two of the biggest stars of radio sports, and Harry saw right away where he wanted to go.

Before you could say "testing, one, two, three," Harry was up to his limber lips on the college radio station. When spring came around, he launched the first of his many promotions—getting MSU football coach Charlie Bachman named to coach the squad for the annual College All-Star Game held every August in Chicago. Some say that most of the names signed to the numerous petitions Harry delivered were actually penned by Harry himself while perusing a few dozen telephone books. Be that as it may, Bachman came in a strong second thanks to Harry's drumbeating.

More important than whether Bachman was put in charge of the collegians, at least as far as Harry was concerned, was that his hustle impressed G. A. Richards, who owned both the Detroit Lions and radio station WJR. Richards put the still-undergraduate Wismer on the air five nights a week as the "Lions' Cub Reporter," and Harry was on his way. The next year, Harry picked Detroit U. coach Charles "Gus" Dorais as his all-star candidate, and this time he pushed him over the top. In 1941, Harry cemented his position as a Big Man in Detroit by marrying Betty Bryant, a favorite niece of Henry Ford.

Seeking new worlds to conquer, Harry moved to Washington, DC, in 1942 where he broadcast Redskins' games and perfected his act. For one thing, he was a consummate name-dropper and no name was too big. "As I said to Harry Truman the other day . . ." or "My friend Bob Taft told me . . ." were great conversational gambits to turn heads and hush rival voices at any cocktail party. Another of Harry's ploys was to congratulate everyone he met—senator, screen star, taxi driver. He figured that nearly everyone had just won something, accomplished something, or completed something and would be pleased to have Harry take note. But mostly Harry moved inexorably ahead in the world with an upbeat, nonstop, self-assured verbal assault that would leave lesser mortals gasping for air. A short, plump ball of energy, he filled a room, in Bob Curran's phrase, "with a suffocating ebullience."

To be fair, he wasn't all bluff, bluster, and balls. In the 1950s, when Harry owned stock in the Redskins, Halfback Vic Janowicz's career was ended by an auto accident. Harry got the press going about the shoddy treatment the 'Skins gave Janowicz as soon as he was of no further use to them. Eventually, he provided the young man with some funds out of his own pocket. He also raised some of majority owner George Preston Marshall's hackles by criticizing the team's lily-white hiring policy.

And to continue to be fair, Harry had a bad situation being stuck in New York's Polo Grounds. And he didn't have Hunt's or Adams's millions to fall back on when the going got rough, which it did practically from the Titans' first day of existence. Harry said he'd lost $1,200,000 in his first two years. Sometimes he quoted a higher figure, but then Harry was always a little wobbly on numbers.

To be *completely* fair, he brought most of his troubles on himself. His practice of asserting phantom attendances and his habit of headline-making announcements that were forgotten a day later cost him any credibility he may have had when he arrived. His public feud with Joe Foss showed that he had no allies around the league, and his humiliating treatment of pro football icon Sammy Baugh left him looking mean-spirited as well as cheap. His "ticket office"—Harry's apartment with tickets laid out on his bed and a Swedish-speaking maid making sales—reeked of fly-by-night.

"Curly" Johnson, a Titan who arrived in 1961 and stayed through 1968, recalled: "We were playing the San Diego Chargers back when they had a great team . . . and we were beating them, like 17–14. There were about three minutes left in the game, and it was getting pretty dark out. So the official comes over to our coach, Bulldog Turner, and tells him to phone upstairs and get the lights turned on. Anyway, Bulldog calls up, and Harry tells him. 'We're doing just fine in the dark. Keep it that way.' See, it would have cost Harry $8,000 to turn those lights on."

The AFL desperately needed a competitive team in the country's largest TV market, but the Titans threatened to pull the whole league into a black hole. The league was learning that "If you *can't* make it there, you *can't* make it anywhere."

Wismer did find one way to save money in 1962. He stopped paying his bills. Two and a half months into the season, East Stroudsburg College, where the Titans trained for six weeks, was still writing pleading letters for what was owed them. Curly Johnson was given a $1,500 check for reporting. It bounced. "Later in camp, the team was scrimmaging, and Turner told me I couldn't scrimmage. So I asked him why, and he said, 'Between me and you, we're gonna make like you're a troublemaker and get rid of you because we can't pay that bonus.' "

When the players' pay was late in September, they threatened a strike until Wismer came up with the money. One day in San Diego, the charter bus didn't show up to take the players back to their hotel after practice because the bus company hadn't been paid. By late October, the trainer was running out of tape and the socks weren't being laundered. The public relations firm representing the team quit for lack of payment. In November, the team's paychecks bounced. The league announced it would assume the costs of running the Titans for the remainder of the season. While the Titans-as-business drew headlines, the Titans-as-football-team drew only apathy. Wismer continued to announce crowds of 20,000 or more, but the actual attendance *totaled* a mere 36,161 for seven home games. Traffic accidents were better attended than some Titans' games.

At one point, Bud Adams handed Wismer $10,000 in cash to use as he saw fit. Harry threw his arms around Adams and cried. "The ship is sinking!" he sobbed.

As November wore on, Wismer began making new announcements about the imminent sale of the team. One day he proclaimed a group headed by Frank Leahy would buy the team and move it to Long Island, but no one ever heard of that one again. Harry said he'd sell most of the shares for $1,750,000 but retain a minority interest. Nobody wanted Wismer as a partner in any percentage, Joe Foss told the press.

The AFL player draft came and went on December 2 with the Titans picking LSU halfback Jerry Stovall and 26 other collegians they had no chance of signing until the finances were straightened out. The season dragged to an end with the Titans in last place in the standings as well as at the box office. Still no sale.

At last, on March 28, a five-man syndicate composed of David A.

Al Davis.

"Sonny" Werblin, Townsend B. Martin, Leon Hess, Donald C. Lillis, and Philip H. Iselin purchased the franchise for $1,000,000. A month later, the new owners hired Weeb Ewbank, the man who'd won the overtime '58 NFL championship as Colts coach, as the new head coach of the team they rechristened the Jets. The Titans became just a bad memory.

On December 16, 1962, the Oakland Raiders defeated the Boston Patriots 20–0 before 8,000 close friends at Candlestick Park. It was both Oakland's first win and last game of the season, leaving them with a record 1-13 record. In ten years of American Football League football, no AFL team would compile a worse won-lost mark.

The Raiders went coach-shopping. For them it was a seller's market and all no-sales. The list of prospective coaches who turned them down would fill a good-sized playbook. The Raiders were floundering, with apparently no idea which way to go and very little money to do it with. They looked like a new coach's one-way ticket to being unemployed and probably unemployable within a season. One prospect who just said no several times was Al Davis, then comfortably ensconced as one of Sid Gillman's assistants at San Diego.

That Davis would soon be a pro head coach *somewhere* seemed obvious. He'd been moving up for more than a decade. After a nondescript three-sport career at Wittenberg College and Syracuse University, he'd landed as line coach at little Adelphi College in 1950 and immediately began making waves with technical football articles in several coaches' magazines. Drafted into the army, he coached the Ft. Belvoir, Virginia, football team to, among other things, a squad-game victory over the University of Maryland's national champs. He spent 1954 on the Baltimore Colts staff learning the pro ropes, then took a job as line coach at The Citadel. Before joining Gillman with the Chargers, Al spent three years as line and defensive coach at USC.

Under Gillman, Davis was known as a teacher and master recruiter who convinced such stars as Lance Alworth, Earl Faison, and Paul Lowe that their futures lay with the Chargers. Oakland was used to waving as their most prized draft choices departed for the NFL, so Davis's powers of persuasion would certainly be welcome. In fact, the only knock Oakland part-owner Wayne Valley heard was that Davis "would do anything to win," certainly a useful quality for a team with only three victories in two years.

But though Oakland was ready for Al, Al wasn't ready for Oakland. "I had a good job, and I didn't need the money," he said later. Why jump out of the feather bed into the fire? The Raiders had been drifting downstream for three years. Were they at last ready to settle on a direction and stick to it? Would they spend the money? Could they be patient?

Wayne Valley assured him yes, yes, and yes. Davis would be in charge. He'd have the support and bankrolls of the owners. And he'd have a three-year contract. On January 15, 1963, Davis was named head coach and general manager of the Oakland Raiders.

In some ways, what Davis wrought in his first year with the Raiders resembled the Lombardi miracle in Green Bay. In some ways, it was better. Like Lombardi, Davis first had to change his team's attitude. But where the Packers could look to a golden past, the Raiders had never been any good. It was a little early for the motto, "Pride and Poise." There wasn't anything to be proud of. But Davis, from the first, stressed poise. If the team could accomplish that, the pride would come. "No matter what the scoreboard says, keep your poise," he told them. "Remember, you're the Raiders of Oakland."

At Green Bay, Lombardi had inherited a large talent pool just waiting for the right man to shape and lead. Davis's pool wasn't so deep. He had a mismatched pair of quarterbacks in steady Tom Flores, who had recovered from his lung infection, and streaky Cotton Davidson. Other leftovers included a good runner in Clem Daniels, and a great center in Jim Otto. A few others were keepers, but mostly the Raiders needed a complete overhaul. More than half the players on 1963 roster were first-year Raiders.

Otto remembers that Davis "brought some older athletes in who still had some football in them and mixed them with younger guys. And through hard work—a *lot* of hard work—we started building a team."

A key addition was receiver Art Powell, who'd played out his option with the Titans. Big, fast, and able to catch anything thrown within his zip code, Powell was said to play just as hard as he was in a mood to on any given day. Davis convinced him to sign with the Raiders, and Powell had a fantastic season, catching 73 passes for 1,304 yards and 16 touchdowns. The Raiders' reputation as a haven for "difficult" players and for getting superior production from them began with Powell.

According to Jim Otto, the Raiders' reputation as the league's black hat brigade missed the point. "If there was a mystique or anything involved with being the 'bad boys,'" he says, "it was just that we played hard, solid football the entire game. In the fourth quarter, we could do things no other team could do because we'd been doing it all week in practice.

"We played hard, tough football in the beginning of the game, in the end of the game. And for some of the guys, in the bars after the game."

To shore up the league's leakiest defense, Davis got hard-nosed middle linebacker Archie Matsos from Buffalo. Rookie tackle Dave Costa and leftover end Dalva Allen were solid up front. With people finally making tackles in front of them, safety Tommy Morrow and cornerback Fred Williamson, the future movie star, improved to all-league status.

The team gained confidence by winning three of its five preseason games, the first time the Raiders had had a winning exhibition record. Then they opened the regular season with surprising wins over Houston and Buffalo. Two games in, Davis had doubled the win total of '62. But then Clem Daniels sustained a deep thigh bruise that knocked him out for four games, crippling the running attack. They lost four straight, the last three on a dismal eastern road trip. Through it all, Davis harped on poise, poise, keep the poise.

The Raiders returned to Oakland, Daniels returned to the lineup, and victory returned with a 49–26 pasting of the Titans. The next week, the impossible happened. Oakland topped the Chargers 24–23 at Balboa Stadium. The unlikely Raiders were back to .500. They roared down the stretch to six more wins, including another triumph over the Chargers, 41–27. On December 22, they outlasted Houston in a shoot-out that would have done the Earp boys proud, 52–49, to finish an astounding 10-4. Ironically, San Diego, whom they'd beaten twice, lost only one other game and won the division.

Nevertheless, it was a heady season along the Bay. The quarterback tandem of Flores and Davidson threw 31 touchdown passes between them, with Art Powell accounting for more than half. Clem Daniels was named the AFL Player of the Year as he set a new league record with 1,099 rushing yards. Fans were blithely predicting a championship in '64.

Al Davis knew better. There'd be no bushwhacking unwary opponents in '64, and his team still had too many gaps. One coach insisted that nine Raider starters ranked last in the league at their positions. At a banquet honoring his team, Davis pulled no punches: "You've got to understand. It isn't realistic to hope for all good bounces, to think of a title in 1964 or 1965. We're building."

By 1967, the building phase would be complete. But by then, Davis was off the sideline and up in the owner's box.

———

Houston was finally deposed as eastern AFL champ in '63. In fact, the Oilers fell to a losing record. Oiler fans insisted the cause could be found in the injuries that limited runner Billy Cannon to seven quarters and knocked star defensive end Don Floyd out of the last five games. The truth was that the team wasn't growing with the league. Players who'd looked pretty good only three years ago were now average or less, even though they played at the same level. George Blanda could still throw at age 37 and Charley Hennigan and Willard Dewveall could still go and get 'em, but the less glamorous positions were falling into the doldrums.

With an opening at the top, the Buffalo Bills under Lou Saban made a grab for the brass ring. Preseason poop said they'd make it. The Bills had quarterback Jack Kemp for a whole season and the league's newest ultimate weapon in 246-pound fullback Carlton "Cookie" Gilchrist. For a time, they even had a dangerous breakaway running threat in Roger Kochman. But Kochman suffered a leg injury so serious it not only ended his career, it nearly cost him the leg. And Kemp, still laboring under the charge that he couldn't win the big games, drew fire for on one hand passing too often and on the other hand being too willing to pull down the football and scramble.

Gilchrist, who set a new pro rushing record in December with 243 yards against New York, "did his own thing," in the parlance of the time. Controversial and outspoken, Cookie came close to matching his thousand-yard '62 season with 979, but his performances were less consistent. And his habit of speaking his mind began to wear thin on Saban. One day the coach fired him right on the practice field. Of course, things got fixed up, but after the season, Gilchrist demanded to be traded.

The Bills staggered out of the blocks, going 0-3-1 before they righted their ship. In the meantime, Boston forged ahead on the strength of a swarming defense, Babe Parilli's arm, and Gino Cappelletti's toe. The Bills and Patriots finished in a tie, both at 7-6-1, setting up a play-off for the eastern crown. In snowy War Memorial Stadium, Kemp lost another big one, 26–8.

Out west, the transplanted Chiefs-né-Texans were shocked when rookie runner Stone Johnson suffered a fatal injury in a preseason game. The trauma seemed to carry into the season, as the talent-laden team never got on track. In November, they even allowed themselves to be shut out by New York.

San Diego survived a pair of losses to surprising Oakland and an astounding rout by Denver—when the Chargers gave up 50 points—to take the western title. The supercharged Chargers could score from anywhere. The backfield boasted long-distance threats in Paul Lowe, who rushed for 1,010 yards, and Keith Lincoln, whose 826 yards gave him an average gain of 6.5 yards per carry. Receiver Lance Alworth, after an injury-plagued rookie season, became all-world as a sophomore, averaging 20 yards a catch. Triggering all this high-powered artillery was a quarterback new to the AFL but not to American fans. Tobin Rote had starred for the Packers and Lions in the 1950s, indeed he'd been the quarterback when Detroit

Paul Lowe.

downed the Browns 59–14 in the 1957 NFL Championship Game. A contract dispute sent him to Canada, where he continued to hone his passing skills until Sid Gillman lured him to San Diego. With Rote at the helm, the Chargers threw fewer passes than any team in the league, but they got better results, leading the AFL in completion percentage, average gain, and touchdowns per throw.

The Chargers' defense was spotty. Earl Faison, Ernie Ladd, safety Dick Harris and company shut people down most weeks, but every once in a while they could crack apart. In San Diego's three losses, they gave up 125 points.

The championship game turned on whether Boston's blitzing defense could stop the San Diego offense. In two previous meetings during the regular season, the Pats had lost but held the high-powered Chargers to a total of 20 points. Could they do it again? On the second play, the 30,127 people in Balboa Stadium knew the answer. No.

Keith Lincoln took a handoff from Rote and zoomed through the Patriots' middle for 56 yards. He was so keyed up, he went to the sideline and threw up. Rote quarterback-sneaked for the touchdown a few plays later. As soon as the Chargers got the ball back, Lincoln roared around end for 67 yards and the Chargers' second touchdown. The Patriots bravely answered with a touchdown of their own. But when Paul Lowe scored the third San Diego touchdown of the opening quarter on a 58-yard burst, Boston was ready for the fork. It was 31–10 at the half. The San Diego defense teed off on the Boston passers in the second half, knowing that the Pats had no choice but to throw or surrender. Lance Alworth added to the Chargers' touchdown parade with a 48-yard reception from Rote. Then Lincoln scored again on a 25-yard pass from John Hadl, and Hadl closed the touchdowning as Rote had opened it by sneaking into the end zone.

The 51–10 blitz set all sorts of offensive records, and Keith Lincoln had the best day of anyone with that surname since Gettysburg. He ran for 206 yards, averaging 15.8 per carry. He caught seven passes for another 123 yards, giving him a combined yardage of 329. And just for variety, he tossed a pass himself. And completed it for 20 yards.

Fans all over the country watched in awe. Many believed for the first time that an AFL team, or at least *this* AFL team, might actually be able to contend with an NFL club. Certainly the Chargers believed so. Had it been possible, they'd have challenged NFL champion Chicago to a showdown.

"That was probably our greatest team," Sid Gillman admitted. "There was no better end than Lance Alworth and no better lineman than Ron Mix. Those are Hall of Fame guys. There was no better guard than Walt Sweeney and no better pair of running backs than Keith Lincoln and Paul Lowe. Our championship game . . . was perfection. I really felt we could have beaten the Bears."

SID GILLMAN: "IT'S THE THROWING THAT PERMITS YOU TO RUN"

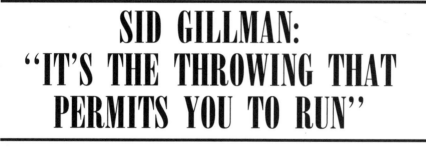

Sid Gillman is the acknowledged master of the passing game. His designs and innovations have been studied and copied by every modern pro coach, and it's reasonable to say that he and Lombardi were the two most influential coaches of the 1960s. That, even more than his 123 career pro victories, his five AFL division titles and 1963 championship, or his 1974 selection as coach of the year, earned him enshrinement in the Pro Football Hall of Fame in 1983.

His decision to cast his lot with the American Football League in 1960 after five years in charge of the Los Angeles Rams brought credibility to the league. The AFL's critics could sneer all they wanted about its minor league status, but they couldn't explain away Gillman's involvement.

———————

"Joining the Chargers seemed to be a great opportunity—the fact that Barron Hilton owned the club and I had the chance to become head coach and eventually the general manager and run the whole show. Frank Leahy started out as the general manager, but Frank got sick right quick. Something happened to him. I don't know what, but he had to give it up. I had the opportunity not only to coach but to completely run [the team]—to control my destiny—much more than I did with the Rams.

"I had some experience in the National Football League, and I put it to what I thought was good use. In the first couple of seasons, I was the only head coach in the league who had coached a major professional team, and to some, that helped give the league credibility. Someone said, 'He taught us how to go big league.' I hope I helped. Some of the teams, the Titans in New York and Denver, for example, took a while to get moving. But the Chargers were never a minor league team.

"We were successful the first two years on the field although we didn't draw well in Los Angeles and moved to San Diego in our second season.

We didn't win the championship, but we won the division both years. But then in 1962, we had a terrible year with injuries. Paul Lowe broke his arm and was lost for the season. Earl Faison, Lance Alworth, Chuck Allen, Charlie McNeil, Wayne Frazier all missed more than half the season. Twenty-three players missed at least two games with injuries. We lost three quarterbacks in one game. Ran out of quarterbacks! I had to sweep the floor and look around for a quarterback. I had five days to get one and we absolutely couldn't find one anyplace. That was one of our major problems. We lost Jack Kemp. We lost John Hadl. Every quarterback we had we lost. Try to play this game without a quarterback!

"Kemp ended up in Buffalo, and some have suggested that's why we went out and got Tobin Rote the next year. But I would have taken Rote anyway. I was from the National Football League, and he had been very successful in the NFL. He'd been playing in Canada, and he was ready to come back to the USA. To get him, we had to flip a coin with Buffalo, who held his rights. I called heads and it was heads. So we were able to get him.

"The 1963 team with Rote at quarterback was I think my best team. That was one of the greatest football teams of all time. Going into the championship game against Boston, we knew we were going to win. I'll tell you why. Their defense dogged—blitzed—on every down. It was feast or famine for them. That was Marion Campbell, who coached their defenses. You know, it's an amazing thing, I worked with him for about three years when we were with the Philadelphia Eagles, and he went from using an all-out blitz in '63 to being ultraconservative with the Eagles.

"The Patriots dogged so much in '63 that if we put somebody in motion—and we put a lot of people in motion, moved a lot of people—it screwed up their coverages. That was our game plan. If they were going to dog somebody, then we were going in motion. What it did was it changed their order, changed their assignments, and they had a lot of people running around like crazy. So we were the ones who had the feast.

"The whole American Football League started to get strong from that point on. There was a lot of money—a great deal of money—behind it. Every owner·except Harry Wismer in New York (and he didn't last very long) went out and spent money for talent. That's what it's all about. To be successful, you have to have the best available talent. And for the AFL it really started at about that time.

"Of course, back in the NFL, Vince Lombardi was having great success. Vince and I were great friends. As a matter of fact, I brought Vince in to coach at West Point in 1948. I was the line coach for Red Blaik at West Point at the time. I'd replaced Herman Hickman, who went on to Yale. One day Blaik pulled me aside. He said I needed an assistant. He'd invited this guy in and wanted me to interview him. If I wanted him there, we'd hire him. He said the fellow had been coaching at a small Catholic high school in Brooklyn. So Vince came over for a couple of days and we became friends. Then I left to go to the University of Cincinnati and they hired Vince, but not to take my place. He was an extra coach. Murray Warmath replaced me and he was actually the one who hired Vince.

"Well, later we were both in the National Football League. Vince was with the Giants and I was with the Rams. When I'd go east, I'd stay with Vince, and when he'd come west, he'd stay with me.

"Then, early in 1959, we were at a league meeting in Philadelphia. I went into the men's room and there was a guy there I hadn't seen since I was in college at Ohio State and working at a department store in Columbus. I was shocked to see this guy there in Philadelphia. We'd been friends in school and I asked him what he was doing. He said he had his own department store in Green Bay and he was looking for a coach. He was the chairman of the selection committee to find a coach for the Packers. I asked him if he'd be interested in Vince and he said he would be.

"So I went back out and found Vince. I said, 'Vince, there's a buddy of mine out here looking for a coach for Green Bay. Would you be interested?' He said yes he would. I said, 'I'll talk to him and make arrangements for you two to get together.' Now, I don't know that that's what got the job for Vince, but I think I played a part in his getting it."

———

When Gillman talks about his Chargers teams of the 1960s, there's pride in his voice. But when he gets into the nuts and bolts of designing an offense, he becomes more animated and speaks more quickly. Here, among the Xs and Os, is where his mind moves into overdrive.

"Lombardi's signature play was the power sweep. I used a quick toss. To a lot of people, they looked the same. In fact, Red Hickey, who coached the San Francisco 49ers, said the first time he saw the 'Lombardi Sweep' was when I ran it with the Rams. There was a difference though. Lombardi ran an option sweep; ours was predicated on getting outside.

"What Lombardi did was set up an option based on the tight end's block. As the halfback came across for the ball, he didn't run at full speed. He came with controlled speed so that he could key the block of the tight end on the linebacker. If the tight end took him out, the ball carrier broke inside. If he took him in, the ball carrier broke outside. Paul Hornung was made to order for that kind of sweep. He wasn't a speedster. He had good speed but not intense speed. With Lombardi's sweep, because of the option aspect, the line was loosened up a little bit. It was inside-outside on the block for his tight end.

"Our sweep came across with intense speed. We were designed to get outside, and our tight end was lined up tight. He was to drive the line-backer in so we could get outside and then cut back downfield. But our ball carrier was taught that when he hit the end area as he took the ball with intense speed, he still reserved the right to bring the ball back in if it wasn't clear outside. We were predicated on speed. Get there first. That was our total commitment. Anybody who couldn't run, couldn't play for me. Our two tackles, Ron Mix and Ernie Wright, had to be fast to lead the toss and they had to be able to pass protect.

"I've always felt that in order to run you've got to be able to throw. It's not the running that permits you to throw, it's the throwing that permits you to run. I'm tired of hearing coaches say that the first thing they were going to do was establish the run. So the first series it's three snaps and out. After that the stuff hits the fan. They start throwing the ball right quick because you can't run if you can't pass.

"We developed passing lanes. We worked out what we called a 'field balance' system. The field is divided into several areas. First, from the sideline out to the numbers on the field is what we called the 'number area.' Inside the numbers to the hash marks is the 'hook area.' And the hash marks are six yards apart, and that's the 'hash area.' Then, starting from the other sideline, you've got the same thing, number, hook, and hash areas. That gives you six areas to throw into. We wanted to make sure in our field balance that there was always someone to throw to.

"It's like a basketball game where you never have two people in the same spot. We didn't want two receivers in the same area. There's a guy on the outside; there's a guy in the number area. Put the tight end in the hash area. And then coming in from the other side, the same thing. If we could maintain that field balance, it made pass defense next to impossible.

"We put a tight end into the hash area and challenged anybody to cover him and that area. We drilled on that. Put the tight end in the area, say go ahead and cover him, and the quarterback takes a five-step drop and fires that ball in there. The depth of the drop was determined by the release our tight end could get.

"Our receivers followed very definite patterns. The system demanded that. Here's one example. We had a comeback call. The two outside receivers would run fly patterns and then comebacks in the outside or number areas. The tight end was in the hash area. Then our two backs knew what was available to them and were in the hook areas. Well, now we had mirror patterns across the field. And this gave our quarterback, know-ing this, the ability to pick out all his receivers quickly and throw to the open man.

"We were never confined to throwing to the weak side or the strong side. Even our receivers didn't know who the hell was going to get the ball. But we had five receivers going down the field in defined areas. And our quarterback, based on knowing where they are going to be, throws to the man with the least amount of coverage.

"Now we had the theory of vertical throwing. We just had to have a consistent quarterback throwing our 'ups.' We were going to attack the defense for all 100 yards. We had a field 100 yards long and 53 and 1/3 yards wide, and our formation was going to demand that the defense cover every inch of that field. We were always the widest team on the field. Our outside receivers forced their defensive backs to cover 53 and 1/3 yards wide and all the way down the field. And, good field balance made it possible for our quarterback to get a good read and throw to the man with the least coverage.

"We tried to give our quarterback simple and well-defined areas to throw in. Then before he got the snap, he had a reasonably good idea of where he was going to throw.

"That was our theory. The LA Raiders still go on that—and it still works."

7 GEORGE HALAS'S YEAR

In 1963, 68-year-old George "Papa Bear" Halas was the last still active of those intrepid pioneers who sat on running boards in a Canton, Ohio, auto showroom in 1920 and designed the National Football League out of hope and faith. Back then, he and a very few others had held the absurd belief that professional football might become more than a small town, pass-the-hat, ugly stepchild of college football—perhaps might someday even rival professional baseball for the spectator's begrudged and grungy dollar. In 1963, a lot of people were saying ol' George had been right all along.

In November, *U.S. News & World Report* said, "One of the strongest American business booms now under way is that in pro football." The NFL had taken 33 years—until 1952—to reach two million in attendance. Six years later, the league passed three million. In 1962, the four million barrier was shattered. *U.S. News* predicted another increase in 1963, a prediction that proved accurate when attendance rose to 4,163,643.

As for competing with baseball as the new national pastime, the article pointed out that the average NFL crowd was over 42,000 and that baseball drew five times as many people over a full season. But baseball played 12 times as many games and sold its tickets for one-third the price. In Cleveland, the baseball Indians drew 562,000 over an 81-game home schedule; the Browns in seven home games plus a preseason exhibition game topped them with 570,648.

The league's growing popularity was underlined by season-ticket sales. The Giants sold only 17,000 season tickets in 1956 when they won the league championship. Seven years later, they had to cut off sales at 51,000 to save a few seats for single-game customers. The only way to get a season ticket in Green Bay, the league's smallest city, was to wait for someone to die and will you one.

Not only were the stands packed, but Sunday afternoon found millions

"Papa Bear"
George Halas.

of fans in front of their TV sets. Television revenue for the NFL had jumped from a $50,000 deal for the whole league in 1951 to a contract that paid each team $325,000 in 1963.

Operating costs were up, of course, particularly salaries. Cleveland's Jim Brown was the highest-paid at $45,000, almost twice the biggest paycheck in the mid-1950s. Nevertheless, with money flowing in and the future bright, *U.S. News* insisted, "Even most of the losers win at the National League box office."

———

The year kicked off with an ugly situation in Cleveland. It's a truism that every coach is hired to be fired, but it had never happened to Paul Brown. In a triumphant career that stretched from Ohio high school championships at Massillon, through a number-one ranking at Ohio State, wartime wins with the Great Lakes Training Center team, and an unprecedented string of titles with the Cleveland Browns, the dapper little coach had seemed exempt from failure. To most fans he *was* the Cleveland Browns. Why, the team had even been named after him!

But on January 9, the earth stood still. Cleveland owner Art Modell, refusing to use the word "fired," announced that he was "removing" Brown from his duties as coach and general manager. Brown was a minority stockholder and his contract had six more years to run at a reported $75,000 per. Modell said Brown was "agreeable" to remaining as vice president and would perform unspecified "other duties" to fulfill his contract. In effect, the Cleveland owner was kicking his employee upstairs to an empty attic. For most NFL fans, it was the first they heard—or at least noted—that anyone other than Paul Brown had the final say on anything in Cleveland Brownsville.

How could such a thing happen?

All Modell would say was, "The only reason I will give for the change is that I believe it will serve the best interests of the Cleveland Browns."

From the time he'd organized the Browns for their first season in the All-America Football Conference in 1946, Paul Brown had made every important decision from players and plays to uniform design. His cool, aloof manner—some would say arrogant—kept all but his closest friends at arm's length, but his dictatorial control won football games. He'd so dominated the AAFC through four straight championships that the league died for lack of competition. In 1950, Brown and the Browns moved smoothly into the NFL and into another championship. Two more league crowns and six more division titles followed, but there had been none since 1957.

Brown had been football's most innovative coach in the post-World War II period, pioneering a new passing game, inaugurating detailed study of films, concentrating his offense by calling all plays from the sideline and communicating them to his quarterback with "messenger" guards. But five years without a championship had produced whispers that "the game has passed him by." The most damning criticism was that Brown's offense was predictable. Significantly, some of the grumbles came from Cleveland players chafing under Brown's totalitarian regime.

"It's no good to play under a feeling of tension, of suppression of the individual," Jim Brown told a reporter. "I like to have freedom of expression."

The Browns had suffered only one losing season in their history—way back in 1956. But their disappointing 7-6-1 mark in 1962 was cutting perilously close to .500.

Paul Brown and Modell were at odds during the 1962 season over Ernie Davis, the former Syracuse All-America halfback. Davis had starred for

Paul Brown.

three seasons with the Orangemen, beginning in 1959 with the school's national championship team. Jim Brown had helped recruit Davis to his alma mater, and Davis had responded by breaking most of Jim's records. Powerfully built at 215 pounds, with good speed and a tremendous work ethic, Davis, in 1961, became the first black athlete ever to win the Heisman Trophy. When Paul Brown traded Bobby Mitchell to Washington for Davis's rights, Cleveland fans considered it a bargain. A few critics also felt that in committing to a big-back, Lombardi-like offense, Paul Brown was for once following another coach's lead, but most slavered at the thought of Jim Brown and Ernie Davis in the same backfield.

Davis was a PR man's dream—soft-spoken, always polite, ever modest, a former student leader, and best of all, marvelously talented. He was almost too good to be true.

And then, in one of football's most tragic ironies, Ernie was diagnosed as having leukemia during training camp for the '62 College All-Star Game. By then, the young star's relationship with Modell had grown beyond the normal owner-player association. When his disease went into remission in October, Modell wanted to activate Davis. He knew that Ernie would never play in a game, but he thought that simply practicing with the squad might help him. Paul Brown, despite his chilly reputation, was never unsympathetic to Davis's situation. But realistically, he felt he needed to be able to use every player on his 36-man roster to win. Brown won that battle, but in January he lost the war.

His abrupt dismissal made Brown, perhaps for the only time in his career, a popular figure with sportswriters, as Modell was generally cast as the villain of the piece. In truth, it was no more than a clash of two strong-willed men over which would have the final word. In such disputes, sympathy traditionally goes to the coach, but the smart money rides on the owner. In the long view, Modell did what was best for Modell, probably what was best for the Cleveland Browns, and surprisingly, what was ultimately best for Paul Brown.

In May of '63, Davis stopped by the Cleveland Browns offices to tell them he was going back into the hospital for a while. He betrayed no bitterness, no despair. He was the same calm, upbeat, young man Art Modell had grown to admire. Only later did Modell realize that his visit was Ernie's way of saying goodbye. On May 18, a little over five months after Paul Brown had been fired, Ernie Davis died in Cleveland's Lakeside Hospital.

————

Only a week before Ernie Davis died, the football world was rocked by another death. In Baltimore, fun-loving Gene "Big Daddy" Lipscomb, the legendary 290-pound defensive tackle, died from a drug overdose. To the average football fan in 1963 America, drugs were something that happened only in sleazy back alleys to the dregs of society. Never to star athletes.

Worse, "Big Daddy" wasn't just any star. His size and skill made him an all-pro with the championship Baltimore Colts teams of 1958–59, and he was still a force at 34 with the Pittsburgh Steelers. His size and sense of humor made him popular with fans. TV announcers could hardly get through one of Lipscomb's games without quoting his self-professed method of tackling: "I just gather 'em all up and peel 'em off one by one 'til I find the one with the ball."

To this day, Lipscomb's friends energetically deny his overdose was self-induced. They insist he was clean, indeed hated needles of any kind, and theorize that he was the victim of a mugging. The chief medical examiner cited a half dozen needle marks on "Big Daddy's" arm and closed the case. Whatever the truth behind the tragedy, fans were shocked by the juxtaposition of football and drugs.

————

Pro football lives in mortal fear of a fix scandal. Any suggestion that a game might not be played on the up-and-up causes nightmares of the whole edifice tumbling into the same category as pro wrestling. Fans in the stands and in front of TVs must believe the big hits on a football field are real collisions of bone, muscle, and plastic instead of the spectacular tumbling exhibitions of the mat world. Happily, the NFL had emulated Caesar's wife since 1946 (when two players were suspended for not reporting a bribe offer). But late in 1962, odious rumors began swirling.

San Francisco offensive tackle Bob St. Clair was said to be somehow keeping time with mob figures. Chicago Bears fullback Rick Casares was said to be keeping bad company. And Colts owner Carroll Rosenbloom was suspected of placing bets. In early January, news leaked to the press that

Bob St. Clair, playing without a face mask, leading the blocking on a 49ers run.

George Halas had asked the league to look into some things he'd heard involving "a member of a Midwestern team."

On the afternoon of April 17, Commissioner Rozelle announced he had suspended indefinitely two of the NFL's greatest stars—"Golden Boy" Paul Hornung of Green Bay and "Bad Boy" Alex Karras of Detroit—for betting on games. Both were consistent all-pros, and Hornung had been MVP in 1961.

The spectre of "fix" leaped to most minds, but Rozelle tried to allay that by introducing his report with three general conclusions: "There is no evidence that any NFL player has given less than his best in playing any game. There is no evidence that any player has ever bet against his own team. There is no evidence that any NFL player has sold information to gamblers."

He also set the record straight on St. Clair. As St. Clair recalls, "I invested in an oil well, and one of the other investors—who I didn't even know—was in the Mafia. Right away, in the newspapers, I was 'guilty by association.' The FBI showed me a picture of one guy and asked if I knew him. I said, 'Of course. That's Louie.' It turns out he was a bookmaker back in the 1940s. Anyway, I was completely cleared." The league's investigation also cleared Casares and Rosenbloom.

What then had the miscreants Hornung and Karras done? They'd bet on their own teams to win and on teams in games they were not involved in themselves. To many fans that didn't sound so bad. Merely putting their money where their muscles were, right?

Analysts were quick to point out the jeopardy of a player placing himself in thrall to gamblers, the possibilities for leaks of "inside" information, and even the fact that a player's pattern of bets might tip interested parties to the likely outcome of a game. What would gamblers make of a situation wherein a player who'd bet on his team all season *didn't* bet on a game? And since most bets were made on point spreads, might a kicker like Hornung try for a field goal to widen a lead when running out the clock would be better strategy? Of course, Hornung didn't make the decisions as to when the Packers would or would not try for field goals, but there was always the danger that . . .

In Detroit, Alex Karras didn't see any danger at all and threatened to bring suit against the NFL. "I haven't done anything that I'm ashamed of and I am not guilty of anything," he said. Surprisingly, it had been Karras's own admission that he bet on games during a TV interview that had helped fuel the NFL's investigation.

According to Rozelle, Karras met "individuals described by Detroit police as 'known hoodlums' through a business associate. He continued as-

Alex Karras.

sociating with these individuals after learning of their backgrounds and habits." The NFL investigation had found no evidence of criminal wrong-doing on Karras's part, but his choice of friends constituted a "guilt by association" cloud that enveloped much of the Detroit team.

Rozelle cited a report in which Karras, guard John Gordy, end Darris McCord, and linebacker Wayne Walker supposedly traveled in the company of "known hoodlums." It turned out that Walker and McCord weren't involved at all, and the traveling consisted of Karras and Gordy returning from a 1962 preseason game in Cleveland on a bus chartered by some of the bad guys. Gordy apparently had no more than a nodding acquaintance with his hosts.

When Lions coach George Wilson received a police report on the affair, he ignored it, possibly because he knew that some of it was erroneous. Nevertheless, his failure to forward the report to the league office, as well as a certain laxness in passing out sideline passes, cost the Lions a $4,000 fine. "In a case like this," Rozelle explained, "I hold the club responsible for the action of its employees."

Five other Detroit players were fined $2,000 each for making $50 bets on the '62 championship game between the Packers and Giants. Gordy, Walker, defensive back Gary Lowe, end Sam Williams, and all-pro linebacker Joe Schmidt had assembled at the Florida home of one of Karras's buddies to watch the game on TV and placed bets through the friend during the contest in what was, according to Rozelle, "basically a group action . . . of extremely rash judgment but one abnormal for each [player]." The fines were the maximum possible under the league constitution. They look paltry by today's standards but represented a sizable chunk of a player's salary in 1963.

Karras, of course, would lose all his 1963 paychecks at least. The 250-pound defensive star had made "at least six significant bets" on NFL games since entering the league in 1958. Four of them had been for $50. One, his Florida party bet, had been for $100, as had an earlier bet on the Lions against Green Bay during the past season.

Hornung, one of the league's most visible players, was the biggest catch of all. Between 1959 and 1961, the former Heisman Trophy winner had regularly placed bets—some up to $500—on college and pro games through an unnamed West Coast businessman. Rozelle specifically noted that the businessman was a personal bettor, not a bookmaker. Hornung, he said, had generally broken even but one year won $1,500.

Unlike Karras, Hornung readily and contritely admitted his error.

When asked if Hornung's betting had anything to do with his limited use by the Packers in 1962, Rozelle explained any absences by Hornung had been because of a knee injury. "Green Bay never was advised not to play Hornung," he said. That Green Bay games were often left off the betting line in some cities was due to "uncertainty about Hornung's condition and also the club is a team that runs up 49–0 scores."

In truth, the Packers had beaten both the Bears and Eagles by exactly that score in 1962.

It was easy to blame Hornung's suspension when the Packers failed to win the NFL's Western Division title for the first time in four years. But the world of might-have-beens is populated by if-onlys. Favored by everyone and his grandmother to promenade to another championship, the Packers lost only two games in 1963. That was enough.

The Bears opened the season at Green Bay with an astonishing 10–3 win over the Packers. "We both played lousy," Vince Lombardi said, "only we played lousier." For once the Packer coach was mistaken. As the season gained momentum it became obvious that the Bears' victory in the opener was no fluke. Admittedly quarterback Billy Wade's nickle-and-dime passing attack lacked flair, and the running game was out of the Woody Hayes school—three yards and a pile of grunts. As victories piled up, the offense earned the phrase not yet coined: "Winning ugly." But when the other guys had the ball, the Bears became a thing of beauty. This Chicago team had a DEE-fense!

Even in losing years, Chicago had been rough. Guys like huge defensive end Doug Atkins and gritty linebacker Bill George could make opponents pay for yardage by the bruise. But other teams found ways to avoid the Bears' predictable all-out blitzes. By the '60s, what had worked so well a decade before only lent fuel to a rising complaint in Chicago that Halas's best years were over. Perhaps he'd caught the same bug as Paul Brown, but Halas didn't have to worry about an impatient boss. He owned the Bears himself.

Halas handed assistant coach George Allen more control of the defense. Though Allen would later win fame as "The Future Is Now" man, in the early '60s he saw the Bears' future as the zone defense. In 1962, Allen began assembling and drilling. The results were spotty at first, but Chicago pitched three shutouts in their nine wins. In '63, Allen's men were ready. Only the front four led by Atkins crashed in all the time. The rest of the defenders harried rival quarterbacks with rugged unpredictability. The best linebacking trio in the league—George flanked by Larry Morris and Joe Fortunato—might blitz, might stay put, or might even drop off to cover a receiver. Given the extra help, the secondary of Richie Petitbon, Rosey Taylor, Bennie McRae, and Dave Whitsell turned into accomplished pass thieves. The Bears intercepted 36 enemy tosses and recovered 18 fumbles. Meanwhile, the play-it-safe offense did its darndest not to screw things up. They turned the football over a stingy 25 times for a golden plus-29 ratio. It was a simple formula, but good for eight wins in the first nine games. Only an incredibly uncharacteristic performance at San Francisco in week six marred the record.

Still, the dream was expected to evaporate on November 17 when the gory, storied, and equally eight-victoried Packers came to town. Surely, Green Bay wouldn't "play lousy" this time.

The Bears proved that *everybody* played lousy against the Chicago de-fense. Hornung's replacement, Tom Moore, managed to rush for 50 yards, but thousand-yard-man Jim Taylor got a mere 23. And when Green Bay passed, Bear defenders had a field day, picking off five errant aerials. Chi-cago's 26–7 win put them firmly in the lead for the division title.

Then they almost blew it. They needed Mike Ditka's spectacular run after a short pass to tie the Steelers 17–17 on November 24, the day most of the country mourned President Kennedy. The next week, they let the Vikings tie them by the same score. Fortunately for the Bears, ties didn't

Mike Ditka.

count in the standings. Two wins in the last two weeks gave them an 11-1-2 mark to edge out the Packers at 11-2-1. The defense held season opponents to 144 points—the lowest team total since 1950, when teams played two fewer games.

———————

If the Bears' defense was the immovable object, the New York Giants' offense was the irresistible force. Pro football's once dominant defense of Andy Robustelli, Sam Huff and company had slipped a tad, but a souped-up pass attack more than made up for any loss. Riding the 37-year-old arm of Y. A. Tittle and the receiving of Del Shofner, Frank Gifford, and Joe Morrison, the Giants had amassed 440 points. Yat threw a then-record 36 touchdown passes.

With his new-found "freedom of expression" under Cleveland coach Blanton Collier, Jim Brown achieved new heights as a runner. Although Collier had much of Paul Brown's ability as a master planner, he was a very different personality from the martinet Brown. Warm, soft-spoken, a father figure, he praised instead of castigated. He let quarterback Frank Ryan call the plays on the field. The offense still revolved around Jim Brown, but Collier installed a system wherein Brown could "read" the blocking as he approached the line of scrimmage. If, for example, his tackle found it easier to take his man in instead of out, no problem. Brown took the available hole. "Blanton gives us the opportunity to play instinctive ball," Brown said.

Whether it was Collier's system or Collier himself, Brown rushed for a new yardage record—1,863 yards in 14 games, more than a mile. Although that total has since been eclipsed by Earl Campbell, Eric Dickerson, and O. J. Simpson, Campbell and Dickerson gained their yardage in 16-game seasons. Only Simpson, who rushed for 2,003 yards exactly ten years later, surpassed Brown's 133 yards per game average, and he had 42 more rushing attempts than Brown's 290. Spurred by Brown's running, Cleveland won its first six games before being gunned down by the Giants, 33–6, in Cleveland. After that it was nip and tuck until Detroit put the Browns out for good in the season's next-to-last game.

———

Any fan still unsure of whether pro football was a business or a sport got his answer on Sunday, November 24, 1963. While the rest of the nation observed a stunned day of mourning for President Kennedy slain in Dallas only two days before, the National Football League conducted business almost as usual. Obligatory moments of silence were observed and halftime entertainments and marching bands were cut, but otherwise the games continued. The product was sold.

And the fans bought it.

Although crowds were described as "subdued and listless" in the early quarters, they were nonetheless typical in numbers. Hundreds of telephone protests were handled by team offices Sunday morning, but attendance at seven NFL games Sunday afternoon wasn't noticeably down. In Milwaukee, Green Bay had its normal sellout of 45,905 for an easy victory over hapless San Francisco. The Rams and Colts drew 48,555 in Los Angeles— about what had been expected—for a game that meant nothing in the standings. Only 4,000 fewer Minnesotans than the norm showed up to watch the Vikings outduel the Lions, 34–31. The Browns had been slumping and the Cowboys were confirmed losers, but 55,096 loyal Clevelanders trooped into Municipal Stadium.

In Philadelphia, Mayor James H. J. Tate tried unsuccessfully to have the Eagles-Redskins game postponed, and Eagle owner Frank McNamee refused to attend. But a capacity crowd of 60,671 saw two tailenders play.

Across the state before 36,465 fans, the Steelers and Bears tied 17–17—a result that helped both clubs. After the game, Chicago's Mike Ditka, whose bull-like run stretched a short pass into a 63-yard gain to set up the tying field goal, expressed the mood of most players: "I think everyone felt something. Not having known the man, however, I think he would have not wanted it postponed. So we go out on the field, and it's business to us, and after the first kickoff all you think about is the Steelers."

Those who supported the NFL's games-as-usual policy generally started with the premise that John Kennedy had been an avid sports fan and built to a conclusion involving insight into his supposed wishes for the National Football League. For the most part, those who found distasteful the idea of "playing" in the face of national tragedy probably wouldn't have spent their Sunday afternoon near a football anyway.

The New York Giants offered refunds to all ticket-holders who chose to express their sense of loss by staying home, but the team announced it had received no such requests before the final gun. 60,800 turned out at Yankee Stadium to watch the Giants and Cardinals.

In attendance was NFL Commissioner Pete Rozelle, the man who'd made the decision to play the games. Twenty-seven years later as he left office, Rozelle called his decision to play on that day the greatest regret of his years as commissioner, but on that November day in '63 he said, "I discussed it with some owners and then decided. I did not feel it was disrespectful to the memory of our late President that the games were played. I went to church this morning and paid my respects, and I'm sure so did most of the people who came to Yankee Stadium."

Several Monday morning game accounts described the players as "sleep-walking" or otherwise seeming unable to marshal full intensity. "Big men were playing a boy's sport at the wrong time," Arthur Daley of *The New York Times* wrote. He compared the ambience at Yankee Stadium to that at the Polo Grounds on December 7, 1941. But New York quarterback Y. A. Tittle said he had no trouble getting up for the game. "When all those guys pile on you, you don't have time to think of anything else."

Daley pinpointed the exact moment when the New York crowd became caught up in the excitement of the game as six minutes into the second quarter. That was the first time Tittle had to signal for silence. "From that point on," Daley wrote, "the fans bubbled as noisily as usual. They were caught up by the growing excitement, and thoughts of their grief were swept aside. If that be an indictment, it would take a learned psychologist to offer interpretation."

Lay psychologists emerged on both sides of the issue. Some extolled the merits of a few hours free from mental anguish; others praised the catharsis of giving vent to grief. All in all, Daley spoke for fans and writers across the country: "It was not a satisfying afternoon. Under the circumstances, how could it be?"

Satisfactory or not, the afternoon cost the NFL next to nothing in its growing prestige. The American Football League, which respectfully pushed its schedule back a week, received only a few kind words for the gesture. If anything, the tacit admission that AFL games weren't more important than a presidential assassination only underlined the young league's second-class status. Apparently the AFL succeeded only in lengthening its championship race. The NFL was on a roll and virtually immune to PR disaster.

––––––––––

On December 29 in Chicago, the slightly favored Giants made their third straight championship game appearance and sixth in eight years. Despite an 11-degree temperature, a crowd of 45,801 packed Wrigley Field.

Allie Sherman, Y. A. Tittle, and Frank Gifford.

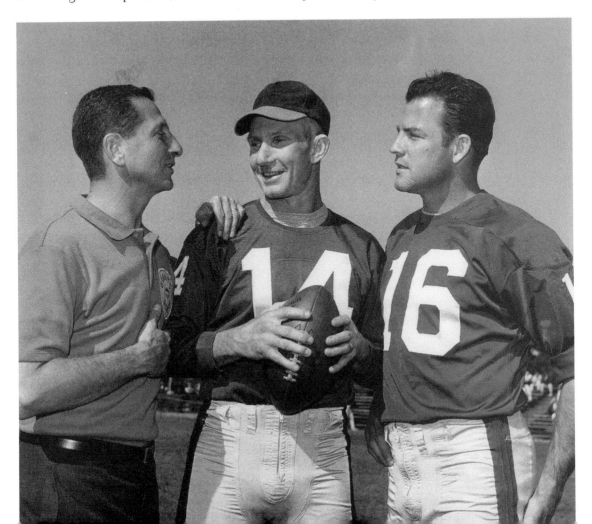

New York got a break early when the Bears did just what they'd avoided all season. Bear quarterback Billy Wade fumbled at his own 41, and defensive back Erich Barnes recovered for the Giants. From there, New York showed little regard for the Chicago defense, moving smoothly down the field. Tittle mixed running plays with an 11-yard toss to Morrison to get to the 16. Then Gifford evaded Bennie McRae in the end zone to take Tittle's TD throw. On the play, the Bears buried Tittle under a just-too-late rush, slightly injuring his left knee. The score stood 7–0 with 7:22 of the first quarter gone.

A few moments later, the Giants were knocking on the door again, but all-pro Del Shofner dropped a Tittle pass in the end zone. What seemed like a momentary reprieve became a turning point for the Bears when linebacker Larry Morris picked off a screen pass and lumbered toward the New York goal line.

"For the first 34 yards I was praying no one would tackle me," Morris said. "Then I was praying someone would. I was getting pooped real quickly." New York guard Darrell Dess knocked him down at the five. On first down, Wade handed off to halfback Ronnie Bull, who blasted to the two. Then Wade sneaked the remaining distance for the tying touchdown.

In the second quarter, Tittle and the Giants drove to the Chicago three before the Bears dug in and stopped them. Don Chandler set up shop at the 13 and booted a field goal to make the score 10–7. After the kickoff, the Giants stopped the Bears again and got another drive going themselves. They seemed about to take control of the game.

Tittle moved his team to a first down on the Chicago 32. Then he flipped a little sideline toss to Gifford who went out of bounds at the 29. That little play turned out to be the biggest of the game. Back at the 40, Tittle lay on the ground in agony. Larry Morris had brushed past two blockers and smashed into him just as he threw.

"His left knee was rigidly set on the ground," Morris explained after the game, "and I slammed him just at the knee. I guess that's what hurt him."

Tittle had a different explanation: "I fell over my own body after that pass. I had slipped going back to pass and just fell badly."

Regardless of the details, Tittle limped off with torn ligaments in his left knee. Under his replacement, young Glynn Griffing, the Giants' drive petered out, ending in a missed field goal.

After two injections to kill the pain, Tittle hobbled back in for the second half, but he couldn't plant his left leg and his throws lacked their normal snap. Late in the third quarter, Bears defensive end Ed O'Bradovich moved in front of a soft Tittle screen pass intended for Morrison at the 24. The six-foot-three, 255-pound O'Bradovich thundered to the 14 before a host of Giants pulled him down.

It took the Bears five plays to negotiate the 14 yards to a touchdown, but when Wade sneaked over from the one behind center Mike Pyle, Chicago went in front for the first time.

More than 17 minutes remained in the game, but Tittle was on one leg. Gallantly he rallied his troops, but he couldn't put his weight into his desperate passes and they floated invitingly. Twice the Bears intercepted him in the end zone, the last time with only ten seconds left.

Although Tittle's courage was admired, his five interceptions crippled New York's offense and led to both Chicago touchdowns. He completed only 11 of 29 passes for 147 yards. Chicago's Wade was even worse—10 of 28 for 138 yards—but he avoided any interceptions and scored both Bears touchdowns on sneaks.

With his sixth league title in hand, George Halas quieted the critics who'd said he was over the hill, at least for a while. In a sense, the Bears' victory was a vote for good, old-fashioned, rock-'em sock-'em football, as his immovable object defense proved superior to the Giants' irresistible force—at least when the force was hobbled on one leg.

SAM HUFF: "IT WAS JUDGMENT DAY!"

8

One of the landmarks of the 1960s was *The Violent World of Sam Huff*, broadcast on the CBS program *The Twentieth Century* on October 30, 1960. Although ratings show that only one out of four American homes tuned in, over the next couple of days everybody was talking about it. What CBS did was fit the Giants' middle linebacker with a minimicrophone and follow him around with a camera through several weeks of training camp and an exhibition game (played in Toronto, Canada, no less!) against the Chicago Bears.

By modern, minicam, instant-replay, slo-mo standards, the *World* was pretty tame—even all the cursing was edited out—but at the time, the close-ups of colliding bodies and, even more, the *sound* of colliding bodies, caused a revelation. New York fans had been chanting "Dee-fense!" for years. Now the whole country got an eye and earful of what it was like to play defense in the National Football League.

Curiously, by making him the most famous defensive player in the league, *World* may have hurt Huff's career. There's always a contingent anxious to pounce on the mighty and label them "overrated." Huff notes that he was named all-pro in 1959 but not in 1960, when he had a better year. And he had to wait 13 years after his retirement in 1969 to be named to the Pro Football Hall of Fame, while Joe Schmidt and Bill George, the players with whom he was most often compared, were elected in five.

———————

"The Giants drafted me in the third round in 1956. Tom Landry, who coached the defense, put me at middle linebacker in a 4-3 defense. I hadn't expected that. At West Virginia, I'd played guard and tackle both ways, offense and defense.

"You need a good tackler at middle linebacker on a 4-3 defense. The way it's set up is to funnel everything toward the middle. You need someone in there who can stop the run. Howard Cosell talked about that on television, only he made it sound derogatory. Like, no wonder Sam Huff makes so many tackles; it's just the defense. Well, of course it's *in* the defense. Nobody can make tackles if all the plays are run *away* from him. But in a 4-3, you need the right man in the middle. Your best tackler. It's one thing to say everything's funneled to the middle; it's something else when you see what's funneled is Jim Brown or Jim Taylor or Larry Csonka.

"Look at the guys who excelled at middle linebacker. I wasn't the only one. Bill George, Joe Schmidt, Ray Nitschke, Chuck Bednarik, Willie Lanier. All in the Hall of Fame. All great tacklers. We were put in the middle of 4-3 defenses because we could do the job.

"The same year the Giants drafted me, they also got defensive end Jim Katcavage and kicker Don Chandler, so I guess you'd have to say it was a pretty good draft. New York traded to get Andy Robustelli from the Rams and Dick Modzelewski from the Steelers that same year. Rosey Grier, Jim Patton, Emlen Tunnell, Dick Nolan, Cliff Livingston, and Bill Svoboda were already there. It was a great defense. The best ever put together up till then. Maybe the best ever.

"It was also the first defense the fans really recognized and cheered for as a unit. They'd yell 'Dee-fense!' After a while, they started introducing the defense before the game instead of the offense.

"We won the championship in my rookie year. We beat the Bears, a good team, 47–7 in New York. Then we played in the 1958 and '59 championship games. And almost the same defense was there when we played in the 1961, '62, and '63 championship games. Landry had gone to coach Dallas, so Robustelli and Patton coached the defense. I helped. Em Tunnell was out in Green Bay, but we added Erich Barnes, a great cornerback. Essentially it was the same defense for eight years and six championship games.

"Then, and I still don't know why, Allie Sherman started trading us all away. He sent Livingston off after the 1961 season. Then he traded Rosey Grier to the Rams after '62, and that was the start of the 'Fearsome Foursome' out there. He sent Dick Modzelewski to Cleveland, and he helped them win a title in '64. He traded me to Washington and the Redskins won twice as many games as the year before. In 1965, he sent Erich Barnes to Cleveland where they won division titles. Sherman sure helped a lot of teams around the league! I saw him on ESPN. They asked him why he traded away the best defense in the league. You know what he said? 'My daughter asks me that same question!' I'm still waiting to hear the answer!

"So, in 1966, the Redskins are getting ready to play the Giants at Washington. That week I looked at films of the Giants' defense. I never did that before. I always studied an opponent's offense because that's what I had to stop. But this time you might say I had a *specific* interest, so I looked at their defense. It was the worst pro defense I ever saw in my life! A little later, I was interviewed by Kyle Rote on WNEW and he asked me how we'd do. I told him we'd score 60 points. He thought I was crazy.

"We're warming up, doing calisthenics, before the game, and our coach Otto Graham walks by. He says the usual stuff, and I say, 'Otto, we'll kill them today. No mercy.' He says he'll just be happy to win by one point. 'Otto,' I said, 'it's in the bag!'

"To me, it was Judgment Day. November 27, 1966. Sherman had traded away the greatest defense in football. Well, let's see how it is to play without a defense. We scored 72 points, which is the NFL record for a regular season game. At the end, we had 69 and kicked a field goal. Otto was criticized for running up the score, but you know who sent in the field goal team for those last three points? Ol' Sam Huff. Otto was busy with something or other, and I told them to get in there and kick. Seventy-two points!

"I played through 1967 and then retired. But then, when Vince Lombardi became coach at Washington in 1969, I came back for a year because I wanted to learn to be a coach. He almost killed me. He really worked us right from the start—took all the fun out of training camp. But he told us we had to be the best-conditioned team on the field. He said most football games were won or lost in the last two minutes of the first half or the last two minutes of the second half, and the team that was in the best shape usually won at those times. He was right, but, oh, it was hard!

"I played with and against some of the greatest players of all time. The best—the greatest running back, bar none—was Jim Brown. But Taylor and Csonka were great, too.

"When the American Football League started in 1960, the players in the NFL—and I was one of them—kind of looked down our noses at it. We thought of it as a minor league. Well, it *was* a minor league when it started—throwing the ball all over the lot and all. So we didn't think a whole lot of it. What we didn't realize was what a difference having a second league would make for players. When I started, we were pretty much at the mercy of the owners. If you didn't like the contract they offered, where were you going to go? We weren't allowed to have agents. But then the AFL started making a difference. It gave players another option. Salaries went up.

"And a lot more money came into pro football. I give Pete Rozelle a lot of credit. He knew how to market the game. He made the Super Bowl a big deal. Rozelle was an owners' commissioner, of course. Bert Bell had been a players' commissioner. He looked out for the players. Rozelle was with the owners, but he did a masterful job of turning pro football into a major sport.

"Another important man was Sonny Werblin. He brought show biz into pro football with Broadway Joe, and he made the AFL important in New York. New York is the media capital, so it was crucial that the AFL succeed there. I give Lamar Hunt all the credit in the world, but he couldn't make the American Football League a major league from Kansas City or Dallas. The league needed New York, and Werblin gave it to them.

"Rozelle and Werblin made the NFL what it is today. Them and, of course, the players."

BUFFALO AND THE COOKIE MONSTER

9

Just by kicking off its fifth season in 1964, the American Football League became the most successful rival ever to challenge the NFL. Longevity was more than an academic concern. The longer the AFL could hang in against the established league, the closer it could climb to parity. With each season, the AFL added another crop of stars that cut deeper into the advantage the NFL held in 1960. Some of the NFL's biggest stars were growing long in the tooth by '64. Of course, the AFL had its own geriatric contingent—George Blanda and Tobin Rote were 36, Babe Parilli was 34—but overall the league was younger than the NFL. And in every season they made a decent showing with their draft picks, the closer they came to equality in talent.

The most famous pro football photograph of the 1960s was snapped in Pittsburgh on September 20, 1964. It shows a stunned and bloodied Y. A. Tittle kneeling in the end zone, his helmet knocked off, his bald head bleeding, after he'd been sacked by Steeler defensive end John Baker. He looks awfully old and terribly tired.

In a nutshell, that's what happened to the New York Giants in '64. The warhorse Tittle was ol-l-l-l-d. He never really recovered from that sacking and, after limping through the worst season of his career, retired. The 1964 season was also the worst in the Giants' history. Sam Huff and Dick Modzelewski had been traded away before the season, and what was left of the defense was suddenly, like Tittle, very old. It gave up a league high 399 points. After winning four division titles in the previous five years, the elderly Giants crashed and finished dead last.

Meanwhile, St. Louis made a try for the brass ring. Coach Wally Lemm had a hot quarterback in Charley Johnson, good runners in John David Crow and Joe Childress, a flock of talented receivers in Sonny Randle, Bobby Joe Conrad, and Jackie Smith, and plenty of strong blockers and

121

Y. A. Tittle.

defenders. The Cardinals tied eventual champion Cleveland early in the season and beat them in December. But in a midseason, four-week span, they lost three games and practically handed the title to the Browns.

Cleveland still had Jim Brown, who ran for 1,446 yards this go-round, but they also had a dangerous passing game for a change. Gary Collins and rookie Paul Warfield were a pair of touchdown-prone receivers, and quarterback Frank Ryan responded with an NFL-high 25 touchdown tosses. Although he got little respect for his accomplishments, Ryan, a certified genius with a doctorate in mathematics, added up to the best quarterback Cleveland had seen since Otto Graham retired.

In the West, Green Bay was favored in preseason to return to the top, but Lombardi hadn't yet completely retooled.

The defending champion Bears were waylaid by injuries to the defense and the shock of the training-camp deaths of runner Willie Gallimore and end John Farrington in an auto accident. They lost three of their first four games, with the Colts blasting them 52–0 in week three. Baltimore, under second-year coach Don Shula, waltzed to the title. The Colts were blessed with football's best quarterback in John Unitas.

Unitas was pro football's favorite Cinderella story. In 1955, after an unspectacular career at Louisville University, he was drafted in the ninth round by the Pittsburgh Steelers, probably because he was a local boy. Ahead of him on the Steelers' depth chart were Jim Finks, Ted Marchibroda, and Vic Eaton. Finks would later become a top pro football executive and Marchibroda would find success as a coach, but the Steelers didn't know that, of course. What they knew was that Finks and Marchibroda were incumbents and Eaton was the team punter. Very sensibly, they cut Unitas. They didn't even let him in an exhibition game. John went home and played semipro ball with the Bloomfield Rams for something like ten dollars a game.

The next year, a fan tipped off the Colts about this terrific semipro. Baltimore telephoned Unitas with the offer of a backup position. His first

Johnny Unitas.

opportunity came when regular George Shaw was injured in a game where the Colts led the Bears 21–20. He fumbled three times and then threw an interception that put Chicago in front 27–21. The final was 56–21.

But Unitas got better—better with every game. Much better. George Shaw never got his job back, and two years later Johnny U. took Baltimore to its sudden-death championship game victory.

Except for the miracles he could work in a football game, Unitas had all the charisma of bib overalls. He was blue-collar all the way. Each year, he showed up the first day of camp, did his work every day, and went home after the season. Had there been a time clock at the 50-yard-line, he'd have punched it. Whether he tossed a touchdown or an interception, he wore the same deadpan expression leaving the field. End-zone celebrations were for kids. If you can imagine Johnny U. leering at a TV camera with his index finger stabbing a "number one," you can conceive the Washington Monument doing a hula. Quote-hungry reporters despaired of postgame locker room interviews with the Colts' super-quarterback. Inevitably, he gave them only politically correct truisms as controversial as a ham sandwich.

Yet, during a game, he was excitement personified—an arrogant gambler who held the outcome in the palm of his hand. The league had passers a tad more accurate, passers who could throw a bit deeper, passers with a smidgen more touch, but Unitas had more than enough of each quality plus the damnedest attitude. No one held the ball to that last millisecond so exquisitely, calculating the infinitesimal difference between a defensive end turning him into rubble and a receiver breaking open. Some thought he waited so long just to show his disdain for frustrated pass rushers. And all that arrogance produced touchdowns in unheard of quantities. He threw for at least one touchdown in 47 consecutive games, football's equivalent to Joe DiMaggio's 56-game hitting streak—only a little harder.

As usual, the Colts' main man in winning the West was Unitas, but halfback Lenny Moore enjoyed a remarkable comeback season. After two straight injury-plagued years, Moore seemed over the hill, and Shula found no takers when he tried to trade him. By midseason, Shula was mumbling the old saw about "the best trades are the ones you don't make." Moore set a new NFL record with 20 touchdowns, 16 by rushing.

––––––––––

The Colts were installed as seven-point favorites for the championship game, but the smart money said that wasn't nearly enough. After all, Baltimore had led the league in total offense while allowing the fewest points. Cleveland had won in a weak division despite finishing dead last in the league in total defense. Baltimore had led all teams in sacking rival quarterbacks. Cleveland was particularly vulnerable to the pass. Baltimore

Lenny Moore.

had Johnny U.; Cleveland had somebody named Ryan. The game would be a blowout.

Don Shula wasn't so sure. He'd been a player for the Browns when Collier was a Paul Brown assistant and an assistant coach under Collier at the University of Kentucky. He knew the old man was capable of exploiting any weaknesses he found in the Colts.

And Collier had found one. While studying films of the Colts in action, he saw that Unitas would drop back to the pocket then shuffle toward his primary receiver. If the Browns' secondary could cut off the primary receiver, Collier reasoned, the defensive line could get to Unitas before he could find his secondary target. He gambled his defensive plan on that slender thread, adding, "I'll take any consequences."

Collier got a break from the weather when a 20-mile an hour wind blew through Cleveland's cold Municipal Stadium on game day. That hurt the wide-open Colts' offense more than the Browns' ground-based attack. Between the wind and Collier's defensive scheme, the Browns held the great Unitas to 95 yards passing on the day and the Colts to zero points. A certain amount of inspiration went into the mix. Browns' defensive tackle Jim Kanicki, hardly a household name, gave the Colts' Jim Parker—arguably the greatest offensive lineman ever—the worst afternoon of his career. Walter Beach, a defensive back of little fame, covered Raymond Berry like a coat of expensive paint.

The Browns were also held scoreless in the opening half, but 40-year-old Lou Groza toed a wind-aided 43-yard field goal early in the third quarter. A short time later, Jim Brown rambled for 46 yards to the Colts' 18, and Ryan hit Gary Collins under the crossbar on a post pattern for six. Before the quarter ended, Collins took another Ryan pass down the middle for a 42-yard score. Cleveland poured it on in the final period with another Groza field goal and another Collins TD reception. On the day, Collins caught five passes for 130 yards to emerge as the offensive star, but the 27–0 victory turned on the defense and Blanton Collier's strategy.

Jimmy Brown, Frank Ryan, and Ernie Green celebrating a Browns victory with head coach Blanton Collier.

By its fifth year, the AFL was losing some of its "put-the-ball-in-the-air-and-be-damned" image. They still threw on average five more passes per game than the NFL, but several teams were developing respectable defenses. And, as every football fan knows, most championships are won with defense. By far, the most respectable "D" in the AFL was played in Buffalo. It couldn't have happened in a nicer place.

Football fans in Buffalo had a long history of NFL-hating. Fans with *really* long memories (and there were still a few around) remembered that way back in 1921 George Halas had talked the league into awarding a championship Buffalo had apparently won fair and square instead to his Chicago team. Halas had argued that a Chicago victory over Buffalo in a postseason exhibition should count, and the league owners agreed. Shortly after the Pro Football Hall of Fame opened in 1963, it received an irate telephone call from a Buffalo woman demanding that all mention of Buffalo be expunged from the Hall unless the NFL returned the "stolen" 1921 championship.

By 1930, Buffalo was out of the NFL, and all its entreaties to be taken back in were ignored. Then, after World War II, the city put in four years as an NFL-hating member of the All-America Football Conference. But, even though it was among the AAFC leaders in home attendance, Buffalo was brushed aside in the merger of 1950. And that was followed by yet another decade of being sneered at whenever the word "expansion" was broached to the old league. Nowhere in the AFL did fans so burn with desire to beat the NFL at its own game.

The Chargers finished atop the AFL West again in 1964, their fourth division title in five years, but it wasn't a cakewalk. At age 36, Tobin Rote hurt his arm, and John Hadl was still developing. Lance Alworth was a big help with 13 TD receptions, and Lincoln and Lowe remained a brilliant combination. Despite some shaky quarterbacking and the lack of a reliable placekicker, San Diego still managed to come in a game and a half ahead of the Chiefs, a team that seemed to have everything but a winning record.

One of the season's most interesting stories was the Jackie Lee *lend*. Desperate for a quarterback, Denver worked a deal with Houston to borrow Lee for two years. From the Oilers' standpoint, it was a way to get their "quarterback of the future" game experience after he'd rusted on the bench for four years. At first, Bronco fans moaned about the prospect of giving up their quarterback two seasons hence, but after they'd watched Lee in action *that* bit of grumbling ceased. Whether he was rusted beyond repair or just grossly overrated, Lee was a bust. By '65 he was third man at Denver, and when he quietly returned to Houston the next year, he went to the bench without passing "Go."

The Jets still weren't ready to challenge, but their attendance nearly tripled with their move into Shea Stadium. The opening game against Denver drew an AFL-record 45,665. An early November meeting with first-place Buffalo brought out 60,300. Jets president Sonny Werblin, true to his show biz background, wanted stars on his field. Linebacker "Wahoo" McDaniel was the Jets' first star, albeit a somewhat manufactured one. A fair defender, he had that great nickname. The Jets' PA man began asking the crowd, "Who made that last tackle?" and the crowd would answer back, "Wahoo!" Soon tackles were being credited to Wahoo when McDaniel was 20 feet away from the play.

Boston made a game try at repeating as eastern champs. Babe Parilli had his finest season, throwing for 31 touchdowns, and slow-footed but sure-handed Gino Cappelletti scored 155 points to lead the league. The Patriots closed strong with five straight victories to edge within a half game of Buffalo and set up a do-or-die meeting with the Bills in the season's finale at Boston.

The weather was frigid and snow covered the markers, but Bills' quarterback Jack Kemp had no problem. The first time he went deep, he hit

Babe Parilli.

Bills quarterback and future politico Jack Kemp.

"Golden Wheels" Dubenion for a 58-yard touchdown. After that, he kept the Bills in front all the way to a 24–14 win and the division title. It was left to all those critics who'd insisted Kemp couldn't win big games to explain what went right.

Coach Saban's Bills were the most solid football team the AFL had yet produced. Although they didn't have as many breakaway threats as the Chargers, there was nothing wrong with an offense that boasted the league's leading rusher in Cookie Gilchrist and Kemp's passes to reliable

129

Glenn Bass or long-distance Dubenion. The offensive line was the league's best, with guard Billy Shaw and tackle Stew Barber as standouts. The defense, led by tackle Tom Sestek, end Tom Day, and linebacker Mike Stratton, held AFL opponents to the fewest points. Because opponents found they couldn't run through the Bills, they threw. But George Saimes, Butch Byrd, and the other defensive backs held rivals to a league-low 46.6 completion percentage while Sestek, Day, and company unloaded for a league-high 50 sacks.

The Bills even had the league's best kicking game, with current TV analyst, then-linebacker Paul Maguire punting for a strong 42.7 average and Hungarian-born Pete Gogolak a placekicking sensation. Gogolak defied all football wisdom by kicking his extra points and field goals soccer-style, with a sideways swipe of his foot. Although some considered it a foreign novelty at the time, Gogolak's way would eventually become the standard booting technique simply because it made for longer, more accurate kicks, something American kickers had failed to discover in nearly a hundred years of football.

One squabble marred the season. Gilchrist became miffed at the Bills' play-calling during a game, apparently because his own impressive skills were being ignored. In the midst of the action, he stalked off the field, told his sub to go in for him, and headed for an early shower. Outraged, Saban cut him. Fortunately, Jack Kemp brought his budding political ability into the mix. He convinced Cookie to return and apologize. Saban accepted and an uneasy truce between the coach and his star fullback held through the rest of the season.

The championship game was at Buffalo. According to Paul Maguire, the Bills came on the field loose because their coaching staff was so uptight it was funny. First, assistant coach Jerry Smith harangued the troops: "The last bit of advice I can give you is . . . Don't forget to remember."

After that non sequitur, head coach Lou Saban took his turn: "The last bit of advice I can give you, men, is . . . Heads up, toes down."

"We were hysterical," Maguire says. "We're walking down the tunnel toward the field laughing like mad. What were those guys saying? But it loosened us all up. We were 15-point underdogs that day, and we kicked their butt. It was the most inspirational thing I'd ever heard."

The game started off like a repeat of the year before when the Chargers slaughtered the Patriots. San Diego's Keith Lincoln ran for 38 yards. Rote passed to Dave Kocourek for 26 yards and a touchdown. The 40,242 fans at War Memorial must have thought, "Here we go again."

But on their next possession, the Chargers were stopped dead by the hit of the year, maybe of the decade. Lincoln swung to his right and lifted his

Paul Maguire.

arms to catch a little pass in the flat. His body was wide open to Buffalo linebacker Mike Stratton smashing in like the wrath of God. *Crunch!* The ball flew away from Lincoln, and Lincoln went away from the game with a broken rib.

With Lincoln out, the Chargers' attack sputtered before the overpowering Bills defense. Meanwhile, Cookie Gilchrist rumbled around the field for 122 yards, and Kemp completed his passes whenever he really had to. Gogolak added a couple of field goals. The Bills were 1964 AFL champs,

131

20–7. After more than 40 years, Buffalo fans finally had a pro football championship, and, if it did not have quite the same pizzazz as an NFL title, at least there was no way George Halas could take this one away from them.

————————

Don Smith is vice-president of the Pro Football Hall of Fame today, but in the early 1960s, he was the crew-cut publicity director for the Denver Broncos. It was not an easy task. The football team and the community coexisted, but seldom did many of the latter turn out at the stadium to cheer the former. And like most such situations, it had to get worse before it got better.

"During the 1964 season, Broncos coach Jack Faulkner was fired. As a reward for getting the Broncos to a .500 record in 1962, Faulkner was made general manager [replacing Dean Griffing] as well as coach. The two hats proved one too many. The Broncos limped out of the blocks in '63 as Faulkner drowned in a sea of GM details while letting his coaching slide. After the first two losses, quarterback Frank Tripucka announced he couldn't move the team any more and retired.

"Mac Speedie replaced Faulkner. In Speedie's first game as coach, the Broncos won. Several times during the game Denver was faced with a fourth-and-one situation and Speedie turned to the crowd to ask them what they wanted. Naturally, they all yelled, 'Go for it!' Well, on that particular day the Broncos made those fourth-and-ones and won the game. The fans thought it was great. Unfortunately, I don't think the Broncos made another fourth-and-short yardage all season. The fans got pretty discouraged. We finished 2-11-1.

"At the end of the season we'd averaged about 16,000 in attendance and we'd sold about 7,900 season tickets. The partners who owned 58 percent of the voting stock got together and decided to sell the team. They had an offer from the Cox Broadcasting Company in Atlanta. On February 15, we were all sitting around waiting to go. The majority owners had stipulated that all the employees of the Broncos who wanted to would go with the team to Atlanta.

"In the meantime, the Phipps brothers, Gerry and Allen, refused to sell their 42 percent of the stock. Cox wanted 100 percent or nothing. When that didn't come through, the majority owners had to sell to the Phippses for a ridiculous price. It seems to me like it was a million and a half dollars, something in that nature. And they got the stadium in the process.

"The city of Denver which had never been very interested up to that time suddenly got all uptight about losing their team. People were suddenly very appreciative of having pro football in Denver.

132

"So, on February 15, the Phipps brothers purchased 52 percent of the stock and saved the franchise for Denver. The next day the annual season ticket sale began with the sale of 143 tickets. That was a record for Denver. It was important enough that when the business manager called me and told me we'd sold 143 tickets, I called the newspapers. The next day we sold 265 and I called them again. By Wednesday we were up to 370 or something like that. Soon we were over 800 a day. On March 5, we had 941 sales.

"Suddenly, Quarterback Clubs sprang up all over the city. They set quotas for themselves and, when they passed them, set new quotas. It was a community function. One bank in nearby Aurora offered no-charge, no-interest loans to season ticket holders. That started a firestorm with other banks offering the same kind of loans. Everybody hustled. I didn't have to call the newspapers anymore. They were calling us. I was chairman of the drive, but I didn't do a thing except sit in my office and record sales. It was an *event*.

"We finally ended up with more than 22,000 season tickets. And that year we doubled our average attendance from about 16,000 to about 32,000."

BILLY SHAW: "THOSE WERE SOME BATTLES"

10

In the best of all possible football worlds, offensive guards would have their pictures on magazine covers, guest on late-night TV talk shows, have kids fight over their bubble gum cards, and publish how-I-won-the-Super-Bowl autobiographies every bit as often as quarterbacks and runners. This, obviously, is not the best of all possible football worlds. In this one, guards labor in obscurity, only hearing their number called when they jump off-sides or hold too obviously. The best an offensive guard can hope for is to play on a championship team. As far as personal fame, there's an occasional all-league selection or the chance to ply his trade in an all-star game or two.

By that limited measure of success, Billy Shaw's career was a triumph. His nine seasons with the Buffalo Bills were blessed by two league championships, All-AFL honors from 1963 through 1966, and nine appearances in the league all-star game. When the all-time AFL team was selected, he was picked for one of the guard positions.

––––––––

"The Dallas Cowboys drafted me 14th in 1961, but that was just an afterthought for the future because I'd already signed with Buffalo, who selected me second. The Bills drafted me to play guard. Dallas and the other NFL teams I talked to were looking at me as a linebacker or defensive end. So I made my decision not by the team or by the league but on what position I was likely to play.

"That was primarily on the advice of my coach at Georgia Tech, Bobby Dodd. I had played both offense and defense at Georgia Tech. College football was trying to limit substitution in the late 1950s. They had a lot of crazy rules that changed every year. You had to play both offense and defense, you could come out once in a quarter and you couldn't return until the next quarter, and so on. I was mainly a defensive player, but it was apparent that I might not have the bulk to play defense in the pros, particularly at tackle or defensive end. My last year of college I'd got up to 235. But Coach Dodd thought that I possibly could be borderline as an offensive guard. I had the speed to play guard—most of the offenses at that time were built around pulling guards—so speed and quickness were a requisite. As it turned out, I got bigger than I thought I was going to get. I played my pro ball at 252. Of course, I'd be a runt if I were playing today.

"In the the '61 draft, Buffalo built its offensive line—drafting me, Al Bemiller, Stew Barber, and Ken Rice. Potentially, Ken Rice, who was later traded to Oakland, was the best football player of all of us. He had size but he had a lot of speed too. I played against Ken when I was at Georgia Tech and he was at Auburn. We were ranked one-two in the Southeastern Conference. In our senior year, the Atlanta Touchdown Club and the Birmingham Touchdown Club gave out the two most prestigious awards for linemen in the SEC. Ken got the Atlanta award and I got the Birmingham award.

"We had quite a battle when we played against each other that year. Then we played together in a couple of all-star games and then at Buffalo for a while. But Bemiller, Stew Barber, and I stayed side-by-side from the '62 season through the championship years and right up through 1969. We would know when one of us got the hiccups.

"Buffalo drafted extremely well for the next couple of years, with Tom Sestek, Jim Dunaway, George Saimes, and a lot of good players. And of course we got Jack Kemp along the way.

"Tom Sestek, a great defensive tackle, and I were good friends, although off the field we didn't move in the same circles. I was married and had a family while Tom was a bachelor, so our lifestyles were different. But at work, we were the best of competitors. I like to think that I had some influence in the way that Tom progressed as a player, and he *certainly* was instrumental in my becoming a better football player. We always chose each other to go against in practice when it came time for one-on-one drills because of the opportunity to improve. Those were some battles. Some I won; but mostly he did. He was one of the finest athletes of that time, and he could play today.

"Buffalo didn't have outstanding speed in the backfield, but we had some durable backs—Wray Carlton, Cookie Gilchrist. They were two big backs but neither had blazing speed. I remember a ball game we played in Houston. I was out in front of Wray and we turned the corner. The Houston cornerback had fallen down, so it became a foot race down the sideline between Wray and me, and I crossed the goal line before he did.

"Raw speed and quickness are two different animals. Cookie had more speed than a lot of people realized, but mostly he was quick. It was a joy to block for him. But you'd better block and get out of the way because Cookie was as big as we were up front and when he hit you in the back— *uh!* That was an incentive to get your man out of the way the next time so Cookie wouldn't hit you from behind again.

"Cookie was probably the best athlete we had. He could have been all-pro at guard or linebacker. In fact, he could have played any position outside of wide receiver or quarterback. Cookie was a free spirit who did his own thing, but within reason. Always within the bounds of teamwork. Well, he *did* stretch that a bit at times.

"Getting Jack Kemp from San Diego solved our quarterback problems. Kemp was one of the most articulate men I've ever been around. I drew a lot of character from him just watching him operate and improve himself. Jack was a great example. He set goals early in his life. As a former congressman and as a member of the Bush administration, he attained some of the goals he set for himself back in the '60s. I may get the chance to vote for him for President in 1996. I think that any player who was concerned about the kind of player he wanted to be after football certainly drew a lot of characteristics from Jack. The greatest compliment I can say about Jack is that he was instrumental in a lot of people becoming better people.

"Paul Maguire is the kind of person that every team needs to stay loose. What people don't realize was that Paul was a better than average defensive football player. He was a backup linebacker for us, and in our time, he was the premier punter. His humor and antics on the sideline made hard practices tolerable. But Paul is the kind of guy who, when the chips are down, you'd want in a foxhole with you.

"Paul is Paul. When he had his heart problem a couple of years ago, I phoned his wife Beverly at the hospital and stayed in touch. It was touch and go for a while. Well, then after Paul got out of the hospital, I phoned the house and got his answering machine. The recording said, 'This is Paul. I'm out walking my heart. I'll return your call when I come back.'

"Even at a time when things are really serious, he still has a lot of humor. He had that way of taking the edge off any situation. I think it helped relax us for the championship game with San Diego in 1964.

"Marty Schottenheimer was another backup linebacker with us, so you could say our reserve linebackers have done pretty well after their playing days.

"On the other hand, Mike Stratton was a great linebacker for us. He was one of our most dedicated players. He had the physical ability—six-three and 240—and he could run with any of the backs. And he loved to hit. It was his hit of Keith Lincoln that made such a difference in the '63 championship game. It put Keith out of the game. A couple years later, Keith joined us and he and I became good friends. We talked about that hit often. He said he'd never been hit harder either before or after. The papers the next day said it was 'The Hit Heard 'Round the World.' It turned the game around.

"People often ask me how Lou Saban was to play for. To be perfectly honest I don't know how good a coach Lou was as far as the Xs and Os. He approached the game as a businessman—as president and CEO—and delegated authority. We had good, dedicated assistant coaches who did all the coaching. The thing I compliment Lou on is that he was a good motivator. He was able to get out of you that little bit extra. I don't want to say that he manipulated people, but he was able to obsess an individual. He had an uncanny ability to get the most out of every player. So when people ask me how good a coach was he, I really don't know. But obviously we were successful.

"Coach Joe Collier was Lou's top assistant. They were two different people. I *know* about his Xs and Os. What Coach Collier can do with Xs and Os is matchless, as far as I'm concerned. He's still a top assistant in the NFL after more than 30 years. Joe was very different from Lou. He was low key and didn't have Saban's motivational skills. But he was a joy to play for.

"A lot of players complained about old War Memorial Stadium. I *loved* War Memorial Stadium. It was old. There's no doubt about that. It was difficult for even the players to find a place to park. But it was close. And it was our home during the nine years I played. It was always full, even in the bad years. I've got nothing bad to say about War Memorial. I had a little bit of speed, so I was able to beat some of the slower defensive tackles to the hot water. If I remember correctly, there were six showers, one urinal, two commodes, a concrete floor, and wood lockers. I felt comfortable there.

"I presently live in a small town in Georgia. Not too long ago, a black family moved in next door to us. Well, I had a little bulldog, and it began gaining weight because the family fell in love with it and they were feeding it too. The poor sucker had gained more weight than I have. So I went over and introduced myself, and they said, 'Well, Mr. Shaw, we know you. You used to park your car in our yard in Buffalo.' It turns out, they lived two blocks from the stadium. The husband worked for AT&T. Later, he was transferred to Nebraska. And then when he retired, they moved to Georgia and ended up next to me. Small world.

"Thinking back on the championship Bills teams, we were probably very average on offense, but that defensive team—and I'm prejudiced—was probably one of the best ever in football. We won championships because of our defense. The credit to the offense was that when given an opportunity, a break, by the defense, we were able to capitalize on it.

"In football, you have a team, and yet there are two teams, an offensive team and a defensive team. Some teams have conflicts because the offense doesn't do something or the defense doesn't do something. We didn't have that. We were a particularly close team. We on offense recognized that we had a tremendous defensive team and if we could put a few points on the board, we'd win. Against anybody!

"I would have loved to play against the NFL teams."

11 BABY-SITTERS, BROADWAY JOE, AND WRISTBANDS

During the late 1960s, the U.S. military attempted to convince the American public (and itself) that it was winning in Vietnam by the meticulous calculation and publication of body counts. Eventually, the theory went, if the inventory of dead bodies grew high enough, the Vietcong would run out of living bodies and peace would ensue. The theory also presumed that all the bodies were active Cong.

To compare the "war" which "raged" between the National and American Football Leagues during the first part of the decade with the bloody conflict in Vietnam that so dominated the second part is an impertinent analogy. Strife in the toy department is never so real or so tragic. Nevertheless, by a curious symmetry, score was kept in the NFL-AFL battle to a large extent with body counts. The bodies in question belonged to healthy young footballers who'd used up their college eligibility and become fair game for the annual league drafts. Each league trumpeted the signings of its draft choices as proof of its present and future superiority.

Counts were manipulated. To proclaim parity, the AFL's eight teams needed to sign fewer choices than the 14-team NFL. High draft picks were more valued for publicity and presumed ability than those of later rounds, but that could be equivocated by drafting "signable" players early. The signing season—the period in which draftees were captured and inked—received nearly as much attention from teams and the media as the game season. Before the pro football war ended, so much money, manpower, and strategy were exerted in improving league body counts that at times the winning of league championships seemed almost secondary.

The NFL was shocked by the number of AFL signings in 1960. Bushwhacked. The older league had gone a full decade merrily drafting and signing with no bidding competitor. A drafted player could always reject the NFL's offer and go north to Canada, but that meant less money usually and less prestige always. Suddenly, with the advent of the AFL, coveted draftees were being offered contracts that matched and sometimes dwarfed NFL numbers. The new league promised it would soon match the old one in prestige too.

Losing Billy Cannon hurt. College football's 1959 glamour boy had the kind of charisma the star-conscious LA Rams always looked for. Ultimately, Cannon would prove too dependent on straight-ahead speed and too lacking in elusiveness to be a great pro running back, but his weaknesses would only be discovered in an AFL uniform.

Hardest hit by the AFL's inroad in 1960 were the Baltimore Colts. As world champions, they were not about to go begging to a bunch of raw rookies. But while the Colts dawdled, the AFL moved. Lost to the new league were Gerhard Schwedes, the all-purpose halfback from Syracuse, future Hall of Fame tackle Ron Mix, defensive end Don Floyd and linebacker Larry Grantham, both of whom became all-AFL, and guard Bo Terrell.

It could have been worse. Buffalo owner Ralph Wilson decided a $3,000 signing bonus was too much for a rookie defensive back from Utah. Rebuffed, Larry Wilson joined the NFL's Cardinals and began a 13-season career that would lead him to the Pro Football Hall of Fame. Big Merlin Olsen took one look at the Denver Broncos' setup in the Frank Filchock era and signed with the NFL Rams for $5,000 less than the Broncos were offering.

By the second draft, both leagues knew they were in a war, and their scouts literally fell all over themselves to get college stars to sign. When a bowl game ended—along with eligibility for a number of players involved—those who'd been drafted were so mobbed by scouts waving contracts and pens they couldn't get off the field. Players on teams not involved in bowl games had their muggings earlier, immediately after their final regular season game.

Lamar Hunt himself handed 230-pound running back Curtis McClinton a check for $10,000 right on the field after his last game for the University of Kansas. Somehow, McClinton mislaid it in the locker room, sparking a frantic search. The check was found and McClinton went on to play eight seasons for Hunt's team.

Drafting and signing a player broke down into three stages. First, determine if a player was signable. There was no point in wasting a draft choice—certainly not a high choice—on a player who was very likely to sign with the rival league. On the other hand, players soon learned that it wasn't in their best interest to commit to one side or the other too quickly. So long as the player might go either way, the offers were likely to improve.

If it seemed likely or at least possible that a player could be signed, the second stage was to draft him. Even a player who might seem irrevocably committed to the other league might be drafted on a high round. After all, he might have a last minute falling out and become available. And if nothing else, the existence of a second offer might force the rival from the other league to spend a little extra money on Draft-Pick A and then make a lower offer to Draft-Pick B.

Sometimes teams outsmarted themselves. The Chargers really wanted Massachusetts tight end Milt Morin, a six-four, 250-pound behemoth with decent pass-catching skills, but when they couldn't get a commitment out of him, they didn't draft him until the third round. Morin signed with the Cleveland Browns who chose him as their first pick.

The third stage, of course, was to actually get the player's signature on a contract. This was the most challenging part, especially when a scout from the rival league was whispering sweet somethings in the player's other ear.

The way around that was to put the player someplace where the other league couldn't reach him.

Otis Taylor, an outstanding receiver from Prairie View, was flattered to be invited by the Cowboys to spend Thanksgiving in Dallas, but when he arrived he discovered that he and a half dozen other players were being held virtually as hostages. "We could see we were being kept away from the other league," Taylor recalled. "They didn't even want you talking to anyone in the lobby. Once they knew you'd talked to somebody, they'd move you to another hotel."

Taylor and the other players were moved four times. Nevertheless, Kansas City scout Lloyd Wells traced him through friends to a Dallas motel. But when Wells tried to see Taylor, he was chased off by NFL guards. Undaunted, Wells went behind the motel, jumped a fence, and found Taylor's room. Like something out of a cloak-and-dagger movie, he tapped on Taylor's window, and when the young receiver opened it, Wells made his pitch. He convinced Taylor to escape through the back window and fly to Kansas City. The next day the Chiefs drafted Taylor and signed him immediately.

The Chiefs had less success with Roman Gabriel. The tall quarterback from North Carolina State was originally Oakland's first pick in the 1962 draft, but the Raiders were in such disarray then that they stood little chance of signing anybody. In desperation, they turned their draft list over to Kansas City in hope of saving the players for the AFL. For weeks, Lamar Hunt tried to phone Gabriel at the college without success. Finally, a call went through to Gabriel's dorm. Hunt introduced himself and began mak-

Otis Taylor.

ing a pitch for the quarterback to join the American Football League. He was encouraged when the voice at the other end of the line seemed interested. For half an hour Hunt answered questions and detailed the advantages of the new league. When the conversation ended, Hunt thought he'd made a strong case, but shortly afterward Gabriel signed with the NFL's Los Angeles Rams. It wasn't until several years later that Hunt learned he'd spent his time talking to Rams' general manager Elroy Hirsch, who was on the spot to sweet talk Roman.

The signing wars made for strange bedfellows. Front office people who wouldn't normally give their intraleague rivals the skin off a grape were willing to hand over a prized draft choice for peanuts just to keep the player within their league. Notre Dame's All-America end Jack Snow was drafted by both the Vikings and the Chargers. Snow, a native Californian, let it be known that he'd had enough of playing on cold, icy fields at South Bend. To keep him out of the AFL's clutches, Minnesota traded his rights to the Rams.

Jack Faulkner, the former Denver coach, was by then a special scout for Los Angeles. When Snow went to New York for an All-America awards dinner, Faulkner signed him and took him to Toots Shor's famous restaurant to celebrate. And as luck would have it, standing at the bar was Vikings coach Norm Van Brocklin.

"You ———— !" growled Van Brocklin. "When we play you next season, you won't catch a pass. Not a one."

By the time the next season rolled around, Faulkner had become an assistant coach for Van Brocklin's Vikings. "I can't recall if Snow caught a pass against us," says Faulkner, "but we beat the Rams in that game and also in a second meeting later on." On the other hand, Snow spent 11 seasons in a Ram uniform and caught 340 passes.

Van Brocklin was never one to mince words. In 1962, the Vikings drafted University of Miami end Bill Miller on the third round and Hunt's Dallas Texans took him on the second. Miller's decision took place in a Chicago hotel where the Vikes and Texans had suites across the hall from each other. Accompanied by his fiancée, Miller went back and forth between the two suites, listening to offers. The warm weather in Dallas won out over the attractions of Minnesota's winter, as far as Miller's future wife was concerned, and a representative was sent over to inform the Vikings. Back across the hall stormed Van Brocklin. "Are you going to let your future be decided by some ———— ?" he screamed at Miller. Needless to say, after that any further importunings by Minnesota were wasted.

In 1964, the NFL threw aside its hit-or-miss signing attempts and organized the "baby-sitters." The NFL didn't call them that, of course; they were league "representatives." Expanding a plan originally conceived by the Rams' Bert Rose, the NFL got together about 80 sitters—"30 of whom were friends of mine," Rose says, "and the rest were recommended by friends." Each sitter was assigned a particular college player in a different part of the country. Months before the draft, the sitter would begin making visits to the player, selling him on an NFL career.

"Almost all of them had one thing in common," Rose remembered. "They were sales oriented. They had to be, since we were asking them to sell the NFL to the best pro prospects in the country." Milt Morin's sitter was Ed King, a former pro player and future governor of Massachusetts.

By the time the draft rolled around, many players and their sitters had become good friends. Oregon halfback Ron Medved even had his sitter as a member of his wedding party.

On the weekend of the draft, the sitters took their players to various NFL cities where games were to be played and stashed them in hotels. Secrecy was intense. Only about 20 draft supervisors at the NFL's secret headquarters knew how to reach the players and their sitters by telephone. If a team wanted to talk to a player before drafting him, it had to reach him through draft headquarters. In one case, Lynn "Pappy" Waldorf of the 49ers called New York from San Francisco and was put in touch with the player he sought. What Waldorf didn't know was that the player was actually sequestered in a San Francisco hotel only a few blocks away—a 6,000-mile phone call to cover less than a mile!

The Jets gave draftee Tom Nowatzke, a fullback out of Indiana, a deluxe tour of Shea Stadium when he came to New York for the Kodak All-America dinner. Nowatzke's buddy, Dick Pollard, went along and was even more interested than Nowatzke. Only when the fullback signed with Detroit did the Jets discover that Pollard, the buddy, was actually an NFL baby-sitter.

The baby-sitting program was an undoubted success, but not 100 percent. Every once in a while, a player who seemed to be all but wrapped up would end up in the AFL camp instead. One sitter almost died of shock: He was walking down Fifth Avenue in New York with three of his charges in tow when they suddenly veered into AFL headquarters. "We just wanted you to get a look at us," they told the AFL office staff.

When all the players had been signed after each draft—and there were seven drafts before the AFL–NFL merger—each league would announce victory. And because there were so many players and signable players tended to be slotted toward the top of each team's draft list, just about every team had something to brag about. A quick check of the consensus All-America lists for the years 1959–65 shows that 38 players went with the NFL and 33 with the AFL. The NFL could boast of more All-Americas, but the AFL had more per team.

The AFL led in signing Heisman Trophy winners four to three, but that needs some explaining. LSU's Billy Cannon was a PR plum at the beginning of the war and led the league in rushing in its (and his) second season. USC tailback Mike Garrett, signed by the Chiefs before the 1966 season, had an outstanding pro career. Garrett, considered too small by most NFL folks, led the Chiefs in rushing in three of his first four seasons and helped take them to two Super Bowls. But Joe Bellino of Navy, the 1960 winner, served his naval obligation and didn't play a game for the Boston Patriots until 1965. He returned kicks for three seasons but never caught fire. John Huarte, the Notre Dame quarterback who came from nowhere to win the 1964 Heisman, disappeared under the avalanche of publicity accorded Joe Namath when they both signed with the Jets in 1965.

If the AFL got only two-for-four stars from its Heisman signees, the NFL was even worse off. Ernie Davis, the 1961 winner, was struck down by leukemia before he could play a game. It turned out that Terry Baker, Oregon State's brilliant quarterback of 1962, had everything but a major league arm. He struggled for three years with the Rams and then went into his life's work. The 1963 Heisman winner, Navy's Roger Staubach, became a Pro Football Hall of Fame quarterback with the Dallas Cowboys, but like Bellino, his pro debut was delayed by his naval commitment. By the time he arrived in Dallas in 1969, the war with the AFL was over.

Of course, it was all a little silly because it usually took several years of pro play before anyone could say whether a draftee was a boom or a bust. And by the time that decision was made, teams were more interested in trumpeting their newest draftees.

The single most important signing during the war was quarterback Joe Namath. For the record, he wasn't the first player chosen by the AFL in the 1965 draft. That honor went to Lawrence Elkins, an All-America wide receiver out of Baylor, who played a couple of seasons with Houston but never justified his high draft status. The Jets and St. Louis Cardinals drafted Namath, but the Cardinals were expected to pass him on to the Giants because it was known Namath hankered to play in New York. According to Jets president Sonny Werblin, "Everyone had him first on their list." The young man from Beaver Falls, Pennsylvania, had damaged knees which might have made some teams leery, but he also had a strong and accurate arm and that marvelous quick release that spelled the difference between a long gain and a sack. And he had something else that Werblin found irresistible—charisma. He was a star.

Werblin's background was entertainment, not football. He'd spent 35 years with Music Corporation of America, once the largest talent agency in the world. When he resigned as MCA president in January 1965, *Variety* said, "No one had better contacts, knew more secrets, swapped more information, flew so many airline miles, ate more meals at '21,' made more deals, or sold so many hundreds of millions of dollars worth of programming." He'd worked deals for Ed Sullivan, Jackie Gleason, Andy Williams, and countless others. He was tuned into the star system. He believed in it. Almost his first act in taking over the Jets was to hire a "star" coach, Weeb Ewbank, the man who'd brought two championships to Baltimore. Werblin wanted a star on the field for his Jets. And, as he said, "Quarterbacks are stars."

Except, perhaps, the Jets' incumbent quarterback. In 1964, the Jets' offense was run by six-foot-five Dick Wood, a competent, strong-armed thrower out of Auburn. Wood had the arm and the brains, but if you look up "charisma" in the dictionary, you'll find a picture of Dick Wood under "antonyms." He definitely wasn't the answer to Werblin's dreams. Time has a way of simplifying. Today, it's remembered that the quarterback before Namath—what's-his- name—was a dismal failure and that Namath

Joe Namath showing off his million-dollar knee to head coach Weeb Ewbank and owner "Sonny" Werblin.

was immediate manna. But here are the passing stats:

		ATTEMPTS	COMPLETION	PERCENTAGE	YARDS	TD	INTERCEPTIONS
1964	Dick Wood	357	168	47.0	2301	17	25
1965	Joe Namath	340	164	48.2	2201	18	15

Namath's edge is only marginal. Of course, Joe had the *potential*, soon realized, of becoming much better and Wood had peaked. Nevertheless, the difference in that first season was, to a large extent, *perceived* rather than real. Charisma.

Everything broke right for Werblin in his quest to produce a megastar. On the night of January 1, a limping Namath was overwhelmingly voted the Orange Bowl's player of the game, after his courageous attempt to rally number-one ranked Alabama against Texas. The next day he signed with the Jets for the stunning figure of $426,000 for three years. Werblin modestly admitted it was the most ever paid a pro athlete in any team sport but insisted that most of it was a signing bonus. Few fans saw much difference between bonus and salary; it all went into Namath's bank account.

"If he's worth $400,000, I'm worth a million," said Dr. Frank Ryan, who'd just engineered the Cleveland Browns to an NFL championship.

A week later, the Jets signed Notre Dame's Heisman-winner John Huarte for $200,000, setting up a nice little three-way competition to see who would emerge as the Jets' quarterback, that guy Wood, Mr. Heisman, or the $400,000 Man. Namath added to the speculation by entering the hospital in late January for a knee operation. Actually, though Wood and

147

Huarte had their backers, Namath was the new Jets quarterback from the moment he signed unless his knee fell completely off. Werblin wasn't about to spend all that money for a warm-up act. Before the season began, Wood was sent off to Oakland. Huarte got hurt and didn't throw a pro pass until 1966, and then it was for the Patriots. Apparently, he'd been drafted as a charisma bail-out if Namath couldn't be corralled and then he was signed as a fall-back position if Broadway Joe's knee was condemned.

Namath, with his good looks, ready quips, and love of New York's night-life, became an immediate media darling. Anyone who would title his autobiography *I Can't Wait 'Til Tomorrow ('Cause I Get Better Looking Every Day)* was a quote-hound's dream. He embodied the fan's ideal athlete—the talented youngster who played hard on the field and just as hard off. Fans drooled over newspaper photos of Joe at some nightspot accompanied by one or another beautiful woman. Obviously, he was having the time of his life—and it showed.

Twenty-five years later during a football game they were broadcasting, NBC's Mel Proctor twitted Joe on air about a curfew-cracking evening out west:

> Proctor: I understand that night out in Denver cost you a little money.
> Namath: Five hundred dollars! Which was a *lot* of money in those days.
> Proctor: But was it worth it?
> Namath (with relish): YES! It was worth it!

Even the prim and proper who disapproved of his life-style knew who he was. Like Barnum said, "As long as they spell your name right." The publicity was pure gold for the Jets, but was Namath worth 400 Gs on the field to them? Was *any* football player worth so much?

Ironically, no Joe (nor Wood nor Huarte) opened at quarterback for the Jets in '65. Mike Taliaferro, who'd backed up Wood for two years, played the whole opener, a 27–21 loss at Houston. But 52,680 turned out at Rice Stadium to watch Joe sit on the bench. The next week, 53,658 packed Shea Stadium. The Jets lost again, but Namath relieved Taliaferro in the second quarter. In week three, another 45,056 showed up at Buffalo's War Memorial Rock Pile. Namath started, completed 19 of 40 for 287 yards and two touchdowns. The Jets lost, 33–21.

Namath didn't engineer a victory until New York's sixth game, and then it was only against Denver. The team was getting better, although fullback Matt Snell, receiver George Sauer, and defensive end Verlon Biggs had as much to do with it as Namath.

So what? This season wasn't about winning, it was about excitement and stardom and putting people into seats. The Jets drew over 50,000 to every home game and were easily the AFL's best road draw. Everybody wanted to see the $400,000 quarterback. By comparison, the champion Bills were dull.

Well, the Bills really *were* dull. Coach Lou Saban finally despaired of ever reaching *rapprocchement* with fullback Cookie Gilchrist and sent him off to Denver for another fullback named Billy Joe, whose chief distinction was that he went by two first names. Sans the Cookie Monster, Buffalo filled its backfield with capable but boring plodders. Then, to make matters even more tedious, regular receivers Elbert Dubenion and Glenn Bass went out for most of the season with injuries, leaving Jack Kemp throwing to—yawn—a couple of journeymen. The Bills' offense spent the season

John Hadl.

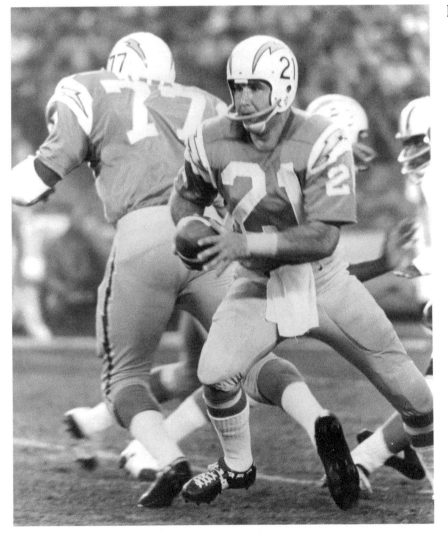

plugging downfield far enough for sidewinder kicker Pete Gogolak to try for a field goal.

It didn't matter. The defense of Ron McDole, Tom Sestek, Mike Stratton, George Saimes, and the rest held opponents to a league-low 226 points and collected nearly 50 turnovers. Besides, the 10-3-1 Bills were the only winning team in the East. The rookie-driven Jets finished second with five wins.

San Diego, with John Hadl throwing and Lance Alworth running, leaping, grabbing for 1,602 yards and 14 touchdowns, won the West for the fifth time in the AFL's six years. Keith Lincoln missed most of the year with injuries, but Paul Lowe was AFL Player of the Year with a new league record of 1,121 yards rushing. The Chargers' defense gave up only one more point than the Bills'. Large Earl Faison and larger Ernie Ladd led the defensive line. In a game against the Chiefs, the 300-pound-plus Ladd made ten unassisted tackles and sacked Len Dawson six times.

In the AFL title game at San Diego, the Bills were predictably dull, but they never let the Chargers past the 24-yard-line. After a scoreless first quarter, Jack Kemp completed an 18-yard touchdown pass to Ernie Warlick. When the Chargers punted on their next possession, Butch Byrd pulled off the one legitimate moment of excitement by scoring on a 74-yard punt return. The second half was enlivened by three Pete Gogolak field goals to make the final score 23–0.

NFL spokesman sneered at the modest 30,361 attendance for the AFL's championship. AFL apologists pointed out that there were barely 30,000 seats in Balboa Stadium where a fan could actually see the game—and those "seats" were concrete slabs. But, they added, better stadiums were coming.

————

On June 1, 1965, Earl "Curly" Lambeau died in Sturgeon Bay, Wisconsin, about 30 miles from Green Bay. Lambeau brought little Green Bay to national prominence during the 1930s with the Packers, the team he founded in 1919 and coached through 1949. He'd won six NFL championships, mostly with a damn-the-torpedoes, throw the ball offense. Lambeau wasn't much interested in defense. "The Little Sisters of the Poor could have scored a couple of touchdowns on us," veteran guard "Buckets" Goldenberg once said. "Curly just figured we'd outscore anybody."

Lambeau's death deprived him of the opportunity of seeing the Packers string three more championships, to give Vince Lombardi five, one less than Curly. But whereas Lambeau's titles had been accomplished with offense, the underpinning of Lombardi's championships was always defense. Bart Starr, Jim Taylor, Paul Hornung, and company made the headlines; Willie Davis, Henry Jordan, Ray Nitschke, and company won the games. That was never more true than in 1965.

In the NFL East, the defending champion Cleveland Browns had it easy. This was Jim Brown's last season (though no one knew it at the time), and the Clevelanders parlayed his running, quarterback Frank Ryan's passing, and Gary Collins's catching into an 11-3 record. Brown rushed for 1,544 yards, his seventh season in nine of over a thousand yards. The Browns were soft on defense, but the East was in a down phase so a real race for the title never materialized.

In the West, the Bears had three first-round draft choices. One of them, Tennessee tackle Steve DeLong, got away and signed with San Diego, but the Bears could hardly grumble. The two they signed were future Hall of Famers, Illinois linebacker Dick Butkus and Kansas runner Gale Sayers—the draft equivalent of hitting the lottery and the Irish Sweepstakes on the same day. Despite the presence of the dynamic duo, the Bears got off to an awful start, losing their first three games. George Halas's team was out of the race before it began, and the offense didn't really gel until 34-year-old Rudy Bukich took over at quarterback from fading Billy Wade. After shooting themselves in the foot at the beginning, the Bears roared through the rest of the season, looking for all the world like the best team in the league—but one that could never make up the head start it had given the Colts and Packers.

In Butkus, Chicago unchained a monster in the middle. He had the size, at 245 pounds, to fend off big blockers and the speed to run down enemy backs or to shadow tight ends. But what put Butkus helmet and shoulder pads above other middle men was his ability to hate. He played with a savage devotion to smashing, crushing, blasting, and otherwise manhandling opponents. "When I went out on the field to warm up," he said, "I would manufacture things to make me mad. If someone on the other team was laughing, I'd pretend he was laughing at me or the Bears. It always worked for me."

Butkus replaced Bill George in the middle of the Bears' defense. After a few rookie mistakes of excess, he began destroying people. He would have been a shoo-in for rookie of the year except for the presence of his teammate Sayers.

Although he was a different kind of back, Sayers was the first runner in a decade who could be mentioned in the same breath with Cleveland's Jim Brown. Like Brown, Sayers forced defenses into special coverages that weakened them at other points. But where Brown was tremendously powerful with good moves and speed, Sayers had blinding speed and moves no one had ever seen before to go with good power. Green Bay tackle Henry

Jordan explained, "Sayers? Sure, I've got a defense against him. I just step out of the way and let Willie Wood hit him. Really, I don't think anybody knows how fast Sayers actually is. Only time I've ever seen him is in the huddle. Once he tucks the football under his arm he's invisible."

Paul Hornung was more serious but just as amazed: "He's simply the best damn athlete I've seen since I came into the pros."

If Sayers wasn't quite in Jim Brown's class in his ability to wear down an opponent by smashing into the line 25 or 30 times a game until something simply collapsed, he was even more of a threat to break away for a touchdown every time he handled the ball. In 1965, Brown led the league in rushing attempts with 289 and caught 34 passes to total 1,872 yards; Sayers ran 166 times from scrimmage and caught 29 passes for a 1,374 total, but he also returned 16 punts and 21 kickoffs for another 898 yards.

Cleveland and Chicago didn't meet in '65, but Brown and Sayers waged a duel for league scoring honors. Brown had the lead until December 12 when the Bears hosted the 49ers. In the first quarter, Sayers took a dinky screen pass from Bukich and turned it into an 80-yard touchdown. In the second quarter, he scored twice from scrimmage on runs of 21 and seven yards, and he added two more TDs in the third period on a 50-yard burst off tackle and a dive over from the one. With five touchdowns already in his personal till, Sayers fielded a fourth quarter San Francisco punt at his own 15 and whirled through the opposition for 85 yards and another score. That TD, Sayers' 21st of the season, broke Lenny Moore's record of 20. He could have had another. Chicago drove down the San Francisco two-yard-line in the closing minutes, but Jon Arnett did the honors to bring the final score to 61–20. Sayers's six touchdowns matched the league record set by the Cardinals' Ernie Nevers in 1929 and tied by Cleveland's Dub Jones in 1951. Ironically, both Nevers and Jones had their big days against the Bears.

Both the Bears and Browns had one game left, with Sayers holding a one touchdown lead over Brown, who'd matched Moore's 20. The Bears had won nine of ten games after their bad start, but they'd only cinched third place and had no chance of finishing higher. Minnesota took them down 24–17, scoring 21 points in the final quarter. Sayers had only one score on the day, a modest two-yard run. Meanwhile, Cleveland was in St. Louis playing a game that had no bearing on their Eastern Division title. The Browns ran up a 17–10 lead in the first half with Jim Brown scoring his 21st touchdown on a three-yard blast. But, at the end of the half, Brown was ejected from the game for fighting with Cardinals end Joe Robb.

Cleveland owner Art Modell was livid. "To rob Brown of a chance to win the scoring title on such an incident is ridiculous. He's been kicked, beaten

Dick Butkus bearing down on Fran Tarkenton.

Gale Sayers, the Kansas Comet, on a 96-yard touchdown dash.

and gouged for many seasons and has never complained, and now when it mattered to him, he has to be kicked out after years of injustice."

Brown soft-peddled his expulsion, terming his altercation with Robb "one of those quick things." Although it marked the second time in his career he'd been booted for fighting, in nine seasons as the busiest running back on the field and most likely target of opportunity, he was never sidelined with an injury.

Sayers, whose 132 points captured the scoring title, didn't have Brown's constitution or luck. A serious knee injury in 1968 almost ended his career; another knee injury two years later did end it. He was called the "Kansas Comet" and, like a comet, he blazed across our vision for a short time and then was gone.

The big bad Bears' big bad start turned the race for the western crown over to the Packers and Colts. In Green Bay, Lombardi had retooled the Pack's offense by shipping perennial all-pro center Jim Ringo off to Philadelphia and big tight end Ron Kramer to Detroit and installing Ken Bowman at pivot and Marv Fleming in Kramer's spot. But neither Jim

Taylor nor Paul Hornung were at their best, and Green Bay had trouble moving the ball. Kicker Don Chandler, picked up from the Giants, helped, but Green Bay's stingy defense helped more. Old hands Jordan, Davis, Nitschke, Adderley, and Wood were still around from the 1962 champs. Lionel Aldridge manned one defensive end and Ron Kostelnik paired with Jordan at tackle. Outside linebackers Lee Roy Caffey and Dave Robinson were all-league quality. The defensive backfield added Tom Brown, a former first baseman in the Washington Senators chain, to go with Doug Hart, Wood, and Adderley.

Baltimore, the defending western champs, had one thing no other team could boast of—Johnny Unitas. The NFL had plenty of great quarterbacks in the '60s: Tittle, Starr, Jurgensen, Ryan, Meredith, Tarkenton, and Brodie, just to skim the cream. But the *crème de la crème* was Johnny U. If he wasn't the best pure passer in the league (and he was close), he was certainly the most effective. But what really set him apart was his ability to get better when things got tougher. No quarterback could bring a team back like Unitas, no one could use the clock better, no one could hit the pass that *had* to be made as often. As a hard-nosed winner, he was much like Bobby Layne, but Layne couldn't pass as well.

Unitas had the league's best fleet of receivers in reliable Raymond Berry, fast Jimmy Orr, spectacular Lenny Moore, and muscular John Mackey, a blacksmith masquerading as a tight end. The offensive line, bulwarked by Jim Parker, was big and experienced. Don Shula, the Colts' 35-year-old coach, had some worries on defense. Two longtime Baltimore stalwarts, end Gino Marchetti and linebacker Bill Pellington, had retired.

The Colts met the Packers at Green Bay in the second week of the season and held a 17–13 lead with five minutes left. Green Bay was without fullback Jim Taylor, halfback Paul Hornung, and quarterback Bart Starr, all out with injuries. The game was practically recorded in the win column— and then the Colts gave it away. In quick succession, three penalties and a botched punt set up a go-ahead Green Bay touchdown. Then, as Unitas the master of come-from-behind, began his inevitable last-ditch heroics, halfback Tom Matte fumbled, leaving Lombardi's crew with a 20–17 win.

Green Bay was 4-0 when they met the Lions in Detroit on October 17. The Lions came out with a vengeance. "We were down 21–3 at halftime," Starr recalled. "They had completely outplayed us, and it looked as if we were going to have a replay of that '62 Thanksgiving Day game. We knew we looked bad that first half, and we determined that win lose or draw we were going to be a better team that second half."

The Packers brought the second half kickoff back to their 38. On the first play from scrimmage, Starr hit tight end Bob Long with a 62-yard

John Mackey.

touchdown bomb. The Pack was back. The defense closed down Detroit completely in the second half. Starr went on to connect on a 31-yard scoring pass to halfback Tom Moore and a back-breaking 77-yarder to fleet receiver Carroll Dale to put Green Bay in front 24–21. As the Lions became more and more frustrated, they began to make mistakes, taking penalties, leaving openings. Late in the fourth quarter near the Detroit goal line, Starr faked a handoff to Jim Taylor. As just about every Lion on the field jumped on Taylor, Starr trotted around end for a game-icing touchdown.

Green Bay had a victory by playing one good half. The next week, they bettered that ratio when they faced Dallas at Milwaukee County Stadium. The Cowboys were still emerging as a respectable team and stood 2-3 at the time, but they had several exceptional players. The defense boasted all-world tackle Bob Lilly, quick linebacker Chuck Howley, and Mel Ren-

156

fro, a great defensive back. On offense: running back Don Perkins, a reliable yardage-gatherer; receiver Bob Hayes, the world's fastest human, and
always a threat; and rookie offensive tackle Ralph Neely, an emerging
all-leaguer. Another rookie, Craig Morton, opened at quarterback.

Early in the second quarter, Morton hit tight end Pettis Norman with a
short pass and a split second later Packer linebacker Lee Roy Caffey hit
him with 250 pounds. The ball rolled loose. Green Bay defender Tom
Brown picked it up and brought it back 27 yards. The Packers eventually
got a 44-yard Don Chandler field goal out of it. Dallas tied the score in the
third period with a Danny Villanueva field goal, but they should have had
a touchdown. The usually sure-footed Perkins broke clear but then stumbled, presumably over a poltergeist. A little later, Renfro was knocked cold
and fumbled as he fielded a punt at his own 22. His own teammate ran into
him on one side just as Packer Fuzzy Thurston clobbered him from the

Bob Lilly.

other. Again Green Bay had to settle for a field goal, but it put them in front. Before the game ended, Taylor scored on a sweep after Willie Davis had recovered deep in Cowboy territory.

The 13–3 win looked better on the scoreboard than on the field. Starr had undoubtedly his worst passing day, completing just four of 19 tosses for a miniscule 42 yards. Since he'd lost 52 yards on five sacks, Green Bay's yardage in passing totaled *minus* 10! "I just had a terrible day," he admitted. "I couldn't have hit anyone with a handful of buckshot. Sure they put on a great rush at times, but even when I had good blocking, I couldn't hit anything."

Taylor, Hornung, and Moore didn't do a whole lot better, accounting for only 73 yards on the ground to the Cowboys' 193. Despite Dallas's rushing total, the Green Bay defense saved the day. Davis, Jordan, and company sacked Morton nine times for 62 yards in losses, recovered three fumbles, and picked off two interceptions. When a reporter suggested to Lombardi after the game that his team had been lucky, he stormed out of the room.

The Packers were 6-0, but their offense continued in the dumper, scoring ten or fewer points in four of their next five games and losing three of them. The defense and two Chandler field goals saved a 6–3 game at Los Angeles, but with 11 down and three to go, the Pack was 8-3 and trailing the 9-1-1 Colts by a game and a half.

After the week-two loss at Green Bay, Baltimore tore off eight straight wins by simply outgunning the opposition. Unitas was having arguably his greatest season, although saying that is like choosing one out of a set of pearls. A shocking 24–24 tie in the annual Thanksgiving Day game at Detroit didn't seem all that important; the Colts were title bound. But then a not-very-funny thing happened on the way to the flag. The Bears.

On December 5, week 12, the Colts went to Chicago. A couple of Bears tackles, Stan Jones and Earl Leggett, sandwiched Unitas into a torn right knee ligament and ended his season. Without their leader, the Colts lost 13–0. Meanwhile, Green Bay topped Minnesota to move within a half game of the top.

The Colts considered themselves fortunate. Unitas's backup was Gary Cuozzo, a young signal-caller who'd been waiting in the wings for three years. Had he been behind almost anyone but Johnny U., the experts said, Gary would have been the number-one QB already. Earlier in the season, when Unitas stayed on the sideline to nurse a sore back, Cuozzo had thrown five touchdown passes against the Vikings. Predictions were that he would prove his worth once more in week 13 by leading Baltimore to victory in what had become a must-win game with Green Bay.

But the predictors hadn't taken into full consideration the lethal Green

Bay defense, the brittleness of Cuozzo's physique, or maybe Murphy's Law. Cuozzo gave it a good try, but under an avalanche of Packers, suffered a separated shoulder in the third quarter. Green Bay won 42–27 to move into a half game lead in the West. The hard-luck Colts faced their final game, a Saturday affair at Los Angeles, shorn of anyone veteran NFL-watchers would recognize as a quarterback.

For $100, Baltimore picked up 36-year-old veteran Ed Brown, who'd been hanging on as a third-stringer with a Pittsburgh Steeler team that managed only two wins all season. Obviously, that wasn't the answer, but what Coach Shula came up with for a starting quarterback was an even longer gamble. Tom Matte.

Matte had been a useful Colts' halfback for a couple of years, but back in his college days, he had indeed been a quarterback. The only trouble with that was he'd been an *Ohio State* quarterback, and under Woody Hayes's three-yards-and-a-cloud-of-dust approach, a quarterback was just a running back who sometimes handed off. The only passes Matte had fired of late were the rare halfback-option variety.

The "instant quarterback" went into the final game with most of the nation looking in on TV. Meanwhile, he kept looking at his wrist, where he had taped a plastic band listing the Colts' plays and his assignments. In obvious passing situations, Brown came in to exercise his ancient arm. One of his tosses went to tight end John Mackey for a 68-yard TD. Matte threw only twice himself and both fell incomplete, but as a *running* quarterback, he was a sensation, gaining 99 yards on rollouts and draws. The Colts won 20–17 to bring their record to 10-3-1.

Not that it figured to make much difference. The 10-3 Packers needed only a win at San Francisco to tuck away the division title. And when was the last time the Lombardi men failed in the clutch? On Sunday, Green Bay had things well in hand, 24–17, with two minutes left when 49ers quarterback John Brodie began to move his team. The clock was at 1:07 when receiver Vern Burke made only his second reception of the season good for a touchdown. Tommy Davis, who missed extra points as often as Pavarotti misses a high note, tied the game and the Western Division up into a 24–24 bundle. In 1965, the NFL did not yet have any fiendishly clever tie-breaking procedure for deciding division titles. The western crown would have to be gained the old fashioned way—by earning it in a play-off. And this time, Matte was completely on his own; Brown had joined the Colts too late to be eligible.

The game was scheduled for the day after Christmas in Green Bay. A crowd of 50,484 packed Lambeau Field, most of them screaming for the Packers. The temperature for that time of year in the Bay was better than could be expected: 28 degrees above zero and windy.

Almost immediately the Packers were in trouble. After the opening
kickoff, Bart Starr tossed a short pass to Bill Anderson, who caught it at the
25. But a Colts cornerback wrestled the ball away from him, and linebacker
Don Shinnick scooped it up and headed toward the goal line. Starr was the
only man with a chance to stop him, but safety Jim Welch smashed him
out of the way with a shoulder to the ribs. Shinnick scored: 7–0 Colts.

Starr was helped from the field, done for the day with badly bruised ribs.
The Packers were forced to go with *their* back-up quarterback, Zeke Bratkowski. "Brat" had been around the NFL for more than a decade, never
able to win a number-one job. Nevertheless, he was brainy, cool, and a
good passer. He was also one of those quarterbacks like Earl Morrall and
George Blanda who thrived best in relief.

Defense dominated the first half, but late in the second quarter, Bratkowski lobbed a screen pass to Hornung, who took it for what looked like
a 49-yard gain deep into Colts territory. But one of the Green Bay blockers
had been a little too antsy. The ineligible-receiver-downfield penalty
brought the ball back and the Packers punted.

It was Baltimore's turn. Starting at his own 25, Matte coaxed his team
down the field on a drive that even included a Matte-to-Lenny Moore pass

good for nine yards. The drive stalled at the eight, but Lou Michaels kicked a field goal to give the Colts a 10–0 lead at the half.

Green Bay opened the second half strong, stuffing the Colts' offense. When Baltimore punter Tom Gilburg got a high snap, the Packers were on him to take over at the 35. Bratkowski immediately called for a long pass. Carroll Dale took it at the two with Colt Jerry Logan draped all over him. Two plays later, Jerry Kramer cleared the way for Hornung into the end zone.

Throughout the second half, the Packers continued to move the ball. The Colts bent but didn't break. Twice Green Bay drives were stopped by interceptions. Then Green Bay got a break. Colts end Billy Ray Smith sacked Bratkowski for an eight-yard loss at the Packers' 42. But an official ruled that Smith had shown a little too much enthusiasm. After a brief debate as to whether Smith had clouted Bratkowski on the helmet with an open hand (he said) or a fist (the official said), Green Bay had a first down at the Baltimore 43. Eight plays later, it was fourth down at the 15 with a little over two minutes to go. Don Chandler came in to kick the chip shot field goal to tie. Starr, injured ribs and all, held.

The kick wasn't one of Chandler's best. It climbed sky-high and twisted to the right. In fact, he seemed to think he'd missed it and turned away. But field judge Jim Tunney liked it and signaled it good. To this day, there's not a Baltimore fan who'd agree. Baltimore kicker Lou Michaels doubled as a defensive end and was on the field at the time. It was his expert estimate that the kick "was at least three feet wide." Chandler later admitted, "It wasn't a real good kick, but I couldn't tell." In the unbiased opinion of Colts owner Carroll Rosenbloom, "There was no justice out there today." Nevertheless, the game was tied, 10–10. For the second time in NFL history, a post-season game went into overtime.

Green Bay won the toss, but they couldn't do much on offense. Neither could the Colts until their second possession, when three straight quarterback draws by Matte moved the ball 22 yards to the Green Bay 37. There the Packers' defense stiffened and threw the Colts back to the 40 by fourth down. Michaels had the leg to hit from 50 yards out, but he didn't get a real chance to show it. The snap bounced to holder Bobby Boyd, and by the time he controlled it, Michaels's timing was destroyed. His kick fell far short.

The Packers took over at their 20. Bratkowski was ready. Two passes mixed in with some typical Green Bay line smashing got the ball to the Colts' 18. In came Chandler, and this time there was no question. His 25-yard boot split the uprights. The clock said 13:39 had elapsed and the Packers were 13–10 champions. They'd beaten the Colts three times.

Matte had put up a game fight, running for 57 yards on 17 attempts and completing five of 12 passes for 40 yards. For Joe Montana a bad day, but not so shabby for an instant quarterback. Matte will never make the Pro Football Hall of Fame, but his trusty wristband is already there on display.

The Colts took little solace in "game fights." "We lost," Baltimore defensive back Bobby Boyd said. "That's all that matters. I'd rather get beat 503 to 0 than this way."

The NFL wouldn't admit it publicly, but two rule changes before the next season stemmed from Tunney's controversial call on Chandler's game-tying field goal. Two officials were required to stand near the goal line to make the call, and the uprights were extended another ten feet into the air to make high kicks easier to judge.

The actual championship game was anticlimactic. Cleveland owned the league's best record, but the competition in the East hadn't been much. The NFL's two best teams had already met in the Western Division play-off. Like the play-off, the championship game was played at Lambeau Field, this time a muddy mess that made straight-ahead running the order of the day. A three-inch snow stopped just before kickoff. The Packer ground crew cleared the white stuff nicely, leaving the field exposed to a steady drizzle. Cleveland hung in for the first half and trailed only 13–12 at intermission. Early in the first quarter, while the field was only slick, Starr connected with Carroll Dale on a 47-yard touchdown pass that accounted for more than a third of Green Bay's pass yardage on the day. Chandler converted. Cleveland quickly matched the TD. Gary Collins took a 17–yard scoring pass from Frank Ryan. There followed what was perhaps the play of the game. The snapback for the extra point was wide and the ball rolled loose. Lou Groza, Cleveland's 41-year-old "Toe," who'd been kicking professionally since 1946, picked up the football and threw what was probably the only pass attempt of his long career. Miraculously, he completed it to Bobby Franklin, his holder, but Franklin was tackled six yards short of the goal line.

As field conditions worsened, Groza and Chandler each kicked two field goals to complete the first half scoring. The second half was all Green Bay, as dominating ball-control offense added ten more points and kept the Browns' offense on the sideline. Jim Brown, in his final game with Cleveland, gained only 50 yards on a minuscule 12 carries. Taylor and Hornung, looking about five years younger than they had all season, rushed for 96 and 105 yards respectively.

Lou Groza.

JIM TAYLOR: "SOMETHING YOU DETERMINE BY CHOICE"

12

During the 1960s, Jim Taylor came to epitomize the line-blasting full-back—a throwback to Bronko Nagurski. He truly enjoyed smashing into people, particularly when he could level them by hammering them with a lethal left arm chop smashed downward on the helmet of a would-be tackler. "They don't tackle real low so that arm helps," he said. "Maybe you'll get an extra yard or two. Over a season, that's the difference between an 800-yard and a 1000-yard season."

For five straight seasons—1960–64—Taylor rushed for over a thousand yards. In 1962, he led the NFL with 1,474 and a then-record 19 rushing touchdowns.

Of all Green Bay's great players of the Lombardi years, Taylor, in 1976, was the first to be enshrined in the Pro Football Hall of Fame.

"I came to the Packers in 1958 with pretty good credentials. I'd been All-America at LSU and Most Valuable Player in the Senior Bowl. Green Bay drafted me on the second round. But then I sat on the bench for the first ten games of a 12-game schedule. Scooter McLean was the coach. He'd been an old Chicago Bear running back, but I think he was with Detroit when the Packers hired him. Green Bay was grasping at straws after a lot of losing seasons, and McLean had a reputation as a good assistant coach. He may have been in a little over his head as the head coach. We didn't have a very good season. We only won one ball game, lost ten, and tied one.

"I finally got my chance in the final two games when we played out in California against the Rams and the 49ers. Up till then I'd had kickoff returns and gone down on kickoffs and punts, all on special teams. We lost both of those California games, too. But, to the best of my knowledge, I gained over a hundred yards in each game. I ended up with only 240 yards rushing for the season, almost all of it in those last two games. I just wasn't given the opportunity until then. But after that, I felt I could make it as a running back in the National Football League.

"Then the next year Lombardi came in. He'd been an assistant in New York. He knew just what kind of system and what kind of organization he was coming to. He gave a lot of leadership, and he was very determined and disciplined.

"He'd go to the blackboard and put up a play like the sweep and he'd go over it and over it and over it for 45 minutes—teaching each player all the little minute things that would make that play work. It was like going to kindergarten where they teach you one, two, three, four, five, A, B, C, D. Just keep it very simple and go over it again and again.

"He was very efficient and very punctual. When there was a meeting, you had to be there five minutes early. It was kind of like the military with a drill sergeant.

"It was quite a change from the year before, but you condition yourself to know what the ground rules are. Everybody accepted it. He said that's how the Green Bay Packers were going to be run, and you either do it that way or leave. You go by all the rules.

"He was very fair and didn't have any favorites or pets. He had one set of standards. Everybody was treated the same. He was the most impartial, unbiased person I've ever known. That's what I admired about him. Human beings have a right wing and a left wing. Most can't give you one standard and they can't live by it. But this was one quality he had as a leader and as a coach. He made you respect him—kind of like a man's man."

Taylor usually ranked second to Cleveland's Jim Brown in rushing and on the annual All-NFL teams. But on one count, it was no contest—Jim Taylor blocked.

"I was a little small for a fullback by NFL standards. Actually, I was smaller than Paul Hornung at halfback. I weighed about 214 and Paul went, I believe, about 218. Size has no bearing on whether you're productive or not. In Lombardi's system, one running back always blocked for the other. So I'd carry 20 times a game with Hornung blocking, and he'd carry maybe ten times with me blocking. I had to be the more durable back as far as running the ball. I was the workhorse. I had to get 4.6–4.8 yards per carry. Hornung didn't have the durability to carry 20 times and maintain that average. He only needed ten carries to be effective. But he did lots of blocking when I carried the ball, and I blocked for him when he carried.

"In the Lombardi system, we worked at possession. We weren't going to break off a sweep for 20 or 40 yards very often. There weren't a whole lot of other teams going to do that either. We were consistent. We were going to run at you—defy you. We were going to get those four, five, or six yards every time with our offense. Lombardi said you won by beating the other team at its strength. We'd line up and defy the other team to stop us. And they never did, not in the eight years I played for him."

San Francisco cornerback Abe Woodson: "Jim Taylor was a harder runner than anybody. When he carried the ball, he went after defensive backs. Most people ran away from a tackler. Not Taylor. Even if he had a clear path to the goal line, he'd look for a defensive back to run over on the way."

Fans and sportswriters constantly compared Taylor with Jim Brown even though they were very different kinds of runners. Brown ran straight up but had to be tackled low. With more breakaway speed than Taylor, he was a greater threat to break off a long run. He had a way of relaxing when opponents had him in their grasp that helped him avoid injuries and could lull a tackler into a mistake.

Taylor ran close to the ground and fought for every inch, pitting his strength against the bigger men who tried to bring him down. Each play was a mini-war. Sam Huff said Jim would have made a great linebacker.

Taylor and Brown had four face-to-face meetings. In October 1961, the Packers and Browns each led their divisions with 3-1 records when they squared off at Cleveland. Green Bay turned what was expected to be a close game into a 49–17 rout, as Taylor ran for 158 yards and scored four touchdowns. Brown settled for 72 yards, as his team was forced to pass once they fell far behind.

The second meeting hardly counted. In January 1964 at Miami, the Pack beat the Browns 40–23 in the late and unlamented Runner-Up Bowl—a rinky-dink television show between the division second-place finishers the NFL concocted and foisted on the public for several years. Taylor played only the first half and gained 44 yards. Brown ran only 11 times for 56 yards.

A truer test came the following November at Green Bay. Taylor, playing with banged-up ribs, was held to 63 yards in 22 carries compared to Brown's 74 for 20, but Taylor led a second-half comeback that gave the Packers a 28–21 victory over the championship-bound Browns.

Their final confrontation was, of course, the 1965 championship game—Brown's last in a Cleveland uniform. Playing on a muddy Green Bay field, Brown was held to 50 yards. Taylor, with 96, was named the game's most valuable player.

Taylor's totals for the four meetings were 361 yards on 83 carries and seven touchdowns. Brown had 252 yards on 59 attempts and a single touchdown. Realistically, the Packers were the stronger team overall, and Cleveland was blown out of three of the four games, severely limiting Brown's running chances. Nevertheless, Taylor demonstrated Packer defensive tackle Henry Jordan's thesis that "he did better when he went against the better fullbacks in the league."

Jordan, who had been friendly with Jim Brown in Cleveland, regarded both fullbacks as "extremely intelligent. When I was at Cleveland, Brown and I often had long discussions on subjects ranging from art to social problems. Taylor shunned the spotlight, allowing his delightful wife, Dixie, to occupy it for him. He liked to give the impression he was a rough, tough, country boy and mumbled a lot, but if you got him talking finances, he came out bright and clear."

––––––––

"I was just a player. I enjoyed football. I enjoyed contact. I guess it's unusual, knowing that you're going to have some pain and have some suffering, and looking forward to it. And have a very strong positive attitude. You're focused on your position and your job, and once they give you that football—hand off to you—you're focused on picking up yards for the Green Bay Packers football team.

"I just tried to be the best possible football player I could be down in and down out. Maybe some players don't have that same attitude. Winning is part of the reward, but there's no guarantee that you are going to win, that you are going to be a Pro Bowler. There's none of that going to happen for sure.

"People evaluate on a scale. After you work hard and you accomplish something—maybe win two or three games—then you lose two or three and you're right between a rock and a hard place. You have to ask yourself why are you losing? Why can't you overcome that? Why can't you bear down and work harder and focus more?

"Everybody can't win. I accept that. There are going to be half winners and half losers. But still there's something inside, something you determine by choice—whether you're a winner or a loser. If you accept being a loser, that's what you're going to be. It's that thing inside of you that can make you a winner. It's not your legs that gain the yards.

"Everybody has size, everybody has speed, everybody has strength. There were another thousand or ten thousand football players who had the same opportunities I did. They all had average ability. They all had legs and arms and a heart, but they still did not produce as I did.

"And by choice."

PEACE AT LAST

13

One thing was clear by 1966. The American Football League wasn't going to go away. The five-year, $36-million TV deal the league signed with NBC in January 1964 made that plain. When the deal was announced, an NFL owner who didn't care to be named grudgingly admitted it gave "the other league substance." The Namath signing in '65 was further proof that the AFL was a fact.

More evidence of the AFL's health was Joe Foss's announcement (right after closing the deal with NBC) that the league planned to expand. Although he didn't give a timetable, he said a dozen groups had applied for franchises. "I'm sure this will be increased soon," he added. "We have received applications from four groups in Philadelphia, also others from Chicago, Los Angeles, Cincinnati, Columbus, Montreal, Atlanta, and Portland, Oregon." LA had been tried and found wanting, and butting heads against the Bears or Eagles seemed to make little sense, so it soon became clear that the AFL had its eye on Atlanta, a growing market in football-mad Dixie. In the spring, it came out that Leonard Reinsch, president of Cox Broadcasting, would receive an AFL franchise to put a new team into Atlanta's new county stadium.

This galvanized the NFL to get off the pot. Reinsch had a verbal commitment from Atlanta's mayor for use of the stadium, but the head of the stadium committee wanted to hold out for an NFL team. On June 30, 1965, a 15th NFL franchise was awarded to 41-year-old insurance executive Rankin M. Smith for $8.5 million. The team would commence operations in Atlanta in 1966. The South had always "belonged" to the Washington Redskins with a wide southern radio audience. The Redskins' Dixie fans had even been given as the reason Washington was the last NFL team to hire a black player, though owner George Preston Marshall's personal racism probably had more to do with it. The Marshall of old would have fought any move by the league into "his" territory. And the Marshall of old might have been able to make it stick. But after suffering a stroke in 1962, G.P.M. seldom left his bed. By 1966, the Redskins' decisions were in other hands. He died in 1969.

Expanding to Atlanta was an obvious slap in the face of the AFL, but the Other League rebounded nicely in August 1965 by awarding a ninth franchise to Miami, for $7.5 million. The owners of the new team, which would play in the Orange Bowl, were little-known Minneapolis lawyer Joe Robbie and well-known television star Danny Thomas. Whatever the AFL might have lost in preferred real estate, it had picked up in glitz.

The NFL's old guard—the ones who'd been in the football business when the players still wore leather helmets (or no helmets)—were losing influence, and they were the ones who most resented the upstart AFL. Marshall's illness pretty much silenced one of the strongest, most hard-headed leaders. Right or wrong, Marshall had been a powerful force. Halas was still there, along with Art Rooney and Wellington Mara, but as each new expansion franchise was added, and Atlanta was the third since 1960, the voting majority at league meetings shifted toward the newcomers, men who'd made their wealth in areas other than football—men more likely to make decisions based on good business practice without being haunted by pro football's past when mere survival was precarious.

Perhaps the shift in the NFL's balance of power helped prod George Halas toward a little show of force in early 1966. Just before Christmas '65, the Los Angeles Rams fired Coach Harland Svare after a last-place 4-10 season. Before you could say reindeer on the roof, George Allen phoned Johnny Sanders, one of the Rams' staff men, with the suggestion that the next LA coach should be that bright young fellow George Allen. The Monday after Christmas, Sanders passed the suggestion on to Rams' owner Dan Reeves, who saw merit in it. One problem. Allen was at that moment employed as an assistant coach with the Chicago Bears. In fact, he was a very visible assistant coach, having received much of the credit for molding the Chicago defense that had been so dominant in the Bears' 1963 championship. Reeves told Sanders to tell Allen to ask George Halas for permission for Allen to talk to Reeves. With all that telling and asking, something was bound to get snafued in the translation.

Allen got back word that Halas had okayed his negotiating with the Rams, and on January 9, he was hired. And George Halas exploded.

"A flagrant case of tampering with a coach under contract," he called it. Allen had two years to go on his Bears' contract.

According to Reeves and Allen, Halas had first given permission and then rescinded it. He added, "I can't believe George Halas will stand in [Allen's] way."

170

Oh yeah? "I'll see you in court," said Halas.

Regardless of who had told whom to ask whom about what, Halas had the law on his side. Allen was under contract to Chicago, and as the court said, that was that. Then having flexed his muscles and made his point, Halas told the Rams they were welcome to Allen. He may have had second thoughts when Allen's Rams beat the Bears 31–17 at LA in the season's second week.

That was a footnote. The biggest news of 1966 was the escalation of the NFL-AFL war.

As the two leagues squared off each year, there was only one clear winner—the players. Since the emergence of the AFL in 1960, the number of available jobs had nearly doubled and the players' compensation for knocking each other down on Sunday afternoons was steadily climbing. The media focused on what they considered the absurd sums paid to untried rookies, but veterans inevitably saw their salaries rise too. On a purely emotional level, many AFL players might have welcomed peace if it allowed them the chance to knock those uppity NFL players on their cans. And many NFL players yearned to put the upstart AFLers in their place. But on a practical level, the war could have continued into the next century as far as the players were concerned.

Bonus signings of Namath-extravagance reached new levels in 1966. Tommy Nobis, the All-America linebacker, was induced to sign with Atlanta for a reported $600,000. Green Bay got runners Jim Grabowski and Donny Anderson as designated heirs to Taylor-Hornung for an estimated million between them. Kansas City paid USC's Mike Garrett $400,000. Namath joked he "was born a year too soon."

For the owners, the war was bad. It forced them to pay the hired help considerably more than they cared to. NFL owners longed for the good ol' days when they could simply draft a linebacker and then give him the option of signing or going to work for the County Road. AFL owners, though they'd never enjoyed that position, could easily see the advantages. It was such a senseless waste to load the new kids up with dollars before they proved their worth.

Another problem owners faced, while not as obvious as the dollars and sense question of salaries, was the increased difficulty in building a winning team. When any number of key draft choices might disdain signing with your club, it increased the likelihood that gaping holes would remain unfilled. If you needed an offensive guard in the good ol' days, you just went out and drafted a couple of likelies and then let one or the other win the job in training camp. But while the war raged, you had to be pretty sure the guard you drafted could do the job and then you had to sign him. Teams were drafting not on the basis of the best available football player,

George Allen.

171

but on the basis of the best available football player they could sign. Tex Schramm, the Dallas Cowboys general manager, was particularly upset in 1966 when he passed over Grabowski, a hotshot fullback from Illinois, because the kid seemed headed for Houston in the AFL. Eventually, Grabowski was drafted and signed by Green Bay.

The mess didn't end with getting a draftee to sign your contract. Once you had him wearing your colors, you had to keep him around for a couple of years to justify all the money you'd spent, even if he proved a lummox who could barely chew gum and run a 5.8 40 at the same time. All that meant scouting costs were up too. Revenues were climbing, of course, by way of ever-larger attendances and TV contracts, but too much of the intake was flowing right back out.

The war was both good and bad for fans. They had a lot more football to watch. More heroes, more touchdowns, and a far likelier chance that a team played within driving distance. But on the whole, fans wanted peace. Most fans held some loyalty to one league or the other based on where their favorite team played. They saw prized draft choices slip away and bemoaned their loss, certain that had the athletes in question been signed a championship would have followed. It mattered not how many gifted football players were garnered by their team; there was always a tragic load of might-have-beens for the ones that got away. Fans also wanted to see some sort of super championship game between the leagues.

As to settling the war, neither players nor fans had any power to bring peace. The only ones who could continue or discontinue the conflict were the owners. And they weren't talking to each other.

The NFL registered a clear-cut victory in signing their 1966 draft choices. The older league signed 174 of its 232 draftees; the Other League got only 83 of its 181. There were 111 players who were drafted by teams from each league. The NFL got 79 of them, the AFL only 28, and four went unsigned. The NFL also had perhaps the showier names, including Texas linebacker Tommy Nobis, Illinois fullback Jim Grabowski, and Texas Tech halfback Donny Anderson. Anderson (who'd been drafted as a future in 1965), Grabowski, and Minnesota lineman Gale Gillingham all signed with league champ Green Bay. Them that had seemed to be them that was getting.

Washington raised some eyebrows by drafting Princeton placekicker Charlie Gogolak on the first round. No one had ever gone that high for a kicker before. Charlie was the younger brother of Pete Gogolak, Buffalo's sidewinder kicker.

The AFL's poor draft and lingering resentment over losing Atlanta as an expansion team were enough to tip the scales against Commissioner Joe Foss. The former fighter pilot had survived Harry Wismer only to run afoul of Sonny Werblin. The New York owner complained that Foss was inaccessible, that he was always "en route" and Werblin never knew where.

In January, Foss probably lost the support of Houston's Bud Adams when he invalidated a trade that would have sent Chargers' defensive stars Earl Faison and Ernie Ladd to the Oilers. He cited as his reason "tampering" by Adams and hit the Oiler owner with a $25,000 fine. Naturally, the Chargers weren't thrilled with the trade cancellation either. Sid Gillman had never been a Foss admirer, but, though Sid had a free hand in running the team, Barron Hilton did his own voting at league meetings. Nevertheless, no Charger official was likely to be happy about the development. Faison and Ladd had played out their options and would become free agents on May 1.

By early 1966, the Dump Foss movement had grown to the point where it was only a matter of time. On April 7, Foss cut to the chase and resigned as AFL Commissioner.

To replace him, the Other League tabbed Al Davis. One thing no one ever accused Davis of is settling for the status quo. Give him an inch and he'll make his status quo-er than yours. Here, they gave him a whole league. He'd insisted on dictatorial powers, and the upshot was "Look out, NFL!" Davis was a hawk. The cold war that had revolved around rookie signings, TV ratings, and nasty words was about to heat up.

Certainly Oakland Al was on a hot streak. Only four years before, he'd been a relatively unknown assistant coach with the Chargers. Since then, he'd saved the Oakland franchise from the abyss and turned the Raiders into one of the league's best teams. The turnaround he'd wrought in Oakland was sometimes compared with the one performed by Lombardi in Green Bay, and if you didn't count Vince's three league and four division titles, the comparison had some viability. Before taking office, Davis gave up his long-term contract as coach and general manager of the Raiders. When questioned by newsmen, he brushed aside problems with the NFL as not among his immediate goals and objectives. "My goal is to make the AFL the best league in football," he told them. "My first job is dedication to the growth of the league."

Actually, his first job was to help break up a scuffle between one of the owners and a newsman. Bud Adams and *Houston Post* sports writer Jack Gallagher got into it over an attempt by a *Post* photographer to get a picture of Davis and some of the league officials.

Davis had soft-pedaled the competition with the other league in his first statements, but soon declared war. He began talking about expanding into Chicago and Los Angeles. It was no secret that several AFL owners favored moving into larger markets and had urged Lamar Hunt to relocate the

Chiefs to Chicago and the Phipps brothers to shift the Broncos to Los Angeles. Expansion teams squaring off against the Bears and Rams would almost certainly be money-losers at first, even though they might improve the AFL's position when it came time to negotiate the next TV contract. But the only immediate reason to expand into existing NFL markets was to injure the older league.

However, the first real shot fired, as opposed to tough talk, came from the NFL. On May 17, the New York Giants dropped what the *Baltimore Sun* called "a 10-megaton bomb" by signing Pete Gogolak, Buffalo's erstwhile sidewinder kicker.

"He sought us out," Wellington Mara told reporters. "There was no bonus involved." Gogolak had played out his option and was free to sign with anybody he cared to, but the perception was that he'd been stolen by the NFL. No one had jumped leagues since Willard Dewveall went to Houston in 1961. Since then, in an unofficial coexistence policy, a player signed by one league stayed in that league until no other league team wanted him.

The Gogolak defection wasn't greeted with universal cheers among other NFL owners, many of whom feared repercussions. For example, the Lions held draft rights to Faison going back to 1961, and as a new free agent he

Pete Gogolak.

was fair game. But when asked if the Lions had contacted Faison, General Manager Edward Anderson said, "We felt it wasn't a good policy and that it could trigger something. This came about suddenly. We will have to do some thinking about it."

Muggs Halas, son of George Halas, said nearly the same thing about Ernie Ladd, to whom the Bears held draft rights: "We have to think it over and after we do we'll issue a statement in a couple of days."

If Wellington Mara thought he could rub Pete Gogolak in Al Davis's face and remain unscathed, he was rudely awakened the next day when the Associated Press reported that at least four Giants players had been contacted by the AFL. The AP named back Steve Thurlow, end Bobby Crespino, and center Greg Larson as having been approached by the Chargers and back Tucker Frederickson as a target of the Oilers. Next, a Detroit radio station reported the AFL's expansion Miami team was after all-pro tackle Alex Karras and several other stars. In the next week or so, if every story or rumor was true, the AFL sang its siren song for everybody in the NFL except Pete Rozelle. Dick Young of the *New York Daily News* wrote that Ralph Wilson of Buffalo had shown an NFL owner two checks for $500,000, one made out to Dick Butkus and the other to Gale Sayers. "If you raid Gogolak, I'll have these checks certified and go shopping. I can write a hundred checks like these." Wilson denied the story, but if the war was to come down to matching dollar for dollar, the NFL would have trouble keeping up with men like Wilson, Werblin, Adams, Hilton, and Hunt.

However, Davis's war strategy was actually much more practical. He zeroed in on selected NFL stars—somewhere between a half dozen and two dozen—and offered them lucrative contracts for 1967 if they'd agree to play out their options in 1966. His primary targets were quarterbacks.

On May 27, the Raiders claimed they'd corralled Rams quarterback Roman Gabriel. The Rams counterclaimed that Gabriel had signed a three-year contract to stay with them.

That one seemed headed for court, but the $750,000 Houston promised 49ers quarterback John Brodie looked solid. Within days the rumor mill had several other NFL stars, including Paul Hornung and Mike Ditka, headed for the AFL. Who might have lined up with whom in 1967 will never be known, because in early June signing rumors were replaced by rumors of a merger. And these rumors were right.

Newspaper wisdom at the time credited Al Davis's tough war policy with bringing the NFL to the bargaining table. The older league hadn't just blinked, the columnists said, it had flinched. The columnists were wrong. In point of fact, Davis had nearly kept the merger from happening.

Tex Schramm, the Dallas Cowboys' president–general manager, had been watching the war with growing alarm. When many teams based their 1966 draft choices on whom they could sign instead of whom they needed, he knew it was time to do something drastic. Otherwise, both leagues would become unbalanced, with the richer clubs picking up all the plums. Teams that survived on only their football earnings, like Pittsburgh, would be left in the dust.

Schramm moved. He called Lamar Hunt and set up a meeting for April 4—three days before Joe Foss resigned.

The Schramm-Hunt meeting, surely as historic as the famous 1920 conclave in a Hupmobile garage that started the NFL, had its own vehicular overtones. Hunt was scheduled to fly from Kansas City to Houston, and responding to Schramm's urgency, he agreed to stop off at Love Field airport in Dallas. There by the statue of the Texas Ranger in the lobby, he met Schramm. The two men who'd fought for three years over Dallas's football loyalties walked to the parking lot unnoticed and sat in the front seat of Schramm's Oldsmobile to thrash out the outlines of a merger.

Surprisingly, they were in agreement on many issues. But they still had to sell the idea to their leagues. Over the next several months, negotiations among Schramm, Hunt, Pete Rozelle, and an AFL merger committee with Billy Sullivan and Ralph Wilson were conducted primarily over the telephone. According to Hunt, the biggest obstacle was personal antagonism. These bitter enemies of six years were looking for a way to climb into bed with each other. And each side was sure the other was intent on rape.

The Gogolak signing confirmed the NFL's deviousness in AFL minds. Wilson and Sullivan began to think that Hunt was being led on by the NFL—led on to some down-the-road slaughter. Meanwhile, Wellington Mara got plenty of complaints from his fellow NFL owners, most of whom knew about the ongoing Schramm-Hunt talks.

Al Davis's deals with Brodie and maybe Gabriel nearly derailed everything. In some NFL minds, it proved the AFL was laying a trap. And even if Hunt was on the up and up, Davis was obviously going in a different direction. So who was running that store anyway?

On Memorial Day, Hunt was in Indianapolis for the 500. He spent almost all his time on the phone talking to Schramm and Rozelle. By June 6, they had it worked out. The announcement came two days later: the NFL had approved the deal unanimously; the AFL had accepted with the Jets and Raiders dissenting.

The terms:

1. All existing franchises would be kept.
2. A championship game would be held after the 1966 season, in January '67.

Lamar Hunt and Pete Rozelle sharing a sideline after ending pro football's cold war.

3. The leagues would continue to play separate schedules until 1970, at which time teams from each *conference* would play a single schedule. Until then, teams from either league would meet only in postseason and preseason games.

4. The whole shebang would be presided over by one commissioner—Pete Rozelle.

5. Each league would add an expansion franchise in 1967. Two other expansion teams would be added sometime later.

6. Beginning in 1967, the two leagues would hold a common draft. Between them, they'd spent $7 million corralling 1966 draft choices from each other, but now the bonanza was over for the players.

7. The AFL would pay $26 million to the NFL (to go to the Giants and 49ers) for the right to impinge on franchised territory.

Al Davis resigned as AFL commissioner and went back to Oakland. He could have stayed on as league president, of course. "Generals win wars," he said. "Politicians negotiate peace." Davis was no politician. He told Billy Sullivan he'd been "sold down the river." Milt Woodward was appointed president. Although the AFL was no longer the Other League and after 1969 was no league at all, loyalties continued. To this day, you can find plenty of "AFL people" who long for the days when their league was separate and (in their minds, anyway) equal.

The merger wasn't quite out of the woods yet. Turning two leagues into one presented a few antitrust problems that required some legislation out of Washington. Rozelle went down to the nation's capital and talked nice. To absolutely no one's surprise, the necessary legislation was signed into law in October. Find a politician who'd vote against the Super Bowl!

By midsummer, 1966 was already one of the most significant years in pro football history. What could the playing season bring that wouldn't be anticlimactic?

The expansion Miami Dolphins got off to an auspicious start when little Joe Auer, drafted from Buffalo, returned the opening kickoff of their first game all the way for a touchdown. After that it was mostly downhill for the rookie-castoff combo. Injuries so decimated the quarterback position that Coach George Wilson was finally forced to start his son George Wilson, Jr. Junior justified his spot on the roster but was obviously not the long-range solution.

The Boston Patriots bounced back from a rotten 1965 to challenge Buffalo. Fullback Jim Nance had been so fat in his rookie year that the coaches threatened to switch him to offensive guard. For '66 he slimmed down to a svelte 240 pounds and set a new AFL rushing record with 1,458 yards. He wasn't nifty, but his straight-ahead power and newfound speed made a nice complement to Babe Parilli's passes. The Pats knocked off the Bills twice during the season, 20–10 at Buffalo and 14–3 at home. All they needed to take the Eastern crown was a win over the Jets at Shea in the final regular season game. Instead, the defense, which had been stellar most of the year, caved in to Namath and company, wasting a near-400 yard performance by Parilli in a 38–28 loss.

Meanwhile, Buffalo closed the season by beating Denver to give them their third straight Eastern Division title. Lou Saban had resigned as coach after the 1965 season to return to college coaching at the University of Maryland, but Assistant Coach Joe Collier had taken over and knew which buttons to push. The main Buffalo button was still defense. All-AFL Tom Sestek nursed an aching knee, but Jim Dunaway and Ron McDole took up the slack in the line. Linebackers were Mike Stratton, Harry Jacobs, and John Tracy, backed by future coach Marty Schottenheimer and punting

Jim Nance.

specialist Paul Maguire, who also served as team comedian. Defensive backs George Saimes, Butch Byrd, Hagood Clarke, and Tom Janik helped hold opponents to the lowest completion percentage in the league. Jack Kemp still quarterbacked the offense. After throwing to make-do receivers the year before, he had Golden Wheels Dubenion back healthy and a fine rookie receiver in Bobby Crockett. Another rookie, slasher Bobby Burnett, led the team in rushing, but the Bills still lacked a big-play breakaway threat. Nevertheless, throw out the two losses to Boston, and Collier's Eastern champs looked stronger than Saban's two previous AFL champions.

Barron Hilton sold controlling interest in his Chargers to a group of 21

179

businessmen headed by Gene Klein and Sam Schulman for $10 million. The new owners got Sid Gillman's expertise, John Hadl's passing, and Lance Alworth's sensational receiving. They also got a defense that their sisters could run on. The 7-6-1 record was better than a stick in the eye but disappointing after so many division titles.

During the short time Al Davis fought the good fight as AFL commissioner, life went on in Oakland. So they hired John Rauch as head coach. Then Davis returned as managing partner, Rauch's boss. Surprisingly, the two worked together well, although every time Rauch made a substitution or called a play, the media looked up at Davis's box to see if he'd pulled a string. Quarterback Tom Flores threw 24 touchdown passes, but the offense was spotty, and much of the blame fell on Flores, who had a head for quarterbacking but not the arm that Davis wanted for a vertical offense. In Davis's philosophy, completing four straight passes of seven yards each wasn't as good as connecting on one out of four—if the one completion went 60 yards for a touchdown. When the Raiders finished 8-5-1, in second place again, Davis decided to go shopping for a bomb-thrower.

It was a great year for Lamar Hunt. His league became an equal partner with the NFL and his team dominated his league. After several years in the doldrums, seemingly jinxed, the Kansas City Chiefs blew through their season with an 11-2-1 mark. Their defense was first rate. Defensive backs Johnny Robinson and Bobby Hunt tied for the AFL interception leadership with ten each. Bobby Bell was one of the best outside linebackers in football, and young bulls Buck Buchanan and Aaron Brown bulwarked the line. The offense scored a league-high 448 points. When Mike Garrett signed for one of the last big bonuses before the merger, some questioned whether at five-foot-nine and 195 pounds he could live up to his Heisman Trophy. No problem. Garrett gave the Chiefs the outside threat they'd needed to go with inside runners Curtis McClinton and Bert Coan. And with a reliable running game grinding out the yards, quarterback Len Dawson could pick and choose when to sling his darts to reliable Chris Burford or spectacular Otis Taylor. In his second season, Taylor joined Alworth, Powell, and Maynard as one of the league's premier receivers, averaging more than 22 yards every time he caught a pass. Dawson, the league's top passer, threw 26 touchdowns.

There was more on the line than ever before in the championship game. This wasn't just for the league crown; the winner would face the NFL's champion in the first interleague championship game. Kansas City had the better season record, but Buffalo was two-time champion and had split a pair of games with the Chiefs during the season. The Bills also had the home field advantage.

180

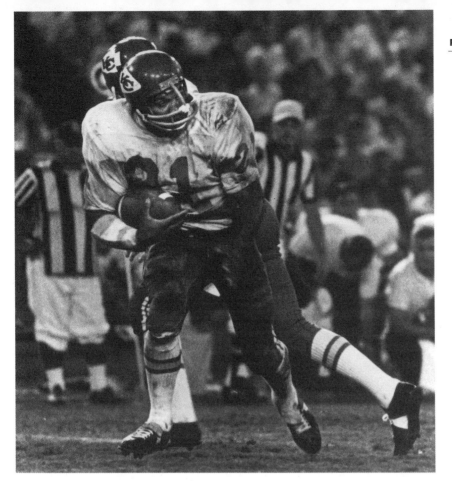

Mike Garrett.

The Chiefs scored first on a 29-yard pass from Dawson to tight end Fred Arbanas. The Bills came back to tie the score before the first quarter ended on a 69-yard Kemp-to-Dubenion pass. The Chiefs jumped back into the lead early in the second quarter when Dawson hit Otis Taylor for a TD. But once more the Bills drove down the field, looking to tie. Then, in the shadow of Kansas City's goal posts, the Chiefs' defense executed the play of the game. Johnny Robinson intercepted a Kemp pass in the end zone and raced up field 72 yards. A few moments later, Mike Mercer kicked a 32-yard field goal to make the score 17–7. Instead of in a tie, Buffalo found itself two scores behind at the half. Kansas City shut down the Bills in the second half, and Mike Garrett scored two fourth-quarter rushing touchdowns to make the final 31–7.

Bring on the NFL!

―――――

With the addition of the expansion Atlanta Falcons, the NFL's Eastern Division numbered eight teams—the same size as the AFL had been until

181

1966. Eight teams competing for a single division crown and with only 14 games to resolve the race meant that most fans had little to look forward to by mid-October, when their local heroes dropped out of contention.

In his third year of an unprecedented 15-year contract as coach and general manager, Joe Kuharich brought the Eagles in at 9-5, their best record in five years. A strong no-name defense and a grind-it-out ground attack, featuring Tim Brown, Earl Gros, Tom Woodeshick, and Izzy Lang, made up for a poor year by passer Norm Snead.

Cleveland fans wondered if there was life—or at least victory—after Jim Brown. The Great One had planned to retire after the 1965 season, but by the next summer, he was waffling. When training camp began, he was in England shooting a movie, *The Dirty Dozen*. After some pointed comments by owner Art Modell as to Jim's deciding on his priorities coupled with a threat to fine him $1,000 for every day he missed camp, Brown quite sensibly bid goodbye to football in favor of Hollywood. Surprisingly, the Cleveland running attack kept right on truckin'. Leroy Kelly had spent two years returning kicks and sitting on the bench waiting for Brown to take a breather. Given the chance to start, he made the most of it, finishing second in the league in rushing with 1,141 yards. He didn't have Brown's power, but he was quick, clever, and determined. His 5.5 average per carry and 15 rushing touchdowns were certainly Brownish. Ernie Green, heretofore a blocker for Brown, got to run more often and averaged 5.2 per carry.

At the same time, Dr. Frank Ryan had the best crop of receivers of his career. Paul Warfield came back healthy to go with Gary Collins and rookie tight end Milt Morin. Green and Kelly were also good receivers. Counting his blessings, Ryan threw a league-leading 29 touchdown passes. Unfortunately, 29 or older was the age of most of the defensive regulars. The Browns started slow, losing two out of three, and ended slow, losing two out of four, to finish in a second-place tie with the Eagles at 9-5.

The NFL's best offensive show was in Dallas. Tom Landry had started from scratch in 1960 and built an original. Three times the Cowboys topped 50 points in games on their way to a league-high 445. Dandy Don Meredith, Bullet Bob Hayes, and rugged Ralph Neely were at the tops of their game. Steady Don Perkins was joined at running back with a surprise star in Dan Reeves, who'd been riding the bench for two years after being signed as a free agent. A quarterback at South Carolina, he didn't have the arm for the pros. But then his size was only middling and he was slow afoot, so his future as a running back wasn't all that bright either—until he got his chance to show what his heart and head could accomplish. Amid the Cowboys' collection of Blue Chippers, he came off Blue Collar. He plugged for tough yards off tackle, paddled around end, threw a mean option pass,

182

Leroy Kelly.

and caught passes in traffic. The Cowboys had the league's most complicated and varied offense, and Reeves fit in perfectly. All told, he scored 16 touchdowns evenly split between rushing and passing.

Defensively, the Cowboys had all-pros in tackle Bob Lilly, linebackers Chuck Howley and Lee Roy Jordan, and defensive backs Cornell Green and Mel Renfro. With all their offense, they also led the Eastern Division in fewest points allowed.

But for all their talent, the season wasn't a waltz for the Cowboys. The Redskins were a particular thorn. In November at Washington, Meredith sneaked for a touchdown and fired two bombs to Hayes—one for 95 yards—to build up a 21–6 lead. Then Sonny Jurgensen got cranking. By the time there were less than two minutes left, the Cowboys trailed 30–28 with the ball on their own three. Meredith passed and scrambled his way downfield. A late hit by Washington linebacker John Reger tacked 15 yards onto the drive to put the ball on the Redskins' 12. Danny Villanueva kicked a

183

Sonny Jurgensen.

chip-shot field goal for the win. Jurgensen had accounted for 347 passing yards, but Dandy Don had 406.

A month later, the same two teams met in Dallas. In a wild game, the lead changed hands three times and the score was tied four times. This time it was Jurgensen who led the last-ditch drive. The score was tied 31-all with two minutes left when he took over at his own 46. He surprised the Cowboys by staying on the ground. Three running plays moved the ball to the Dallas 22. As the clock ran out, Charlie Gogolak kicked the winning points from 29 yards out.

———————

In the West, everyone tried to catch the Packers. Baltimore, the number-one contender, lost its opener at Green Bay and fell further behind by losing its fourth game to the Bears at Chicago. Although Don Shula's team trailed all the way, the Colts remained one of the league's stronger teams primarily due to the presence of Johnny Unitas. Bouncing back from his 1965 injury, Johnny U. had a generic Unitas season with 2,748 yards gained and 22 touchdowns. His uncharacteristic 24 interceptions stemmed in part from the Colts' lack of a dominating ground game and the necessity of throwing the ball more often than was prudent. Raymond Berry, Jimmy Orr, and John Mackey remained a strong trio of receivers, but Lenny Moore slumped and was obviously nearing the end of his career. The Baltimore defense was growing old—older still when 40-year-old Gino Marchetti came out of retirement to lend a hand late in the season—but it stayed effective. Moving young Mike Curtis from offense to outside linebacker provided a shot in the arm.

Finishing just behind the Colts at 8-6 were the Rams with their first .500-plus season since 1958. New coach George Allen installed an unspectacular offense built around the running of veteran Dick Bass, the short passes of Roman Gabriel, and the field goals of Bruce Gossett. It was a far cry from the glory days of the 1950s when Waterfield and Van Brocklin threw bombs to Hirsch and Fears.

The Rams' strength was on defense. The Fearsome Foursome of Deacon Jones, Rosey Grier, Merlin Olsen, and Lamar Lundy was already in place when Allen arrived. Behind them, he filled in with veterans—a tactic that would become his trademark. For linebackers, he lured 30-year-old Jack Pardee out of retirement, signed 35-year-old Bill George after the Bears let

Deacon Jones (75), Merlin Olsen (74), Roger Brown (78), and Lamar Lundy (76) behind Olsen, the Los Angeles Rams' Fearsome Foursome.

him go, and traded for veterans Myron Pottios and Maxie Baughan. Another important acquisition was Irv Cross, a veteran cornerback. Deacon Jones had many virtues, but modesty was not among them. "I'm the best defensive end around," he declared. "I'd hate to have to play against me." For those who question his ranking of himself, the Deacon can point to his 26 quarterback sacks in 1967 and 28 in 1968. Both numbers are in excess of the "official" record of 22, set by Mark Gastineau in 1984, the first year sacks became an official, leaguewide stat.

Allen, with his defensive bent, was a perfect match for Jones. "He was the greatest coach I ever played for," Jones says. "He believed in discipline and conditioning. Totally dedicated. He would work 24 hours a day at that film projector, and he would come up with something against anybody."

Green Bay cruised through a serene 12-2 season. Bart Starr was again the league's most efficient passer. Rookies Donny Anderson and Jim Grabowski saw occasional action while Jim Taylor, Paul Hornung, and Elijah Pitts carried the running load for one more season. The Packers scored an adequate number of points—more than adequate considering the defense. The Packs' defenders limited opponents to an average of under 12 points per game. Lombardi rounded up the usual suspects—Davis, Jordan, Kostelnik, Aldridge, Nitschke, Robinson, Caffey, Wood, Adderley, Brown—added in cornerback Bob Jeter, and produced a classic.

The NFL Championship Game provided a variety of contrasts. The Cowboys had the league's best offense, the Packers the best defense. Dallas was a young team just arriving, Green Bay had been at or near the top for eight seasons. The Cowboys were spectacular, the Packers almost never made a mistake. Coaches Landry and Lombardi, both Giants aides in the '50s, were ice and fire. But Landry, the epitome of cool, ran a hot team. Lombardi, the era's most charismatic coach, ran a team of technicians.

The smart money was on the Packers. Green Bay's defense would shut down the Dallas offense. And Dallas, in its first championship game, would make critical mistakes. The smart money was half right.

As soon as Green Bay got the ball, it drove 76 yards to score, Pitts taking a 17-yard pass from Starr for the touchdown. On the ensuing kickoff, Cowboy Mel Renfro fumbled. Jim Grabowski swooped in, picked up the ball, and dashed 18 yards for a second Green Bay touchdown.

Dallas bounced back and got two touchdowns of its own before the first quarter ended, moving through the famed Packers' defense like it was manned by mere mortals. In the second quarter, Carroll Dale found himself isolated on Cornell Green and took a Starr pass for a 51-yard touchdown, but the Cowboys' Danny Villanueva got some of that back with a chip-shot field goal. At the half it was 21–17, Green Bay.

Tom Landry.

Villanueva opened the second half scoring with another field goal to narrow the score to 21–20. Then, as the smart money predicted, Green Bay took over and scored twice more on Starr passes. The second score came as the indirect result of a Cowboy mental error when Bob Hayes inexplicably fielded a punt at his one. Dallas's punt from the end zone a few moments later gave the Packers excellent field position. When Bob Lilly got a hand up and blocked the extra point on the second TD, it didn't seem to matter. With five minutes left, Dallas was dead, 34–20.

Or were they? Lombardi knew better. "What the hell . . . what the hell!" he stormed. "One lousy extra point my grandmother could make! Now we got to sweat this thing out!"

On a third-and-20 at the Dallas 32, Frank Clarke broke clear on a deep

Z-in pattern. Tom Brown slipped. Meredith laid it into Clarke's hands. "That catch was the highlight of my career," Clarke said later. "I knew I had Brown beaten, then I looked back and saw Don's arm cocked and the ball coming and I knew it was up to me. I didn't think about the importance of the game or the millions of people watching on television. I just wanted to get that ball in my hands and hold on." Clarke sped the rest of the way for a 68-yard touchdown: 34–27.

Green Bay tried to run down the clock, but they were too conservative, and when Don Chandler punted poorly under a Dallas rush, the Cowboys had the ball in Packers' territory a mere 47 yards from a tie game. Meredith ate up 21 of that with a pass to Clarke, and a couple more by sending Perkins into the line. Then he went to Clarke again. The Packers' Tom Brown knew he was beaten. In desperation, he grabbed Clarke around the waist at the two before the Cowboy could grab the football. Interference! The official put the ball down 72 inches away from the goal line and then signaled for the mandatory two-minutes-remaining timeout.

Meredith went to the sideline to confer with Landry.

Pettis Norman, a good blocker, trotted onto the field to replace Hayes, who blocked about as well as Johnny Belinda sang. It was a substitution Dallas always made when they got inside an opponent's ten-yard-line. But, instead of Hayes, Frank Clarke went out. No one caught the mix-up. Not Landry, not Meredith, not Hayes, Norman, or Clarke. When Reeves slammed into the line on first down, he got only a yard.

On second down, Meredith rolled right and lobbed a pass to Norman waiting to be a hero in the end zone. Norman dropped it. No matter; the Cowboys were offsides anyway. Second and six.

The situation had changed—a perfect time for a timeout to talk things over. Nobody called it.

Meredith called for a pass to Reeves. He didn't know that Dan had caught a finger in the eye on his dash into the line and was seeing double. Reeves didn't argue. He didn't catch the pass either. Third and six.

Meredith rushed a pass to Norman that was complete—but only to the two-yard-line. When Tom Brown brought Norman down, he was holding his face mask, according to photos. Photos don't drop yellow hankies. Fourth and two.

Roll-out! Meredith faked to Perkins to freeze linebacker Dave Robinson, then kept moving with a run-pass option. Robinson ignored Perkins and slanted outside too quickly for tackle Leon Donohue to block him. Hayes had a shot at Robinson. Had Clarke been in he might have got him but Hayes was brushed off like lint. Robinson grabbed hold of Meredith's left arm. With his right, Don launched a pass that fluttered, sputtered, and

nestled right in the hands of Green Bay's Tom Brown. "I noticed Hayes on my left and another receiver on my right," Brown explained. "I just tried to move between them and the ball was there. It made me feel great after my mistakes." Green Bay, 34–27.

Bring on the AFL!

Don Meredith.

———

Both league championships had been settled on January 1, leaving two weeks before the long anticipated first meeting between the NFL and AFL.

Two weeks of unprecedented media hype! Most of it was just as unmemorable and unsubstantial as the stuff cranked out before this year's Super Bowl. Or next year's. An exception were the quotes emanating from Fred Williamson, one of the Kansas City cornerbacks. Fred, who later followed his natural bent into a movie career, had plenty to say about himself (outstanding), the Packers (overrated), the NFL (ditto), and anything else that came to his mind (God knows!). Nicknamed "The Hammer," he explained, "I have broken thirty helmets with my forearm alone. I can't wait to add to my total against the Packers."

Fred's boasts were good copy, but they didn't sway bettors. Green Bay was installed as a whopping 13-point favorite. In wagering shorthand, a 13-point favorite is likely to lose only if the Goodyear blimp lands on them as they leave the dressing room. The Chiefs' Curtis McClinton demurred, saying the Packers should be *maybe* favored by three points. If he'd been allowed to bet, he could have had several thousand takers.

The game, scheduled for January 15 in the 100,000-seat Los Angeles Coliseum, was officially the AFL-NFL Championship Game, but the media was already calling it the Super Bowl. Both NBC and CBS paid a million dollars to telecast. Certainly the fee was super. Even though it was blacked out in the LA area and the weather was warm and sunny, only 61,946 paid to get in—the only Super Bowl not a sellout.

There was no way it could live up to seven years of anticipation and two weeks of industrial-strength tub thumping. It didn't, but the first half wasn't all that bad.

Fears of a blowout were sparked when Green Bay scored in the opening quarter on a 37-yard Starr pass to Max McGee. Kansas City regrouped and came back to tie early in the second quarter when Dawson passed successfully to McClinton for a 17-yard touchdown. By now, Starr had zeroed in on KC's weakest defensive links—tackle Andy Rice, end Chuck Hurston, and cornerbacks Willie Mitchell and (couldn't you die!) Fred Williamson. Middle linebacker Sherrill Headrick was a soft touch on passes too. Skillfully, Starr led the Pack downfield until Jim Taylor burst over from 14 yards out. The Chiefs weren't quite ready for the bone heap. Dawson passed them back into field goal range, and Mike Mercer connected for 31 yards to make the score a respectable 14–10 at the half. Through 30 minutes of football, the AFL had not disgraced itself, was in fact still very much in the game. There was hope for the second half.

In the Packers' dressing room, someone had printed "Know Thyself" on the chalkboard.

Kansas City took the second half kickoff and moved upfield. On third down at the Kansas City 45, Dawson dropped back to pass and the Packers

Buck Buchanan smothers Bart Starr in one of the Chiefs'
few bright moments from the first Super Bowl.

blitzed. Four down linemen and three linebackers came at Dawson—the charge of the *heavy* brigade! Instead of taking a sack like a good little soldier, Dawson tried valiantly to make something out of nothing by launching a pass toward tight end Fred Arbanas. Henry Jordan got a hand on it going up and Willie Wood got both hands on it when it came down. Fifty yards later he was downed at the Chiefs' five. On the next play, Elijah Pitts nipped into the end zone.

The Chiefs were only 11 points down, but the game was really over. "They wouldn't respect our run again," Kansas City offensive tackle Jim Tyrer explained later. "Our play fakes were useless. They knew we had to pass, and they just flew at the quarterback." Dawson was a fine passer, but he didn't have the arm of a Jurgensen or Namath. He needed play-action to open the defense for his darts. Without it, he was meat.

"If you throw, throw, throw against Green Bay, you're going to lose," admitted KC Coach Stram.

Green Bay scored two more second half touchdowns to make the final 35–10 and took a little revenge on Fred Williamson. In the fourth quarter, he was the target of a patented Packer sweep. The Hammer got hammered. After the crunch, he was carried from the field with a broken arm. "I didn't even know he was playing until I saw him being carried from the field," said Lombardi in the most unkind cut of all.

Each losing Chiefs player received $7,500 for his efforts. Each Packer earned twice as much—$15,000—for more than doubling the score. It was good money, more than a few Green Bay players had made for the season, but most of the Packers were blasé about the victory, feeling that the real Super Bowl had been against Dallas two weeks earlier. One writer described them as displaying "about as much emotion as the third shift at the nut and bolt factory on pay day."

As they trooped to the dressing room, someone called out, "Another day and another dollar."

But Willie Wood described a "collective sigh of relief" in the Packers' dressing room. The pressure hadn't been to win. It had been to not lose. Green Bay, the league champion four out of the last six years, had carried the honor of the NFL onto the field against a foe that everyone in their league believed inferior. To lose such a game—well, the potential shame was unthinkable.

Another of Lombardi's postgame statements was quoted almost everywhere: "The Chiefs are a good team. But they don't compare with the top teams of the NFL." The next day he regretted the remark as ungenerous. Ungenerous, but to most observers, true.

Starr, who completed 16 of 23 passes for 250 yards and two touchdowns,

Super Bowl MVP
Bart Starr.

was voted the game's MVP. It could have gone to Max McGee. The
34-year-old veteran had caught only four passes all season. He played only
because Boyd Dowler was injured, but he finished the day with seven
catches—a couple of the circus variety—for 138 yards and two TDs. Or
Willie Wood may have earned it with the interception that turned a close
game into a rout. Or Henry Jordan, who tipped the pass. Or . . .

The Packers were all heroes. For the Chiefs and the AFL, the game
they'd wanted for so long hadn't turned out the way they'd hoped. Now it
was time to learn from their mistakes.

FORREST GREGG: "DISCIPLINE, CONDITIONING, AND ATTITUDE!"

14

When Vince Lombardi called Forrest Gregg "the best player I ever coached," he meant above the shoulder pads as much as below. To no ones's surprise, the former Green Bay all-pro has gone on to a successful coaching career, making a practice of revitalizing teams that have fallen to the depths. In 1976, he was named NFL coach of the year for bringing the Cleveland Browns back to respectability. In 1981, he took Cincinnati to its first Super Bowl and earned AFC coach of the year honors. By the mid-1980s he was back in Green Bay where the Packers had fallen on hard times. Gregg wasn't able to complete his rebuilding program there because his alma mater SMU needed him more. Having been given the "death penalty" for NCAA violations, the Mustangs no longer had any football program at all—the ultimate rebuilding challenge. In Gregg, they found the combination of inspirational coach and honorable gentleman the situation demanded.

Gregg was elected to the Pro Football Hall of Fame in 1977 after a 15-season NFL career. Many regard him as the best offensive tackle the league has seen. All-NFL from 1960 through 1967, he played on all five Packer championship teams. In 1971, his final year, he earned his third Super Bowl ring by helping the Dallas Cowboys to victory.

"I don't know where Coach Lombardi got the sweep. I suppose he brought it from the New York Giants, where Frank Gifford ran it. Other people have their versions of it. But he brought that play in and he really emphasized it. He diagramed that play on the blackboard the first offensive meeting we had. He said, 'If we're going to be successful offensively, this is one play we're going to have to run and run successfully.'

"He had a lot of good things involved in the sweep. One of them was the block the tight end made at the point of attack. With the Green Bay sweep, the tight end would split out about three yards and he just took that linebacker on. Wherever the linebacker went, the tight end took him. If the linebacker went outside, he took him outside, and we ran the play inside. If the linebacker went inside, he took him inside, and we ran outside. He didn't have to push him off the line of scrimmage five yards in order for us to gain.

"Our tight end on the 1961 and '62 teams was Ron Kramer. He was a good receiver and a really strong run blocker—one of the finest tight ends I ever saw. He didn't have a real long career, but, man! he was awesome when he was in his heyday. I don't think there was anybody any better. We had an off-tackle play where he and I would double team the defensive end. Man! that was the easiest job I ever had, just hanging around there with Ron. Sometimes I'd come off and hit that defensive end and then Ron would come down and hit him and you could just feel that guy's feet coming off the ground.

"Key blocks on the sweep were the fullback's block on the defensive end and the pulling guard's leading the ball carrier. Jerry Kramer was probably the best athlete of any of the offensive linemen. He had a lot of injury problems during his career, but he was a fine player.

"I ran a single wing in high school and then when I first went to college. I remember the single wing had a lot of pulling linemen—both guards and the off-tackle pulled sometimes. So, with the tight end and guards and fullback all blocking into the hole, the Green Bay sweep was a power play, like the old single wing. And there was the deception of the T-formation. It was sort of a synthesis of the T's quickness and the single wing's power.

"Coach Lombardi turned the Packers around, but let me give you a little background first. I was drafted in 1956. We had a guy at Green Bay whose name was Jack Vanisi. Jack was the personnel director and he was the guy in charge of everything. He did everything from scouting players to running the draft to signing players—the whole works. And Green Bay had not had a winning season since 1947, so we were drafting at a pretty good position. I thought he did a great job of accumulating talent.

"Basically, the talent was there when Coach Lombardi came. We had a good mixture of youth and age, but one thing we had a lot of was young players who just needed direction. One of the most important things Coach Lombardi did was he put discipline, conditioning, and attitude into the mix, and he kind of pulled everything together. I've tried to stress those things in my own coaching—discipline, conditioning, and attitude! Lombardi got the most out of the talent that was already there. That's what had to be done.

"The 1961 and '62 Packers had great potential. The squad wasn't very big, about 35 players, but the players we had were good. Jim Ringo, Jerry Kramer, Fuzzy Thurston, Bob Skoronski, Ron Kramer, Boyd Dowler, Max McGee, Jim Taylor, Paul Hornung, and Bart Starr. And that was just the offense! On defense we had Willie Davis, Dave Hanner. Henry Jordan was a fine defensive tackle, not big but quick! Ray Nitschke, Willie Wood, Herb Adderley, and on and on.

"Our 1966 team—the first Super Bowl winner—played really well. We played the Cowboys in Dallas for the NFL Championship. That was a close game, and it could have gone either way. We felt a great relief that we had won the NFL Championship again. That was the biggest thing in our lives at the time. But then, knowing we still had another game to play and not really knowing who those guys were, so to speak, and not knowing how good they were, made us apprehensive.

"Remember, when the AFL first started, I think everybody in the NFL sort of supposed it was probably going to be somewhat of a minor league. I think the attitude was 'Well, this will probably pass. We'll just wait and see because we're in the big league and they're in the minor league and they'll probably be a long time catching up to us.'

"But then they started getting competitive with draft choices. Both leagues were drafting the same players. We got a lot of good players, and we knew they were getting some good players too.

"So the thing about that first Super Bowl particularly was that we were playing an unknown. We were playing someone we really didn't know much about. It's hard to really know how good a team is going to be and what kind of competition it's going to be until you've actually played them. It's an uncertain thing.

"One thing we knew, this game would be the first time the two leagues met, and we certainly didn't want to lose.

"We prepared well for the game. We saw a lot of film. We knew the Chiefs had some good ball players. Some of their guys were high draft choices by both leagues. And some of them had played in the National Football League and been cut, but in time those people developed. We thought we could win the game. We were a confident team, but not overconfident. We didn't take the Chiefs for granted. That was one of the things I thought Coach Lombardi did a great job with—keeping our focus on the game, not letting us assume anything.

"And it all worked out.

"The 1960s were a time that professional football would have a hard time duplicating—ever. The other league evolved. Television. Pro football really came into its own.

"I don't know if ever a team will come along like the Packers, with so

many players who were household names. There have been great teams since. The Steelers in the '70s. The 49ers in the '80s. But take the 49ers. Everybody knows Joe Montana and maybe Jerry Rice. After that you start scratching your head. Who were those guys?

"I have people right now that I meet on the street who recognize me or tell me who I am and start talking about the Packers. Maybe their father took them to a game somewhere where we played. They start asking about this guy and that guy. They just like to remember. It's like they studied it. Jon Tenuta, an assistant coach here at SMU, can name every player on that Packer team of the '60s. He was a young kid living in Wisconsin when his father took him to some games.

"It was a unique time in professional football."

ICE

15

As part of the merger agreement, each league was to add an expansion team. The AFL put off their choice for a year, but the NFL got right at it and named New Orleans as its newest member on November 1, 1966. In mid-December, millionaire sportsman John Mecom, Jr., the majority stockholder, was named president. The new team, christened the Saints (as in "When the Saints Go Marching In"), hired one of Lombardi's Green Bay assistants, Tom Fears, as its first coach. Fears had been an all-pro end with the Rams in the 1950s. He had seen the best of times. As Saints coach, he would see the worst. Of all the teams added to the NFL since 1951, none took longer to achieve respectability than the Saints. Their first winning record would not be posted until 1987. By then, of course, Fears was remembered as only the first of nine unsuccessful New Orleans coaches.

The Saints were placed in what was called the Capitol Division of the Eastern Conference. With 16 teams now in the NFL (not to mention nine in the AFL), the league envisioned too many also-rans. The solution was to simply subdivide the Eastern and Western Conferences into two divisions each to produce four division winners, several more contenders, and—best of all—two extra playoff games. And money, money, money, money.

"Interest will be maintained," Rozelle crowed. "No team will finish lower than fourth." Of course, there would now be four last-place teams.

However, if two teams tied for a division title—as seemed more than likely to happen—there'd be no playoff to decide the winner. The schedule didn't allow for that. Instead, the NFL unveiled what would become the bane of sportswriters and fans everywhere in the coming years, the notorious NFL Tie-Breaking Procedure.

The Eastern Conference was split into the Capitol Division, with Dallas, New Orleans, Philadelphia, and Washington, and the Century Division, with Cleveland, New York, Pittsburgh, and St. Louis. The Western Conference was made up of the Coastal Division, with Atlanta, Baltimore, Los Angeles, and San Francisco, and the Central Division, with Chicago, Detroit, Green Bay, and Minnesota. If fans got confused as to which division their team was in, they certainly weren't helped by having all the names start with 'C'. Because all the Eastern Conference teams wanted to play in New York (money, money, money), the Giants and Saints would switch divisions in 1968 and then switch back again in 1969. In 1970, when the merger with the AFL became complete, they'd have to think of something else.

The AFL enjoyed its historic first common draft with the NFL in February. Perhaps "enjoyed" is the wrong word. According to the NFL, the AFL didn't do so well.

"The American Football League had a terrible draft," a veteran NFL scout told Jerry Green of the *Detroit News*. "I don't know where they came out with some of their names." Another NFL man pointed out that there were only 15 "name" players available and the NFL drafted 11 of them.

Some of the NFL "names" didn't come through. Running backs Clinton Jones of Michigan State (Minnesota), Ray McDonald of Idaho (Washington), Harry Jones of Arkansas (Philadelphia), tackle Loyd Phillips of Arkansas (Chicago), and quarterbacks Don Horn of San Diego State (Green Bay) and Steve Spurrier of Florida (San Francisco) spent time in the NFL but were always ranked as disappointments. Lineman Bob Hyland of Boston College (Green Bay) had a long pro career but was never a star. Three of the 11 "names" did very well: Mel Farr of UCLA was an outstanding running back for the Lions until injuries caught up with him and defensive end Bubba Smith of Michigan State (Baltimore) played in two Pro Bowls. Notre Dame defensive tackle Alan Page, drafted by Minnesota, earned a bust in the Pro Football Hall of Fame.

One of the AFL's four "names," defensive back John Charles of Purdue, never made it big, but the other three did okay. Denver got running back Floyd Little of Syracuse, who went on to lead the AFC in rushing in 1970 and 1971. Linebacker George Webster of Michigan State, drafted by Houston, spent only three years in the American Football League but was named to its all-time team. And quarterback Bob Griese of Purdue led the Miami Dolphins to an undefeated season in 1972. He was named to the Pro Football Hall of Fame in 1990.

Besides Griese, three other future Hall of Famers were drafted by AFL teams in '67: defensive back Ken Houston of Prairie View A&M by the Oilers (on the ninth round yet!), linebacker Willie Lanier of Morgan State

Bubba Smith.

by Kansas City, and guard Gene Upshaw of Texas A&I by Oakland. Additionally, running back Dickie Post of Houston, picked by San Diego, led the AFL in rushing in 1969.

So how bad could the AFL draft have been?

The NFL scouts said the real weakness in the AFL draft came in the later rounds where depth was to be acquired. "Even as early as the fifth or sixth rounds, they didn't seem to know what they were doing," Jerry Green was told.

The AFL was far behind their rivals in scouting. NFL teams had contacts, spies, friends everywhere, some going back for decades. George Halas

201

got reports from people who'd played for him in the 1920s. "The AFL thinks it can cover the whole country with two scouts," one NFLer laughed. "Heck, it takes me two weeks to scout one school like Michigan State."

The Dallas Cowboys hadn't been around any longer than the AFL, but they were ahead of everyone else in the use of computerized scouting. Starting in 1961, Dallas first standardized their scouts' terminology so they could tell "mean and mobile" from "aggressive and quick." Then they settled on six factors for ranking football players:

- Character
- Quickness and body control (agility and balance)
- Competitiveness and aggressiveness
- Mental alertness (The Cowboys determined that the best football players had IQ's between 94 and 120.)
- Strength and explosion (factoring quickness into strength)
- Speed

All of their scouting reports were fed into the computer and out popped— they hoped—all-pros. And did the Cowboys get reports! Gil Brandt, their personnel man, seemed to know (and be owed favors by) every college football coach in the country. If there was a potential pro at some little school that not even the NCAA had heard of, Brandt could call the coach by his first name and remember his children's birthdays. On draft days, when names were being taken off every team's big board as selections were made and other teams were shuffling through stacks of loose papers to make their next choice, the Cowboys needed only to push a button.

Obviously, computerized scouting was the wave of the future. Traditionalists hated the idea and grasped at straws. They repeated endlessly the tale of the halfback who ended with San Diego after the Dallas computer said he wasn't a prospect. The kid had a fine year, leading Sid Gillman to quip: "When it's third and three, I can give the ball to a running back, but I can't give it to your computer."

But, in the long run, the computer could find you a *better* running back—and also suggest a short pass for third and three.

A few players had been drafted by more than one team in the years before the merger. They still had to be bargained with, and the AFL broke even whenever money talked. Miami outbid St. Louis for receiver Jack Clancy. Denver won over Cleveland on linebacker Pete Duranko and lost to Detroit on halfback Nick Eddy. Receiver Ray Perkins, the future coach, signed with Baltimore over Boston. Reportedly, Clancy got about $250,000 from the Dolphins. "I'm paying more in income tax this year than I earned before in my entire life," he said. A few days later, Clinton Jones, the Vikings number-one pick, signed for a $40,000 bonus and $20,000 salary. The good times were over for players for a while.

Pro football's owners still jealously guarded salary information, but before the 1968 season, Jack Kemp, who was head of the AFL Players' Association, surveyed AFL players. Out of 400 surveys sent out, 350 came back. Allowing for the players who didn't answer and the fact that some players may have inflated or deflated figures for personal reasons, league salaries broke down as follows by position:

$25,000 - quarterbacks
$23,000 - flankerbacks
$22,400 - fullbacks
$19,600 - halfbacks
$18,600 - centers
$18,300 - ends (split or tight)
$18,000 - defensive linemen
$17,500 - guards, safeties, and linebackers
$16,700 - offensive tackles
$15,900 - cornerbacks
$14,200 - kickers

The San Diego Chargers averaged $20,733 per player for the highest payroll. Then came Boston, followed by Oakland, Kansas City, Houston, Buffalo, New York Jets, Miami, and Denver. The Broncos' payroll averaged only $16,170. The biggest surprise was the wealthy Jets with only a $17,976 average.

The names of players were kept secret, but by matching teams and positions to salaries, the *New York Times'* William N. Wallace made some educated guesses. He decided the highest-paid quarterback was Kemp himself at $45,000. Namath was the highest-paid Jet at $32,000. At least one halfback, apparently either Kansas City's Mike Garrett or San Diego's Paul Lowe, made $38,000. Earning better salaries than Kemp were Boston fullback Jim Nance at $50,000 and Chargers' flankerback Lance Alworth at $55,000. The AFL's highest-paid player at $60,000, Wallace figured, was Chiefs' flanker Otis Taylor.

————

After the Super Bowl loss, Hank Stram told reporters: "I don't think one game is any criterion to decide the strength of two leagues." His was the voice of reason crying in the wilderness. No matter. Except to diehards, the

NFL had proved its superiority. Most football fans endorsed Lombardi's words as he brandished the game ball his players had voted him in the dressing room after the game: "This is the NFL ball and it kicks a little bit better, it throws a little bit better and it catches a little bit better."

The AFL could only wait for another meeting to prove its worth. The chance would come in the summer of '67 when there were 16 preseason exhibitions scheduled in which teams from the two leagues would face each other. The AFL hoped to regain some prestige. The NFL expected to sweep.

The first meeting was set for August 5 at Denver University Stadium between two aggregations that neither league would likely have chosen to carry its banner. The Detroit Lions had been an NFL also-ran in '66, bad enough to get Coach Harry Gilmer fired and replaced by Joe Schmidt. This was to be the Lions' first game under their new leader. The Denver Broncos had been, as usual, the AFL's tailender the previous year, and they also were being led by a new coach. Lou Saban had been lured back to pro football. The Broncos already had one exhibition under their belts, a humiliating 19–3 loss to a Miami team in only its second year. A crowd of 21,228 showed up without great expectations.

The Lions left the field much less smug. Denver won—had beaten the NFL—13–7. The AFL's dominance was shortlived too. They won only two more of the 15 remaining exhibitions. Still, they could take comfort in the thought that it was *possible* to beat an NFL team.

––––––––

Despite brave words about the relative strength of the whole, as opposed to the Green Bay Packers, changes were taking place in the American Football League. Many of its early stars—the people who put the league on the map—were either retired, about to retire, or shunted to substitute roles. Tackle Eldon Danenhauer, for years a lone bastion in the Denver offensive line, missed all of 1966 with a knee injury and retired. Abner Haynes, the plucky halfback who'd brought so much excitement and class to the early Texans-Chiefs, finished 1967 running back kicks for the Jets and then called it quits. Mel Branch, who'd made the first All-AFL team with Dallas in 1960, still started at defensive end for Miami, but you only had to look at Miami's record and Branch's 235 pounds to know the sun was near setting.

Once the 1967 regular season began, the NFL and AFL went their separate ways. Interleague (actually interconference) play wasn't to begin until 1970. Attendance continued to rise in both leagues. The AFL's increase was no doubt helped by the merger, which legitimized it as a major league to some fans. More important, however, were the new stadiums:

Lance Alworth.

Oakland's Alameda Stadium, which opened in September of 1966, and San Diego (later Jack Murphy) Stadium, which hosted its first Chargers game—an exhibition loss to Detroit—on August 20, 1967. The $28 million, 50,000-seat stadium was a godsend to San Diego rears, tortured by the concrete slabs of old Balboa Stadium since 1961.

Jim Nance continued as the AFL's dominant rusher. He cracked, crashed, and crunched for 1,216 yards to lead the league again, but he was pretty much a one-man show as Boston fell to last place in the East at 3-10-1. Boston's collapse enabled Miami to avoid finishing last by a half-game at 4-10, the same as plummeting Buffalo. In New York, Joe Namath became the first pro passer to throw for over 4,000 yards, yet finished fifth when the team voted for its MVP. The Jets entered December at 7-2-1, a seeming shoo-in for the division title. But consecutive losses to Denver,

Kansas City, and Oakland turned them into also-rans. A final-game win at San Diego simply underlined what might have been.

New York's late-season slump left the path open for Houston. This was a very different team from the George Blanda-led scoring machines of a few years earlier. Blanda was in Oakland; this Oiler club won with a tight defense led by rookie linebacker George Webster and rookie safety Ken Houston. What offense there was came from line-plunger Hoyle Granger and scatter-armed quarterback Pete Beathard.

Sid Gillman was rebuilding San Diego with the John Hadl-to-Lance Alworth passing combo as his centerpiece. Hadl continued to improve and Alworth was simply the best that there ever was. The only thing certain about his impossible catches was that he'd make one even better soon after. His 52 receptions for 1,010 yards and nine touchdowns were almost an off-year for Lance.

Gillman had a championship-caliber offense and it got him to 8-1-1 after ten games. But the defense had been San Diego's weakness all season, giving up 51 points in a loss to the Raiders and 31 twice in a tie and a win. The Chargers hadn't been able to stop a run or rush a passer since the glory days of Earl Faison and Ernie Ladd. In their last four games—all losses— San Diego was blitzed for 148 points.

After a long spring and summer hearing about how they were embarrassed in the Super Bowl, the Chiefs got a measure of revenge with a 66–24 exhibition win over the Bears. Some said that the Chiefs so admired that victory that they forgot to play the season. It was true that the 9-5 record was disappointing and Kansas City could never string more than three wins in a row together. It was also true that only three end-of-season wins after they were eliminated from the western race allowed the Chiefs to climb safely above .500 and into second place. But Kansas City's up-and-down performance was mostly the result of Coach Stram's efforts to repair some of the weaknesses Green Bay had revealed in the Super Bowl by feeding rookies and other newcomers into his lineup. Willie Lanier and Jim Lynch upgraded the linebacking. Ernie Ladd was an improvement over Andy Rice at defensive tackle. The biggest impact among the newcomers came on special teams where "Super Gnat," 155-pound Noland Smith, terrified opponents with his kick returns. He led the AFL in kickoff return yardage. Norwegian-born Jan Stenerud began his long career as a super sidewinder kicker by leading in field goals.

Meanwhile, the Chiefs' established strengths—Len Dawson, Mike Garrett, Jim Tyrer, Bobby Bell, Fred Arbanas, Johnny Robinson, Otis Taylor, and Buck Buchanan—meant they could still put up a winning record while in transition.

The Oakland Raiders had changes too, nearly all for the good. Some had been in the works for a season or two. Billy Cannon completed his transition from washed-up running back into the league's most dangerous tight end. At 215 pounds, he was a bit thin for heavy blocking, but when he set sail downfield no linebacker and few safeties could stay with him. He scored ten touchdowns on 32 catches and was voted all-league. Meanwhile, Hewritt Dixon, who'd been a tight end at Denver without creating much excitement, came into his own as a fullback with the Raiders. Big Hewritt ran for 559 yards and led the Raiders with 59 pass receptions.

The major change was at quarterback. Al Davis went out and got the long-distance passer he craved by sending Art Powell and Tom Flores to Buffalo for receiver Glenn Bass (who was sent on to Houston) and Daryle Lamonica, a former Notre Dame quarterback who'd backed up Jack Kemp for four seasons. Lamonica had the arm and inclination to throw the ball 50 or 60 yards downfield and see what would come of it. His preference for deep tosses quickly earned him the nickname "The Mad Bomber." According to Davis, Lamonica's greatest virtue was his persistence: "If you take a concrete wall, and you stick four nails up there, and you assign a man to each nail, this is what would happen, see. One guy would quit the first day. Another the second. Another the next. But five days later Daryle Lamonica would still be there, hammering that nail into that concrete wall."

Several seasons hence, Lamonica persisted in throwing deep after zone defenses had learned how to turn bombs into interceptions. Eventually, it would cost him his job in favor of dart-thrower Ken Stabler. But in 1967, he was just what Davis and Coach Rauch wanted.

To back Lamonica, Davis brought in 39-year-old George Blanda, who was over the next few years to become known as the best relief quarterback in football. In 1967, most of his time was spent kicking, and with the Raiders' high-powered offense, he got enough opportunities to lead the league in scoring.

The Lamonica trade didn't look so hot when the Raiders lost three of their five exhibition games, including a 48–0 pummeling at the hands of Kansas City. But when the real season opened, Daryle won over the home fans by leading a 51–0 dismantling of Denver. An easy win over Boston and a tight 23–21 victory over Kansas City followed before the Raiders hit the road. Before 63,106 fans at Shea, Namath and company stopped the winning streak at three, 27–14.

That looked like the cue for Kansas City to come on and win the division, but instead the Chiefs lost to San Diego and Houston. Meanwhile, the Raiders began another winning streak with a victory at Buffalo and continued winning all the way through the season. When feature back

Daryle Lamonica.

Daniels went down with a broken ankle in the tenth game, rookie Pete Banaszak picked up the slack without a hitch. Oakland's final 13-1 mark was the best ever compiled in the AFL and one of the best marks ever made by any pro football team anywhere.

Five future Hall of Famers were on the Raiders' roster: Blanda, clutch receiver Fred Biletnikoff, center Jim Otto, rookie offensive guard Gene Upshaw, and cornerback Willie Brown, acquired from Denver. Otto and five others were named All-AFL: Lamonica, Cannon, defensive end Ben Davidson, defensive tackle Tom Keating, and safety Kent McCloughan.

Upshaw, who today heads the NFL Players' Association, was a breakthrough-type guard. Offensive guards needed size, but they also had to be fast enough to lead sweeps. Most of them were around six-two and 240 pounds; Gene was six-five and 255, bigger than some offensive tackles, but still one of the quickest linemen in the league. From the time the Chiefs unveiled their giant defensive tackle Buck Buchanan, Al Davis began looking for a guard with Upshaw's combination of size and speed. "I figured if Buchanan was going to play for the Chiefs for the next ten years," Davis says, "we better get some big guy who could handle him. Those two guys put on some stirring battles over the years."

The Raiders lived by their long passes. Upshaw admitted, "I don't have as much fun pass blocking, but I get satisfaction from it. That's where we separate the men from the boys. It takes a hell of a man to stand in there on pass protection, to take those roundhouse clubs to the head and the butting with the helmets and all that. You've got to keep control of yourself.

"The good protection blocker sits and waits for the defense to make the move and then reacts. You have to be passive and aggressive at the same time. If you charge too hard, some of the quick linemen will get you off balance and skip around you or grab you and throw you. Or you might fire off at the wrong guy and the defense will be in a stunt and another guy will have an open road to your quarterback."

Upshaw's favorite moments were sweeps. "That's my play," he said. "A wide receiver wants to catch a long touchdown pass. A defensive lineman wants to break in to sack a quarterback. I get my satisfaction pulling to lead those sweeps. That's a play where it comes down to just me and the defensive back. If I get him clean, we're going to make a long gain. If I miss him, we don't get a yard.

"I'm weighing 260 coming right at that defensive back. He's 210 at most and 185 some of the time. And he hasn't got a chance. I've got it in my head that whatever he does has to be wrong. If he goes to the outside, I'm going to put him out of bounds. If he goes inside, I'll knock him in. And if he stands there, man, I'm going right over him."

The first quarter of the championship game at Oakland was encouraging for the few Houston rooters tucked in among the crowd of 53,330. Lamonica had suffered muscle spasms and wasn't throwing well. The Oilers couldn't get Hoyle Granger untracked, but the only score for the Raiders was a 37-yard George Blanda field goal. Three to nothing wasn't much to overcome.

Lightning struck in the second quarter. While studying films, Lamonica had noted the Oilers were inclined to slant their middle and right linebackers. "We realized we could seal them inside." At the Oakland 31, Dixon started on a simple sweep. Banaszak and Upshaw sealed off the end and linebacker, and Dixon broke clear. His 69-yard run was the longest in AFL Championship Game history. Well, 10–0 wasn't too much to overcome.

Shortly before the half ended, the Raiders set up for a Blanda field goal try at the Houston 17. Success would still leave the Oilers within two touchdowns of the lead if they could catch a break. Lamonica knelt to hold, but when the ball was snapped, he jumped up, spotted seldom-used tight end Pete Kocourek running alone, and drilled him. The Oilers were dead, 17–0.

When Houston came out for the second half, they had to throw, and that was the weakest part of their game. The Raiders chased Beathard from sideline to sideline. He completed only 15 of 35 on the day. Meanwhile, Dixon and Banaszak swept the Houston ends clean of 260 yards. The final score was 40–7. "King Kong and ten gorillas couldn't beat us today," crowed Raider Ike Lassiter.

Coach Rauch was ecstatic. He told equipment manager Dick Romanski to slice the football into 52 pieces. "I want this game ball cut up so every player and coach gets a hunk of leather tacked to a plaque."

———

When he split the NFL into four divisions, Pete Rozelle's idea had been to produce longer and more intense races that would keep more fans hoping for division titles down to the wire. It worked in only one of four. The Century, Capitol, and Central races were tame all the way.

In the Century Division, Cleveland was getting older (and older!). The Browns were ripe to be taken. Frank Ryan was troubled all season with a sore arm. Tight end Milt Morin was injured. Defensive ends Bill Glass and Paul Wiggin slumped, as did cornerback Erich Barnes. All were over 30. Kicker Lou Groza was 43! When Blanton Collier's crew began the season with consecutive losses to Detroit and Dallas, they gave some encouragement to their division rivals. But then league-leading runner Leroy Kelly and running mate Ernie Green kicked into gear, and the Browns won nine of their remaining 12 games.

The Capitol Division had losers in Washington, Philadelphia, and New Orleans but was stronger than the Century, if only because of the presence of the Dallas Cowboys. The Cowboys' 9-5 record was less than expected, but they were never pressed, and two of the losses came after the Capitol crown was wrapped up in silver, blue, and white ribbon.

Coach Landry put the blame for any offensive slowdown on "significant injuries." Don Meredith missed three games and was physically below par in several others. Multipurpose halfback Dan Reeves limped through multigames. Regular center Dave Manders and backup receiver Buddy

Dial missed the whole season with injuries. But how much offense did a team need when it had Bob Lilly, Cornell Green, and Chuck Howley playing All-NFL defense?

————————

The Central Division wasn't yet the "Black-and-Blue Division" it would become in the 1970s, but the pieces were beginning to fall into place.

Having won four Grey Cups, cool Bud Grant agreed to give up some of his hunting and fishing time to come down from Canada and replace Norm Van Brocklin as Vikings' coach. He opted to turn Minnesota into a defense-oriented team. The linebackers and deep backs needed tuning, but Grant had his cornerstone in a defensive line of Carl Eller, Jim Marshall, Paul Dickson, and super-rookie Alan Page. Of course, there's no gain without pain and the Vikes' 3-8-3 pained. To get the draft choices they

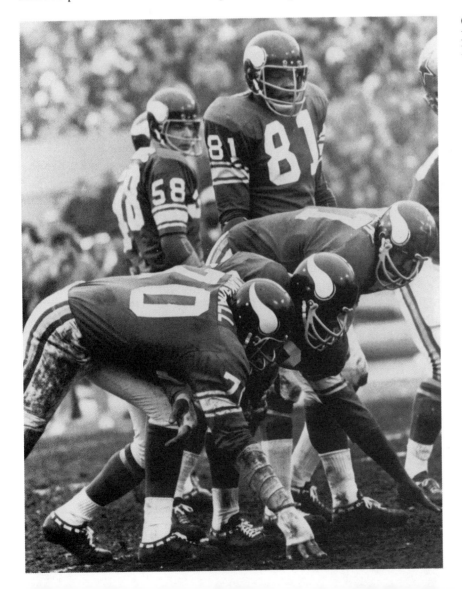

Carl Eller (81) of Minnesota's Purple People Eaters.

needed to build with, Minnesota sent Fran Tarkenton to the Giants and Tommy Mason to the Rams. Mason's departure left the running in the hands (actually the feet) of pluggers Dave Osborn and Bill Brown. This was certainly not a fate worse than death, but it meant that any run of over five yards was cause for celebration. Losing Tark was more serious. His replacement, one-time U. of California sharpie Joe Kapp, came from Canada with Grant and proved to the satisfaction of nearly everyone who saw him that he was incapable of throwing a major league pass. Kapp was a dangerous runner and a clever and daring field general, but his passes often resembled the ducks shot out of the sky by his renowned hunter coach.

Minnesota would have had the worst passing in the NFL had not Detroit with Milt Plum and Chicago with Jack Concannon been on the scene. After a staggering 7-6-1 season, 73-year-old George Halas stepped down as head coach (although as owner he'd still be running the show). He'd coached in the NFL for 40 years and compiled a 324-151-31 record. Don Shula, who started as a near tot with Baltimore in 1963, the year Halas won his last NFL championship, is on line to surpass him in total NFL victories, given today's 16-game season. What seems far less likely is that any ten men will ever achieve the on-field off-field influence that George Halas wielded in the NFL from 1920 to his death in 1983.

Green Bay was the only team in the division with major league quarterbacking (although Bart Starr threw an uncharacteristic 17 interceptions). And with Chicago taking itself out of the race early and Detroit and Minnesota never entering it, the world champion Packers were at no time in real danger of losing the Central Division title; Starr and the defense saw to that. When the Pack beat the Bears, 17–13, in week 11, the crown was cinched.

All of which is not to say everything ran smoothly all the way. This was the season Lombardi decided to revamp his running game. Jim Taylor and Paul Hornung were discarded to New Orleans (Hornung decided to retire) to make room for heirs-apparent Jim Grabowski and Donny Anderson. But after a nice start, the new guys came down with injuries. When Elijah Pitts was also hurt, Lombardi had to scramble for replacements. He found them in journeyman Ben Wilson, Giants' discard Chuck Mercein, and kick return specialist Travis Williams, and the Pack kept right on rolling. Green Bay's continued strong ground game seemed to prove that any competent back could do a good job when running behind Forrest Gregg, Jerry Kramer, Ken Bowman, Gale Gillingham, and Bob Skoronski.

The NFL's one nail-biting race developed in the Coastal Division. Don Shula had a powerhouse going in Baltimore even though some of the old

Don Shula.

tried-and-true parts were nearing their end. Both Raymond Berry and Jimmy Orr were injured most of the year. Berry would retire after the season. Willie Richardson, who'd subbed for five years, and Alex Hawkins, the special teams captain, stepped in and handled the receiving chores with aplomb. Working with a new set of receivers, Johnny Unitas had another one of his terrific years, throwing for 3,428 yards and 20 touchdowns.

Another longtime Colt hero, Jim Parker, limped along on a knee that wouldn't respond to treatment. With the Colts possibly heading for a championship, big Jim might have simply sat around and collected his money. In his years with the Colts, he'd earned nearly every honor an offensive lineman could, but the nickname "Unitas's Bodyguard" said as much as anything. Certainly no one was more deserving of a free ride to a

213

final payday. But late in the season, Parker announced his retirement, allowing the Colts to add a healthy player to their roster: "I can't help the team and I won't deprive 40 guys of their big chance."

"It was one of the most unselfish moves ever made in sports," Shula said.

The Baltimore defense, aided by the play of rookies Rick Volk in the secondary and huge Bubba Smith at defensive end, held opponents to fewer than 200 points for the season.

The Colts opened with four straight victories before being tied 24–24 by Los Angeles. Surprisingly, the Vikings held them to another tie, 20–20, the following week at Minnesota. But then Baltimore got its second wind and rolled over seven straight opponents. Included in the streak was a 13–10 win over Green Bay. With only the 14th game to go, the Colts stood undefeated—11-0-2. Yet they hadn't wrapped up the Coastal Division championship. The Los Angeles Rams were right on their tail.

George Allen's Rams were not the most exciting team in the league. Quarterback Roman Gabriel ran a ball-control offense that won by avoiding mistakes. His short passes, judicious running by Dick Bass and Les Josephson, and Bruce Gossett's placekicking actually put more points on the board than any other NFL team, but much of that was because the defense consistently gave the offense good field possession. While Gabriel threw the fewest interceptions in the league, the Rams' secondary led the league in steals.

The LA defense was a typical George Allen concoction of veterans, veterans, veterans. When middle linebacker Bill George retired, Allen plugged in seven-year veteran Myron Pottios. When big Rosey Grier was hurt in preseason, putting a serious dent in the Fearsome Foursome, Allen swapped three draft choices to Detroit for bigger Roger Brown.

After winning their first three games, the Rams bumped into San Francisco on one of John Brodie's good days and lost, 27–24. The next week, Allen's crew went to Baltimore and tied the undefeated Colts to stay in the race, but the week after that, Washington's air circus put up 28 points and the Rams were lucky to escape with another tie. Having given up 79 points in three games, Allen's defense was creaking and looked ready to crack. Perhaps it just took a while to get those ancient muscles moving, because LA held the next six opponents to a total of 54 points. With two games left, all the Rams had to do to win the division was knock off defending champion Green Bay and the undefeated Colts. Piece of cake!

The Rams-Packers meeting was one of the best games of the year. Green Bay led 10–7 at the half, but Allen, who may have been the first to suggest it was possible to give 110 percent, told his troops: "Close games are won

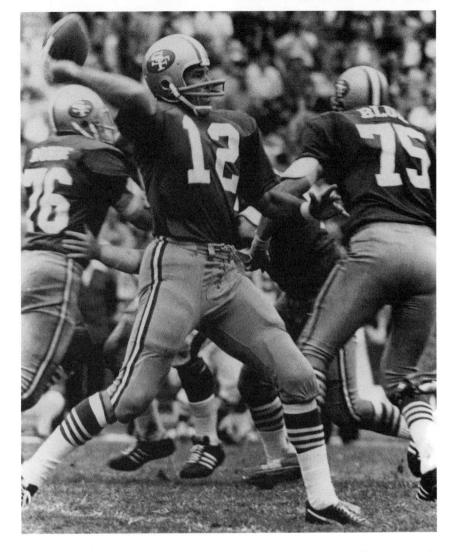

John Brodie.

by attitude . . . *winning* attitude. If we convince ourselves we'll accept only winning today, we'll win."

The Rams returned to the field convinced. They moved down the field to a go-ahead touchdown on short, careful passes. When Gossett added a field goal, LA led 17–10. But on the ensuing kickoff, Travis Williams stunned them with a 104-yard return, his record fourth runback touchdown of the season. The Rams pulled themselves together and, with eight minutes left, regained the lead on another Gossett field goal.

Green Bay drove down the field, eating up the clock. Chuck Mercein capped the nine-play drive with a four-yard slash. Green Bay 24–20. The Rams received but were stopped and had to punt. Only 80 seconds remained. Green Bay ran the ball three times and the Rams called three time outs. Fifty-four seconds left.

Donny Anderson prepared to punt. Tony Guillory, captain of the Rams' special teams, lined up over center. Guillory had never blocked a punt. Anderson had never had one blocked.

Until now.

Guillory shot between center and guard. Blocking back Tommy Crutcher had moved out to stop Claude Crabbe flying in from the outside. Anderson saw Guillory coming up the middle and tried to rush his kick, but Guillory leaped . . . THUMP!

Crabbe picked up the rolling ball and started for the goal line with six Rams guarding him. Anderson looped around the blockers and hauled Crabbe down at the five.

Forty-four seconds to go. Gabriel couldn't find a target and threw his first pass safely out of bounds. On second down, Gabriel spotted Bernie Casey and dropped a feathery bundle of football into his hands for the winning touchdown.

The Rams were still alive. Now all they had to do was accomplish something no other team had done in 1967—beat Baltimore. The Colts were 11-0-2 and the Rams 10-1-2. A Los Angeles victory would leave the teams with matching records, but because they'd tied in their first meeting, a Ram victory would give them the division title under the NFL's tie-breaking procedure.

On December 17, a Coliseum crowd of 72,277 saw Baltimore take a 7–3 first quarter lead, but in the second period, Gabriel hit Jack Snow for a stunning 80-yard touchdown. A few moments later, the noblest Roman connected with Casey for 23 yards and another touchdown. That made it 17–7 at the half. The second half was no contest. The Fearsome Foursome pressured Unitas unmercifully, sacking him seven times. He'd been snagged only 13 times in the Colts' first 13 games. All he could accomplish was one drive good for a field goal. Two of his passes were intercepted. Meanwhile, Gabriel and company matched their first half production with another 17 points. In his second year as coach, George Allen had his troops in the playoffs. George Allen was a genius. The Colts, arguably the best team in the league except for that one day, went home. The question was whispered: "Could Don Shula win the big one?"

Sunny California was a long way off and several dozen degrees warmer than Milwaukee's County Stadium when the Packers took the field for their playoff against the Rams on Saturday, December 23. Just what Lombardi had ordered. While some of the dressing-room warmth lingered, Gabriel threw a 29-yard touchdown pass to Casey for a first-quarter lead. By the second quarter, the Rams cooled, most of the 49,861 fans had begun to shiver, and the Packers were warmed up. Bart Starr handed off to Travis

Williams, who burst off tackle for a 46-yard touchdown to tie the game. From that point on, the veteran Green Bay offensive wall had the Not-Very-Fearsome Foursome in its pocket, as Starr stood unmolested in his pocket while passing for 222 yards and the Packers make-do backs pocketed 163 rushing yards. Green Bay advanced, 28–7.

The next day at Dallas, the Cowboys showed 70,786 fans just how devastating they could be when everything clicked as they demolished Cleveland, 52–14. Coach Landry suggested the inspiration for the slaughter came from Green Bay's win: "After watching the Packers, I felt what they did carried over into this game for us. I never expected to win the game this big."

Dallas took charge right from the start, scoring a pair of touchdowns in the opening quarter. Any dreams Cleveland may have had about getting back into the game were shattered four minutes into the second quarter when Meredith connected with Bob Hayes for an 86-yard backbreaker to

Bob Hayes.

set a new playoff record. "We called an audible," Hayes explained later. "They had a blitz look. Don threw a perfect pass. It couldn't have been more perfect."

Mike Howell, the Cleveland cornerback victimized on the play, maintained, "I don't feel badly. It's to be expected with that guy. I can't compare him with anyone . . . his speed sets him apart."

The World's Fastest Human also returned punts for 64 and 68 yards but failed to score on either. "They had me penned in on the first one, but the second one I stumbled and fell."

In the closing minutes, Cleveland's Paul Warfield scored on a 75-yard bomb from Frank Ryan, but by then, it was only decoration. "I don't think it hurts you to win big," Landry told reporters.

The Green Bay and Dallas victories set up a rematch of the previous year's exciting championship game—a game all of Dallas believed the Cowboys should have won. And had Don Meredith's last-ditch pass nestled in a Cowboy's hands instead of a Packers' . . . well, who knows? But that magnificent contest had been played under Texas skies. This one would be in Wisconsin, a state never designed to host a football game on the last day of December.

As if to prove the point, the temperature on Lambeau Field read 13 degrees below zero at game time. The windchill factor was lower than a badger's basement. Electric heating wires implanted six inches under the surface of the field were supposed to thaw the sod. They didn't work. Much of the field was perfect . . . for hockey. Cold be damned, 50,961 Packer fans showed up, protected by enough layered clothing to shield three, maybe four times as many. Everyone in the place seemed to be shaped like Vince Lombardi.

The temperature was no lower for the Cowboys than for the Packers, but the Packers were accustomed to end-of-season games in igloo conditions. When Green Bay "warmed up," they went about their business as usual. But the Cowboys worried and fretted and considered changing things. Meredith's first few practice passes bounced off his receivers' icy-stiff hands. He noted that across the field Starr was throwing softer passes and eased up on his own, but that just ruined his accuracy.

The first time they got the ball, the Packers drove 82 yards for a touchdown. The score came on a soft, three-yard Starr pass to Boyd Dowler. Business as usual. The cold and the Green Bay defense kept Dallas bottled up. Early in the second quarter, Starr and Dowler combined for another touchdown, this one 43 yards. Green Bay, 14–0. The game threatened to turn into a blowout.

But suddenly Green Bay went flat. "Maybe we started to think more about the cold and the conditions than we thought about our own execution," Starr suggested later. Whatever, Green Bay lost its concentration and stopped moving the ball. Instead, they made mistakes.

Starr went back to pass at his own 26 and was sacked by Willie Townes. The ball came lose. George Andrie picked it up at the seven and skated into the end zone. Shortly before the first half ended, Willie Wood muffed a punt at his 17. Danny Villanueva turned it into a 21-yard field goal. Dallas hadn't made a first down in the half but they were right in it, 14–10.

The Packers began the second half as they'd ended the first—flat. Dallas got to the Packer 13 before Herb Adderley recovered a third down Meredith fumble. The third quarter ended with the score still 14–10.

The Cowboys had been hurting the Packers with Dan Reeves on sweeps. On the first play of the fourth quarter with the ball at the 50, Meredith pitched to Reeves running right. Willie Wood and cornerback Bob Jeter came up to stop the sweep. Suddenly, Reeves, the former South Carolina quarterback, pulled his arm back. Too late, the Packers realized they'd fallen for one of their own favorite plays, a halfback option. Reeves arched a pass to Lance Rentzel running free at the 20. Tom Brown was the nearest Packer and he was nowhere near enough. Rentzel loped into the end zone to put Dallas in front, 17–14. Only eight seconds had ticked off the fourth quarter clock.

For the next ten minutes the teams jockeyed back and forth, Green Bay desperately looking for a comeback score, Dallas just as desperately wanting a touchdown to put the game out of reach. With 4:50 remaining, Green Bay took over at its own 32. The temperature had now dropped to 18 below. Footing was a nightmare. Little clouds formed in front of faces with every breath expelled. Crunch time.

Starr gained six on a swing pass to Donny Anderson. Chuck Mercein ran for seven. On first down, Starr passed to Dowler cutting across the middle, good for 13 yards and another first down, but Boyd was hurt on the play. Max McGee replaced him.

Disaster! Anderson swept right to attempt an option pass, but Townes was too quick and threw him for a nine-yard loss.

Not to panic. The Dallas defensive backs were playing "deep conscious," making certain no Packer got behind them. Starr took what they gave him and tossed two short passes down the middle to Anderson to gain a first down at the Dallas 30. Next he threw to Mercein in the left flat. Dallas linebacker Chuck Howley came up quickly but slipped. Mercein zipped past him down to the 11 before he was knocked out of bounds.

The clock showed 1:11 remaining.

Starr called for a "sucker play." Gillingham pulled right. Dallas tackle great Bob Lilly followed him, taking himself out of the play. Bob Skoronski sealed George Andrie to the outside and Mercein barged through the hole and down to the three. The Packers called a timeout to stop the clock. Then Anderson ran right for two and a first down. First-and-goal at the one.

The Packers huddled quickly. Anderson was stopped for no gain. Green Bay used its second timeout. They came back with Anderson again and he got a foot . . . maybe.

With 16 seconds left, Green Bay spent its final timeout. Lombardi and Starr discussed their options on the sideline. A tying field goal was reasonably certain, although in this cold nothing was *absolutely* sure. Lombardi joked later that he had "compassion" for the crowd and didn't want to keep them there into overtime. A better reason to eschew overtime was the weather and field condition, which could easily give the game away on a break. If Green Bay passed at the one and it fell incomplete, there'd still be time for the field goal. One year before, Dallas had passed in close . . . and been intercepted. Starr told Lombardi he thought he could run it in.

In the huddle, Starr called 31-Wedge—Mercein up the middle. But Starr had no intention of handing off. Ken Bowman snapped the ball to Starr. Bowman and right guard Jerry Kramer drove into the Cowboys' Jethro Pugh, pushing him back. Starr followed them . . . into the end zone!

Jerry Kramer's lead block allowed Bart Starr to sneak into the endzone for the winning touchdown in the "Ice Bowl."

The 21–17, "Ice Bowl" victory put the Packers into the second NFL-AFL championship meeting to be played at Miami. So much emotion had been expended in winning the NFL Championship Game that some experts predicted a letdown for the Packers. Nor would the Packers have Wisconsin's cold as an ally; the thermometer in Florida read 81 degrees higher at game time than had its counterpart at the Ice Bowl. Furthermore, the 1967 Pack, as good as it was, wasn't quite up to the level of the '66 crew. And, according to their record, the Oakland Raiders were the strongest team yet produced in the AFL. The Packers were still favored for the game, by now officially called the Super Bowl, but hopes were for a closer battle than had occurred the year before.

Technically, it *was* closer. The Packers had whipped the 1966 Chiefs, 35–10; they bested the '67 Raiders, 33–14, a six point improvement by the AFL. The stats were closer yet: Oakland trailed in first downs by only 16 to 19 and in total yardage by a mere 293 to 322. Had it not been for three turnovers by the Raiders—two fumbles and a pass interception—the score might have been narrower. Of course, were it not for the ocean, New Yorkers could ride bicycles to Paris. When the game was over, many felt the gulf between NFL football and AFL football was still as wide as the Atlantic.

As in Super Bowl I, the AFL entrant stayed close during the first half, trailing only 13–7 at one point and 16–7 when the gun sounded.

As in Super Bowl I, the Packers made a shambles of the game in the second half, completely dominating the third quarter when they scored ten unanswered points.

As in . . . Bart Starr was chosen MVP, having completed 13 of 24 for 202 yards this time out.

As in . . . a Packer intercepted a pass for a long return, when Adderley picked off Lamonica for 60 yards in the fourth quarter to score the final Green Bay touchdown.

Raiders coach John Rauch was left to explain: "We thought we could do it today . . . but the Packers don't give you many openings." The third quarter was the turning point, he said. "The breaks went against us in that quarter and that's the name of the game." Rauch called the Super Bowl the high point of his 15-year coaching career, but added, "It's always tough to accept a beating, especially when you're not used to it."

But after two heavy-duty Super Bowl losses, it looked like the AFL had better get used to beatings.

CHUCK HOWLEY: "I WAS ALWAYS LOOKING FOR THE BIG PLAY"

16

Mention Chuck Howley of the Dallas Cowboys and the first thing that comes to most fans' minds is the most valuable player award he won while playing on the *losing* side in Super Bowl V. Other fans remember that he was a regular All-NFL and Pro Bowl selection in the 1960s. Few recall that his career ended—the first time—in 1959. Only the AFL and the expansion it forced on the National Football League gave players like George Blanda, Don Maynard, and Chuck Howley the chance to return to football and become headline performers.

Speed and agility were Howley's trademarks. At West Virginia University, he lettered in five sports—track, diving, wrestling, and gymnastics, as well as football. The Chicago Bears made him their number-one draft choice in 1958, and he became a regular linebacker in his first season. Then a knee injury seemingly ended it all.

But with ten new pro football teams operating by 1961, players were needed. And Howley got a second chance.

A successful Dallas businessman today, his name is still seen regularly on national TV—whenever the cameras show the Cowboys's Ring of Honor emblazoned on the stands at Texas Stadium.

———

"The 1960s were a time of terrific growth for pro football—television, the two leagues, expansion. Of course, at the time, you don't think of it in that way. It all just sort of happens. But then afterward, you can look back and realize you were a part of something that was really becoming big.

"I'd played two years for the Bears and then sat out 1960 with a knee injury. Actually, I was retired. I'd satisfied myself that I could play with the pros and I was working back in Wheeling, West Virginia. While I was there, Don Healy, an offensive lineman who'd been with the Bears and then come to Dallas in the expansion draft, suggested to the coaches that

I might be available. The Cowboys took a chance and traded a couple of draft choices to the Bears for me.

"In the meantime, my knee had gotten stronger. In the spring of 1961, I tested it in a WVU alumni game and found it had come all the way back. By then I'd decided there were better things to do in this world than run a gas station. Dallas was a unique opportunity. They'd just gone through their first season and hadn't won a game. People have asked if I considered jumping to the American Football League at the time. In truth, it never crossed my mind. I was just glad to get back to playing ball. I knew the Cowboys could only go in one direction. Up.

"During my first four years in Dallas, we had losing records, but there was that feeling that we were building toward a good team. We had some very good draft choices. Bob Lilly was the number-one choice in 1961, the same year I got there. He was just a great tackle. A fantastic player. And a fine gentleman off the field.

"Then over the next couple of years we drafted George Andrie, Lee Roy Jordan, and Mel Renfro—all of whom added to our defense.

"I think by '63 we had a good defense. It took a while longer for the offense to catch up."

Howley's speed was a constant source of wonder. *Dallas Times Herald* writer Blackie Sherrod wrote a humorous piece in which he explained it all. Howley, he said, was simply confused and thought he was someone else. Like Bullet Bob Hayes.

"Howley assumed Hayes' identity a couple of seasons ago in St. Louis," Sherrod wrote. "Mel Renfro intercepted a pass and fled 90 yards downfield to a touchdown. Renfro, of course, is faster than gossip and no linebacker could stay in his neighborhood. But Howley, in one of his demented quirks, had become Hayes, so he sprinted all the way ahead of Renfro and knocked the last defender out of the way. He pulled the same trick on a Hayes 85-yard punt return last year. Goodness knows who he was impersonating that time."

"Don Meredith, our quarterback, was the kind of player you could admire. A little bit of a playboy, but he could keep the team loose. I always thought he retired too soon.

"Don Perkins was one of the best. A great runner, of course, but he could also block and catch passes. He was a terrific team player too.

"Bob Hayes had so much speed! He didn't have the greatest hands in the world, but they were okay. When he came to the Cowboys, he was a sprinter more than a football player—the first of the real speed-burning wide receivers. No one could stay with him. After him, other teams started looking for really fast receivers. In a way, he changed how football was played.

"We were getting better players every year.

"And we believed in our coaches. Some people have written that Tom Landry is cold or distant, but that's not it. He was reserved. He was always concentrating on what we could do next to give us an advantage. All that action would be going on on the field and everybody on the sideline would be excited, and Coach Landry would be sort of removed from it because in his mind he was about ten or 15 plays farther on in the game. When somebody's deep in thought, he'll appear to be distant.

"No question that our system was more complicated than Green Bay's. The Packers were very direct. You knew what they were going to do. The challenge was to stop them.

"We had confidence in our system. Our defense was the flex. Later on they called it the Doomsday, but that was just a name they hung on it. I think the flex was the finest defensive system of its time.

"Basically the flex is a reading defense. Read and react. Every man on the defense has certain keys he looks for in the opponent's offense. When he sees one of those keys, he reacts immediately. Normally, the offense has all the advantage because they know where the play is going to go. If you wait and let it happen, you're going to get buried. The flex takes some of that advantage away by cueing the defense as to what's happening. Then, if you're fast enough, you can stop it. For example, I would be at linebacker and I'd see the guard on the other side pulling. He'd be coming to get me. But, if I react immediately, I can beat him to the point of attack. And by being there before he expects me to be, I have the advantage.

"The flex was very structured. But after a while, Lilly and I were given a little leeway. We could gamble a little. Dick Nolan, who was an assistant coach for us, said that when I gambled I was right about 90 percent of the time. It's those gambles that produce big plays.

"I was always looking for the big play—the kind that might turn a game around. But that doesn't mean you just go out there and start guessing. I studied films for hours and hours so that when I took a chance, it was an 'educated' gamble.

"Of course, the biggest game I ever had was Super Bowl V. It was just one of those kind of games when I was in the right place at the right time—all the time. Even when I made a mistake and was out of position, I was in the right place. It's a trivia question now—'What player was a Super Bowl MVP while playing on the losing team?' Awards are nice, but some of the trivia players forget that the next year we were back in the Super Bowl and won.

"The game that really stands out in my mind was the '67 championship against the Packers at Green Bay. The 'Ice Bowl'! I suppose that was the coldest game I ever played in. Some of our linemen got frostbite where they had to put their hands down on the field when they went into their stance. But when you're out there playing, you don't really notice the cold so much. Just your face and hands a bit.

"The real difference in that game was the field was frozen. The linebackers and defensive backs couldn't cut or change direction quickly. Bart [Starr] took advantage of that in the second half to keep some drives going. I'm not making an excuse. The field was frozen for both sides. They adjusted to it a little better. But I would have liked to have played them on a field that wasn't frozen."

HEIDI AND JOE

17

Two weeks after Super Bowl II, Vince Lombardi announced his retirement as Packers' coach. His righthand assistant, Phil Bengston, would take over. Lombardi would remain as Green Bay general manager, he told newsmen, but the responsibilities of both coaching and running the team's front office had become too much for one man. The growth of pro football, problems created by the merger with the AFL, and the increasing burden of player relations demanded a full-time general manager, he said.

While all these were legitimate concerns, history would note that Lombardi remained a master of timing. He'd arrived in Green Bay just when a mass of talent accumulated through years of high draft choices was about to blossom—under the right leader, of course. In nine seasons, he'd molded all that inherited talent, along with some key additions he discovered himself, into perhaps the greatest team pro football had ever seen: a regular season record of 89-29-4, six Western Conference titles, five NFL championships, and two victorious Super Bowls. But cracks had begun to show in the 1967 edition of the Packers. Grabowski and Anderson didn't prove they could replace Taylor and Hornung. The defense slipped a little. They lost five games, including their last two regular season starts. Injuries and age were factors. Injuries healed. Age didn't. Eleven of the 22 starters would be 30 or older in 1968. Three regulars would be 35. The wonderful Green Bay Packers were about to emulate the wonderful one-horse shay. Lombardi's parting words should have been *"Après moi le déluge."*

But just as George Halas and Lombardi kicked themselves upstairs, a new, old coach returned to the sideline in the AFL—Paul Brown. Brown's return was no surprise. His reappearance in one capacity or another had been rumored from the day he was fired at Cleveland in 1963. Hardly a coaching vacancy opened that didn't bring up his name. Not that Brown solicited a new job working for someone else. When Paul Brown returned, it would only be under his own terms. He'd be the boss, answering only to himself and God—so long as God didn't try to call the plays.

In the meantime, he still had a contract with the Browns for $80,000 a year and the title of vice-president, but it was made clear that his duties boiled down to one thing—staying the hell away. "It was like a family tragedy," Brown told Ed Hersey of *Newsday*. "I went as far away as I could. It's surprising how much time and distance help you forget. We were out in La Jolla, California." Brown had plenty of time to golf and bask in the sun. Too much time. "It was like chocolate cake. I like chocolate cake—but not every day for breakfast."

He began looking for his next challenge. His son Michael surveyed possible expansion cities and came up with Cincinnati. Perfect. Paul Brown and Ohio football! When the AFL awarded an expansion franchise in Cincinnati to a group headed by Brown in September 1967, the master had allowed he'd "probably" coach the team in its first year. Probably? How many regiments would it take to keep him off the sideline?

Brown's new team was named after a defunct Cincinnati team of the late 1930s—the Bengals. But in a sense, the club might have been named with Paul Brown in mind: After a long winter's nap, the old Massillon tiger was coming out to do battle.

At age 60, Brown had a new challenge, perhaps his greatest. Could the man who had conquered high school football at Massillon in the 1930s, bested college football at Ohio State in the early 1940s, won in service football at Great Lakes during World War II, dominated the All-America Football Conference at Cleveland in the late 1940s, and again triumphed in the National Football League in the 1950s, produce *anything* with an expansion team? Or would he prove that what they'd said about him in his last years at Cleveland was true—that the game had passed him by, that his dictatorial methods were all wrong for modern players, that he was indeed a dinosaur?

Brown would stay as Cincinnati coach through 1975, and he would have an overall losing record for those eight years—55-56-1. By comparison, in his NFL years at Cleveland, 1950–62, his team lost only 49 times. But he'd entered the NFL with a roster of great players he'd put together in the old AAFC. In Cincinnati, he started from scratch.

How did other NFL and AFL expansion teams of the 1960s fare in their first eight seasons? The Miami Dolphins (1966–73) had the best record by far at 61-48-3. However, most of that came in their Super Bowl seasons. The Dolphins did not win more than five games in any of their first four seasons. The Dallas Cowboys, despite playoff seasons in 1966–67, were 44-61-5 in their first eight years. The Minnesota Vikings managed a winning record in their fourth season (1964) but were 40-65-7 overall. The Atlanta Falcons (1966–73) took six seasons to earn a winning record and were 37-69-4 for their first eight. The sad sack Saints were 30-77-5, without once climbing above .500. Brown had the Bengals in the playoffs three times in eight years, their first postseason appearance (and their first division crown) coming in 1970, their third season.

————————

In 1967, the AFL's Western Division was home to three of the league's four strongest teams. San Diego had performed well, but they had lost games to each of the league's other top teams at the end of the season. That tail-end collapse had Chargers' fans wondering what had happened. The truth of the matter was that Sid Gillman had a dreadfully unbalanced team: good offense, no defense. Getting this half-team to 8-2 with four to go had been an admirable accomplishment.

Kansas City, which had given up a mere 170 points in 1967 to lead the league, was also a power. In eight of their 14 games, Chiefs' opponents scored ten or less. Small wonder. The Chiefs had the league's best linebacking trio in Bobby Bell, Willie Lanier, and Jim Lynch; possibly the best defensive line in Jerry Mays, Buck Buchanan, Ed Lothamer, and Aaron Brown, with Ernie Ladd and Curly Culp backing them; a prime cornerback in Emmit Thomas and star safety in Johnny Robinson. The rest of the secondary wasn't in that class, but plenty of teams were worse off.

Len Dawson had led the AFL in passing efficiency again, but '67 hadn't been one of his best seasons, with only 17 TD passes. Part of the decline in touchdown throws could be blamed on an injury that kept Otis Taylor off the field much of the time. Mike Garrett had also been hurt, but rookie fullback Robert Holmes came on strong with 866 rushing yards. The line was burly, big, and boasted all-league types in tackle Jim Tyrer and guard Ed Budde. And, when all else failed, Kansas City could call on Jan Stenerud, who was successful on 30 of 40 field goal tries.

Oakland was favored to return as the AFL's Super Bowl representative in 1968 after compiling the best record in AFL history in '67 with a young team. Some even suggested the possibility of an undefeated AFL season. Those thoughts went by the boards in week five when the Chargers surprised the Raiders 23–14 at San Diego. That left Oakland and San Diego at 4-1, tied for second behind 5-1 Kansas City. One week later, on October 20, the Chiefs playing at home defeated the Raiders 24–10 and dropped them into third place.

KC took the measure of San Diego the next week, 27–20, while Oakland pounded Cincinnati. On November 3, the Raiders turned the Western Division race into a snarl by stopping the Chiefs 38–21 at Oakland-

Bobby Bell.

Alameda Stadium. Both teams went undefeated from there to bring about a tie for the division title.

The Raiders were basically the same team that had won in 1967. One important loss was All-AFL defensive tackle Tom Keating, who sat out the whole season with an Achilles tendon injury suffered in the championship game against Houston the year before. Outside linebacker Bill Laskey also missed most of the season, and cornerback Kent McCloughan went out in mid-October with a knee injury. Nevertheless, the improved play of several veteran defenders, particularly tackle Dan Birdwell, and the development of rookie Butch Atkinson into a hard-nosed corner kept the defense solid. As a matter of fact, the Raiders gave up exactly the same number of points in 1967 and 1968—233.

Fullback Hewritt Dixon played practically the whole season on one leg yet finished third in league rushing with 865 yards. Spectacular Warren Wells replaced steady Bill Miller at split end and gave Daryle Lamonica a better long-distance target for his bombs. Wells caught 11 touchdowns; Lamonica threw 25.

One rookie who joined the team would loom large in the Raiders' future in more ways than one. Offensive tackle Art Shell, a little-known third-round draft choice out of Maryland Eastern Shore, would play 15 seasons as one of the biggest and best. Then, in 1989, he would become the Raiders head coach and the first black since Fritz Pollard in 1921 to hold such a position in NFL history.

On November 17, the Raiders met the Jets at Oakland in what was to become the decade's most notorious game. It was, of course, a game the Raiders had to win if they were to keep pace with the Chiefs in the West. The Jets, on their way to an eastern title, were led by Joe Namath, probably the most famous football player in the world by that time. NBC had a real attraction for its coast-to-coast broadcast.

For once a much-anticipated attraction more than lived up to its advance billing. The Raiders sandwiched a Lamonica-to-Wells touchdown pass between a pair of field goals by the Jets' Jim Turner to lead 7–6 at the end of the first quarter. In the second period, Billy Cannon scored on a 49-yard Lamonica bomb, but Namath came back to sneak one yard for a touchdown. When the conversion failed, Oakland led 14–12.

The third quarter saw more action. New York took the lead for the first time since early in the game on Bill Mathis's four-yard run. Oakland forged back in front with a touchdown run by Charley Smith, and a two-point conversion pass to Hewritt Dixon brought the score to 22–19.

Early in the fourth quarter, the Raiders were driving for another touchdown when Smith fumbled at the three. Namath turned Don Maynard loose on the inexperienced Butch Atkinson. The result was a 47-yard completion followed by a 50-yard touchdown pass to Maynard that put the Jets back into the lead, 26–22. A little more than half of the final quarter was left to play when Turner widened the Jets' lead to 29–22 with his third field goal. Back came the Raiders. Lamonica's 22-yard touchdown pass to Fred Biletnikoff and George Blanda's kick tied the game at 29 apiece.

So far the teams had behaved like two heavyweight fighters, each intent on knocking the other cold. Play was brutal and penalties abounded. The game was running long, but who cared? What a game! Now Namath finessed the ball down the field using the clock and the sidelines. With only a bit more than a minute to play, Turner kicked his fourth field goal—26 yards to make it 32–29 Jets.

Oakland received the kickoff and ran one play. There was 1:05 left. Suddenly, every NBC-tuned TV set east of Denver stopped showing snarling football players on a hundred-yard gridiron and replaced them with a smiling blonde girl in the Swiss Alps. *Heidi* was here! Yo-de-lay-ee-oh!

NBC had scheduled the special presentation of the Johanna Spyri children's classic for 7 P.M. (EST). The Raiders-Jets game was the lead-in. For some reason, NBC assumed that millions of football-loving fathers would remain enthralled when the network's programming switched to a sugary saga designed for ten-year-olds and that all those moppets out there would be heartbroken if Heidi didn't yodel on screen at seven sharp. So when Mr. Clock put his little hand on seven and his big hand on 12, out came the darlin' girl just as scheduled. Can't have those bedtimes of America's tots pushed back a whole minute and five seconds! Those screams of outrage heard in American living rooms didn't come from 10-year-olds.

The switchboards at NBC lit up like Uncle Harry on New Year's Eve. Angry football fans demanded their football game back. Of course, long before a fraction of the calls were answered, the game was over—an apparent Jets victory. Then the final score rolled across the bottom of the screen. When fans found out what they'd actually missed, they really exploded. Eventually, NBC handled tens of thousands of complaints, very few of which were satisfied the next day when NBC president Julian Goodman called it "a forgivable error committed by humans who were concerned about the children."

Children be damned! America had just missed one of the best bang-up endings in football history! With 42 seconds left, Lamonica threw 42 yards to Smith for a touchdown. Then, on the kickoff, the Jets' Earl Christy fumbled and Raider Preston Ridlehuber recovered for another touchdown. Instead of the Jets, the Raiders won, 43–32.

"I missed the end of the game as much as anyone else," Julian Goodman announced. He got no sympathy. Jets coach Weeb Ewbank said he thought the game—not the telecast—should have ended right after Turner's field goal.

Since the *Heidi* debacle, the television networks have gotten their priorities in place. They may switch from a blowout to a closer game in parts of the country not directly concerned, but local fans can watch their heroes to that last kneel down even if the score goes to the moon. And never, *never*, will a game's end be summarily lopped off just to put on entertainment.

Oakland went from *Heidi* to Hi-Ho-Silver (and Black), winning their final four games to move even with Kansas City. With only two divisions to worry about, the AFL still settled divisional ties the old fashioned way.

The playoff was scheduled for December 22 at Oakland. With the Chiefs and Raiders having split their regular season meetings, the playoff outcome was hard to predict—at least until the first quarter.

On the Raiders' first possession, Lamonica worked the team 80 yards down the field on a drive that featured three strikes to Biletnikoff, the final one good for 24 yards and a touchdown. Kansas City couldn't move and shanked a punt to give Oakland the ball at the KC 25. Three plays later, Lamonica passed to Wells for a 23-yard touchdown. On the Raiders' third possession, they drove 70 yards, with a 44-yard Lamonica-to-Biletnikoff pass bringing Oakland's third touchdown of the quarter.

Kansas City got some offense going in the second quarter and took one drive to the Oakland three and another to the two, but in each case they had to settle for Stenerud field goals. When Lamonica tossed his fourth touchdown pass of the game, a 54-yard bomb to Biletnikoff, the Raiders had a 28–6 lead at the half.

Oakland added 13 more points in the second half while holding the Chiefs to nil. The final: 41–6.

————

In the East, New York's 11-3 record gave them the dubious honor of facing their *Heidi* nemesis, the Oakland Raiders, in the AFL Championship Game.

Fred Biletnikoff.

The man who had instituted the star system that brought Namath to the Jets wasn't part of the celebration of their first division title. In May, Sonny Werblin had sold his 23 percent of Jets' stock for $1.6 million to his four partners, Don Lillis, Leon Hess, Townsend Martin, and Phil Iselin, with Lillis assuming the team presidency. Reportedly, the partners had grown tired of Werblin's high profile and wanted the Jets run more by committee. "They said they never had a hand in things, that I did all the talking," Werblin admitted. "Maybe this is true. But where were they five years ago when things were tough?" As for the committee idea: "Show business or sports, I've seen too many companies broken this way."

In slightly more than five seasons at the helm, Werblin had changed the Jets from the league's laughingstock into its most profitable franchise. His price for less than a quarter of the team's stock was $600,000 more than the partners had paid for the whole blooming shebang in 1963. They'd enjoyed their first winning season in 1967. On the other hand, his "star policy" was criticized as disruptive, particularly his insistence that Namath be given special treatment.

Rumors spread that Werblin would resurface with another franchise, possibly in Miami or Philadelphia, but he quickly put the kibosh on that. "Everything's Philadelphia once you get out of New York. I love the action here. Why would I want to leave?"

Phil Iselin became the third Jets president of the year when Don Lillis died in August.

When he took over as Jets' coach in 1963, the year the Titans became the Jets, Weeb Ewbank said it would take five years to win a title. He missed by a year. Ewbank brought his team in at the top of the Eastern Division in his sixth year at the helm. The Jets' climb in 1968 can be traced to three factors. First, the oft-maligned defense improved to the point of being pretty good. They didn't rank with the stoppers in Kansas City, Oakland, or Houston, but they got the job done. Ends Gerry Philbin and Verlon Biggs and tackles Paul Rochester and undersized John Elliott made an impressive forward wall. Philbin was named All-AFL after the season. Larry Grantham, who'd been on the scene since the Titans days, Ralph Baker, and Al Atkinson handled the linebacking. The secondary, supposedly the weakest part of the supposedly weak defense, held up better than it was supposed to. Regulars Randy Beverly, Johnny Sample, Jim Hudson, and Billy Baird intercepted 20 passes among them.

The second factor in the Jets' climb was the return to health by fullback Matt Snell and halfback Emerson Boozer. Both had been injured the previous year. Snell, known for his blocking as much as his running, was on the beam from the git-go and finished with a solid 747 rushing yards.

Boozer, coming off knee surgery, was tentative in the early going. By December, Coach Ewbank had him convinced that he could again cut and wheel as before.

Matt Snell following lead blocker Emerson Boozer.

The third and most important factor for the Jets was the development of Namath into a quarterback. From day one, he'd had the arm; in '68 he added the head. Having Babe Parilli as a backup was a big help. The Babe was in his 17th season as a professional quarterback, and he'd not only seen it all, he knew how to attack it. The combination of Parilli's tutoring, his own maturation, and having an improved team to lead changed Namath from a marvelous thrower into a marvelous quarterback. Ironically, his passing stats fell off from 1967. He completed slightly less than half his passes (49.2 percent), his 3,147 yards gained were nearly a thousand below his record total of the year before, and his 15 touchdown throws were 11 fewer. The proof that this was the new and improved Joe Namath wasn't to be found in the passing stats but in the league standings. The Jets turned in an 11-3 record because he'd learned to use the running game that Snell and Boozer gave him, learned to use his brilliant receivers, George Sauer, Jr., Don Maynard, and Pete Lammons, to their best advantage . . . learned to win.

But when all was said and done, most experts ranked the Jets behind both the Chiefs and the Raiders in overall strength, so outside of New York, there weren't a whole lot of AFL people rooting for the Jets when they lined up against Oakland on December 29 at Shea. The winner would advance to Super Bowl III, and after two humiliating defeats, few doubted the Raiders stood a better chance against the NFL bullies.

Most of the 62,627 in attendance, of course, were with the Jets. And they were delighted when Maynard outmaneuvered Butch Atkinson to take a 14-yard Namath pass for a touchdown less than four minutes into the game. The weather was cold, with wind gusts up to 35 miles per hour, exactly wrong for two teams that lived by the long bomb. Neither quarterback would complete half his passes, yet both would connect on big plays. When Jim Turner added a 33-yard field goal before the first quarter ended, New York had a 10–0 lead.

In the second quarter, Lamonica began to find Biletnikoff. Ewbank had Johnny Sample on Biletnikoff, but he'd warned him that if Fred started to get open, Sample would be replaced by rookie Cornell Gordon. When Biletnikoff caught a 29-yard touchdown from Lamonica, Ewbank jerked Sample.

Moments later, the Jets got a major scare as Namath came to the sideline with a dislocated ring finger. Fortunately, it was on his left hand. "This is gonna hurt," trainer Jeff Snedeker told him. "It already hurts," Namath growled. Snedeker yanked the finger back in place and Joe returned to the game.

Turner and George Blanda exchanged field goals before the half ended with the Jets still in front, 13–10.

Early in the third quarter, Lamonica passes to Biletnikoff and Warren Wells took the Raiders to the Jets' six. Sample came back in for Gordon. In years past, the New York defense would have curled up and died. But not this time. Three plays by Oakland gained only five yards, and they had to settle for Blanda's tying field goal. That tie lasted only until Namath took the Jets on an 80-yard drive. His 20-yard toss to Lammons put New York back in front, 20–13, as the final quarter began.

Another good Raiders drive was stopped short, and once more Blanda booted a field goal. With the lead down to four points, Namath made a mistake. He forced a pass. Atkinson picked it off just inside the Jets' 40 and returned it clear to the New York four. This time Oakland would not be denied. Lamonica handed off to Pete Banaszak, the Raiders' best short-yardage runner, and he plowed into the end zone to put the Silver and Black ahead, 23–20, with just over eight minutes to go.

In the *Heidi* game, the Raiders had come back late and then quickly widened their lead when Earl Christy fumbled the kickoff. This time Christy handled the kick perfectly and returned it to the 35. Namath picked up a first down and then sent Maynard at Atkinson again. Butch was with him stride-for-stride, but the wind took the ball and Maynard adjusted beautifully, pulling it in at the Raiders' six for a 52-yard gain. Namath dropped to pass, looked at Bill Mathis in the flat, looked at George Sauer, looked at Pete Lammons. They were all covered. Maynard flew open, and Namath whipped it to him sidearm. Touchdown!

But more than enough time remained for yet another patented Raiders comeback. Lamonica drove them to the Jets' 26, but a sack stopped the advance and took them out of Blanda's field goal range. A few moments later, Lamonica had his team on another drive. With two minutes remaining, Oakland was at the New York 24.

Lamonica set his two running backs wide on the same side. Jets' line-backer Ralph Baker remembered the set from the *Heidi* game. One back went deep and the other stayed in the flat as an outlet. Now Lamonica dropped back, and Verlon Biggs was after him. The Raiders' quarterback threw quickly to Charley Smith waiting as a safety-valve in the flat, but the

Don Maynard.

toss tipped off Smith's fingers and rolled away. It was a lateral! A free ball! Baker was on it. Jets' ball!

Smith later admitted he hadn't realized it was a live ball, but, "It all happened so fast. I don't know if I even could have gotten to the ball. Baker was on the ball so quickly. You either react or you don't. I didn't."

The Jets ran out the clock to become the 1968 AFL champs.

The bad news for many was that they'd also be the league representative at the Super Bowl. Here we go again!

The National Football League was embarrassed in the 1968 preseason when American Football League teams won 13 of 23 interleague exhibition games. Meetings between the rivals weren't watched as closely as gauges of the strengths of the leagues as they had been in 1967, but the AFL took a few bows anyway. NFLers grumbled about them being "only" exhibitions. Just wait for the next Super Bowl!

All-AFL defensive back Willie Brown believes the new league's ascendancy over the NFL was rooted in their different approaches to pass coverage. NFLers had long scoffed at the AFL as a "basketball league" that could only throw the football around the field like a hot Frisbee, but Brown points out the league's aerial aptitude caused it to develop better defensive backs.

"For about six or seven years in the AFL, we had probably the best secondary people in football," Brown remembers. "In the National Football League, they played a lot of zone coverage. When the American Football League came in, they threw the ball a lot more and they played a lot of man-to-man coverage. You have to have very physical skills and the ability to run to play man-to-man. That was the biggest difference. When we started playing the National Football League, we found that those guys couldn't cover man-to-man. And when they played us, they had trouble because we played man-to-man. That's why we beat them quite a bit before the merger in 1970.

"They had the experience. They had probably more established quarterbacks and offensive linemen. But overall, I think we had a better group of defensive linemen—some teams did."

If any team had a romp through the regular season, it was Dallas. The Cowboys had more of everything than their Capitol Division rivals. Take runners. When Dan Reeves banged up his knee in week four, Coach Landry plugged in Craig Baynham. When Don Perkins needed a rest, rugged Walt Garrison was available. At quarterback, Don Meredith had another excellent year, and his sub, Craig Morton, would have started for several teams. Receivers? Lance Rentzel and Bob Hayes scored 16 touchdowns between them and kept veteran Sonny Randle and young Dennis Homan on the bench. Pettis Norman and future author Pete Gent split time at tight end. Ralph Neely, John Niland, and Tony Liscio starred on the offensive line. Line subs included Rayfield Wright and Blaine Nye. The Cowboys' 431 points led the NFL.

Their 186 points-allowed placed them second. The usual crew of stout-hearted defenders were on the scene: Bob Lilly, George Andrie, Jethro Pugh, Willie Townes, and Larry Cole up front; Dave Edwards, Lee Roy Jordan, Chuck Howley, Dave Simmons, Jackie Burkett, and D.D. Lewis at linebacker; and Mel Renfro, Cornell Green, Mike Gaechter, Dick Daniels, and Mike Johnson in the secondary.

If Dallas had a problem, it was perhaps that it was so far ahead of the others in the division that there was never a chance the Cowboys wouldn't win the title. No foe required undivided concentration. They could win most games with one head tied behind their backs. And so, on occasion, they were upset or nearly upset by a weaker opponent. They finished 12-2, with losses to the Giants and Packers, neither better than a .500 team. After the season, Landry criticized his club for a lack of "mental toughness."

The Browns hardly looked like division winners when they lost three of their first five games. Coach Collier benched Frank Ryan in week four and replaced him with Bill Nelson, the man with tissue-paper knees. Nelson had been picked up in the off-season from Pittsburgh, where he'd never been able to survive very long uninjured. But life at the top was different. Suddenly Nelson had a line that actually blocked, one that included a couple of All-NFL types in Dick Schafrath and Gene Hickerson. Bill not only survived, he prospered. After splitting his first two starts, he pulled one out of a hat in week six—a 30–20 win over Baltimore. That was the Colts' only NFL loss all season, and it started the Browns on an eight-game winning streak that wrapped up the Coastal Division crown.

The biggest question around the NFL going into the season was how the Packers would do with Lombardi as a full-time general manager and Phil Bengston as head coach. It didn't take long to get the answer—not so hot. Green Bay stayed around .500 all season, winning a couple, losing a couple, and never able to put together any kind of winning streak. The Central Division title was ripe for picking, as neither the Bears nor Vikings were able to sustain any momentum. But when the regular season ended, they both sneaked in ahead of the third-place Packers. For the first time since 1958, the year before Lombardi arrived, Green Bay finished with a losing record—6-7-1.

The Vikings and Bud Grant won the Central Division title with a so-so

The Browns'
offensive line
protecting Bill
Nelson's tissue
paper knees.

8-6 record. With two games left, Minnesota was only at .500, but a pair of road wins pushed them ahead of the Bears. Joe Kapp, the much-maligned quarterback, emerged as a fiercely competitive team leader. The Vikings were dead last in league passing, but his wobbly throws often found the mark in clutch situations. He was usually more dangerous when he pulled down the ball and ran with it, showing a gutty knack for hurdling low tacklers and smashing head-on into high ones.

The Vikings' strength remained its defense, particularly the front four of Carl Eller, Alan Page, Gary Larson, and Jim Marshall. The addition of pass-stealing safety Paul Krause cemented the secondary.

The Rams started off like a house on fire and ended up getting burned. They opened the season with six straight wins, as the defense simply overpowered the opposition. Through those first six, the Fearsome Four-some and company held the enemy to an average of less than 12 points a game. For the whole season, they'd set a new league record by allowing a scant 3,118 yards.

On October 27, the Rams lost 27–10 at Baltimore, dropping them into a 6-1 tie with the Colts. Despite a slew of injuries, four victories and a tie followed for LA, but the Colts continued undefeated. With Baltimore scheduled for the final game, the Rams needed to close out the season with two more victories to slip past Baltimore and into the play-offs.

Perhaps too many minds were on the 14th game because the Bears came on strong against them in the 13th. LA plagued itself all day with penalties and fumbles. Usually reliable Bruce Gossett missed a 35-yard field goal try. With the clock running down, Chicago held a 17–16 lead. Roman Gabriel had been knocked cold in the first half, but he returned as the Rams tried to rally. A 32-yard Gabriel-to-Snow pass put the ball at the Chicago 32, close enough to try for a winning field goal but still iffy.

What followed was the most bizarre series of the season. On first down, tackle Charlie Cowan was flagged for holding, moving the ball back 15 yards and out of field goal range. There was less than a minute to play. Gabriel missed three straight passes and the ball went over to the Bears.

Wait a minute! Holding penalty and the down goes over. Three passes and it's fourth down coming up. Right? Incredibly, all six officials on the field had lost track of the down! But by the time it was realized, the game was over and the Bears had won. Admittedly, fourth-and-31 at the Rams' 47-yard-line with five seconds remaining was a long shot at best. But it was one the Rams could never try. Commissioner Rozelle admitted the error the next day and suspended the officials for the remainder of the season. Small consolation for the Rams. With two losses on their record, they could only finish second to the Colts who gave them a third loss by winning the season finale, 28–24.

In three seasons as head coach, George Allen had taken the Rams from last to third-, first-, and second-place finishes. His record was 29-10-3. So it came as a shock when Christmas arrived and owner Dan Reeves fired him. Talk about coal in your stocking!

Reeves criticized Allen for dealing away draft choices to acquire veterans, the "Future Is Now" philosophy that Allen would espouse throughout his career. Others suggested that Reeves was upset with Allen's takeover style and had decided to take back his ball club. Whatever, the firing sparked a mutiny among the troops. Thirty-eight of the 40 Rams players signed a petition demanding the reinstatement of their coach.

On January 6, Reeves called a press conference to introduce the man who would replace George Allen as coach. And out came George Allen.

If Allen was the league's most controversial coach, Don Shula was its most successful—up to a point. Since taking over as Colts' headman in 1963, his regular season mark was 63-18-3. Not even Lombardi had done so well in his first six seasons. But Shula's record had some flaws. In 1964, his team had been upset in the championship game by Cleveland. In 1965, he'd lost the conference play-off in overtime to Green Bay. In 1967, the Colts lost only once, the season finale to Los Angeles, which cost them the division crown. Hence the whispers: Shula couldn't win the big ones.

As it turned out, the Colts didn't have to beat LA in the season finale.

Johnny Unitas was the NFL's all-time Cinderella story, but Earl Morrall was the league's Cinderella in 1968.

As Morrall entered his 13th NFL season, he could complain that he'd never really been given a full chance to show what he could do. He was the Steve DeBerg of his day, the perennial bridesmaid quarterback shoved aside for a hot new property or waylaid by inopportune injuries in a career more checkered than a beanery tablecloth.

So, when the Giants sent him to Baltimore for a fourth-round draft choice on August 25, 1968, it wasn't exactly front-page news. Just a backup to Johnny Unitas's backup, Jim Ward. At 34-years-old, Morrall had had a couple of good seasons a while ago and was a decent insurance policy. But then Johnny U. crippled his elbow in the last preseason game and Ward was also hurting, so the insurance policy was on the hot seat.

He took over for Unitas in the opening game and led the Colts to a 13-1 record, one of the best marks in history. He deftly mixed the running of

Cinderella with a flat top, back-up quarterback Earl Morrall.

Tom Matte, Terry Cole, and Jerry Hill with his own passes to John Mackey, Jimmy Orr, and Willie Richardson to produce 402 points, second only to Dallas's 431. The quarterback that nobody wanted as a regular finished at the top in the NFL's byzantine method of ranking passers, averaged over nine yards for every pass and threw a league-leading 26 touchdowns. UPI voted him the NFL player of the year.

Earl's path was made easier by a powerful offensive line and a defense that held opponents to a minuscule 144 total points. If Shula could break his "big one" jinx in the postseason games, the Colts might go down as one of the greatest teams ever.

The first round of play-offs opened with an upset, but Baltimore wasn't involved. On December 21 at Cleveland before 81,497 delirious fans, the Browns astounded Dallas, 31–20. The game was tied 10–10 at the half, but on the first play from scrimmage in the second half, Cleveland linebacker Dale Lindsey intercepted a Meredith pass and ran it back 27 yards for a touchdown. Moments later cornerback Ben Davis picked off another Meredith throw to set up still another Cleveland touchdown.

The next day, Baltimore dispensed with Minnesota, 24–14. A good crowd of 60,238 showed up, although the Maryland weather was miserable, with the temperature just below freezing and 14-mile-per-hour winds blowing sleet across the field. After 27 minutes of scoreless play, Morrall threw a three-yard pass to sub tight end Tom Mitchell to give the Colts a one-TD lead at the half. In the third quarter, Morrall connected with John Mackey for a 49-yard touchdown, and Mike Curtis ran back a Joe Kapp fumble for 60 yards and another score.

The championship game was held at Cleveland with 78,410 on hand to cheer for the Browns. They had a quiet day. The Browns had handed the Colts their only loss all season, and lightning wasn't about to strike again. The game was scoreless until the second quarter when Tom Matte ran for a pair of touchdowns and Lou Michaels added a 28-yard field goal. In the second half, the Colts matched their first-half point total with another 17, and the Browns matched theirs with another zero. It was the fourth shutout pitched by the Colts' defense and the sixth time they'd held an opponent without a touchdown.

Two weeks later, on January 12, the almost-all-conquering Colts were scheduled to wrap up their season at Miami in Super Bowl III. They were already counting the $15,000 per man that would become theirs at the final gun of what figured to be little more than a signal drill. Not only were the Colts one of the strongest teams in NFL history, but their opponents, the New York Titans—no, Mets—no . . . Well, whatever they called themselves, they weren't even considered the best team in the AFL, that upstart league that had already proved its inferiority by crumbling in Super Bowls I and II.

Gamblers installed the New Yorkers as 18-point underdogs. An 18-point spot was the kind you'd give an apple when William Tell pulls his bow. Saddam Hussein couldn't even get 18 points in Desert Storm. Colts' owner Carroll Rosenbloom had a ten-piece band and plenty of champagne ready for the victory party to be held under a specially built tent at his beachfront home the evening after the game. On the morning of the game, CBS, which would televise it, took measurements and marked camera positions with tape on the floor of the Colts' locker room so they could capture the victory celebration there.

All of which made those statements by Joe Namath in the week leading up to Super Sunday so strange. Why had he said things like there were at least four quarterbacks in the AFL better than Earl Morrall, "including me"? Didn't he know Morrall was the MVP of the NFL? And how could he have been so outrageous as to predict—no, *guarantee*—a Jets victory? Didn't he realize how foolish he would look when the final score was posted?

"Joe believed it. He really thought we were going to beat them," Jets tackle Dave Herman explained later. "And eventually, we all did."

But the Jets' faith was tested when the Colts drove easily to the New York 19 on their first possession, making it look just as easy as the 75,377 gathered in the Orange Bowl expected it to be. Then Morrall missed on three passes, including one dropped by a wide-open Willie Richardson. Surefooted Lou Michaels came in for the chip-shot, 27-yard field goal and *missed* it! The lucky Jets escaped this time.

But a little later, George Sauer fumbled and the Colts took over at the New York 12. Morrall aimed a pass at big Tom Mitchell. The ball was tipped slightly and hit Mitchell in the shoulder pad, then caromed into the hands of Jets' cornerback Randy Beverly. What was happening here?

In the second quarter, Namath mixed off-tackle smashes by Matt Snell and quick passes to George Sauer to take the Jets on an 80-yard drive. Snell scored the touchdown on a four-yard plunge and Jim Turner added the extra point. For the first time in Super Bowl's three-year history, an AFL team had the lead.

The Colts' frustrations continued. Tom Matte tore loose for a 48-yard dash, but Morrall immediately threw another interception. On a flea-flicker, Jimmy Orr jumped up and down all alone in the corner of the end zone, but Morrall never saw him and threw down the middle for his third interception.

Meanwhile, New York stayed with its short game. The Colts kept ex-

Joe Namath.

pecting Namath to try to hit Don Maynard deep and double covered the Jets' receiver. That left George Sauer one-on-one short and an easy target. On the day, Sauer caught eight passes for 133 yards. Maynard didn't catch a pass but was equally valuable by keeping two Colts tied up. Snell, running mostly behind Dave Herman, carried 30 times for 121 yards.

In the third quarter, Turner booted field goals of 32 and 30 yards to widen the Jets' lead. A minute and a half into the fourth quarter, Turner kicked his third three-pointer from nine yards out. The clock had struck 12 on Morrall's Cinderella season. He was able to complete only six of 17 passes with three interceptions. Unitas replaced him in the final quarter and sore-armed 24 passes. With barely over three minutes left to play, he took the Colts to a meaningless touchdown.

Namath, the game's MVP, hadn't thrown a touchdown, but he was 17-for-28, good for 206 yards and no interceptions. More important, he'd *controlled* the game from the opening kickoff. When the final gun sounded, he ran off the field, grinning from ear-to-ear, his index finger raised in the traditional "number one" signal. But to many in the proud NFL, he might well have raised a different finger.

245

WEEB EWBANK: "THE JETS WERE THE TOUGHER JOB"

If you look only at Weeb Ewbank's won-lost record for twenty years as a pro head coach—a good-not-great 134-130—you might wonder how he got into the Pro Football Hall of Fame. There are retired coaches with more wins who'll never be enshrined. But Ewbank was a builder. In 1954, he left a secure position as an assistant to Paul Brown in Cleveland and took over the woebegone Baltimore Colts, then only in their second NFL season. It was the kind of situation that often ends a coach's career. The year before, the Colts had been blitzed for 45 points in three different games. Ewbank's Colts dropped their opener 48–0. Yet within five years, he built the team into the best in the league—champions in 1958 and 1959.

In 1963, Ewbank became head coach of the New York Jets, a team that after three years as the Titans had become the laughingstock of the American Football League. Once more Ewbank prevailed, shocking the football world with a totally unexpected victory in Super Bowl III.

Ewbank was the coach who groomed two of football's greatest quarterbacks, Johnny Unitas and Joe Namath, for immortality, and he's quick to credit them and other players for his success. Certainly no coach wins without good players, but as Howard Cosell said, "When Weeb has a big game to win, he'll win it." Winning big games is Hall of Fame stuff.

———

"I don't think there's anybody who picked up two worse teams than I did with the Colts in 1954 and the Jets in 1963. Artie Donovan always talks about what a lousy team the Colts were before and how tough it was once I came in there. I did a lot of switching. Gino Marchetti, who became one of the greatest pass rushers ever, was an offensive tackle when I got there. Joe Campanella had been an offensive tackle too, and he became a terrific linebacker. We had a lot of switching around.

"But between the two, I think the Jets were the harder job. A lot of the players had stories about checks bouncing the year before. They were worried about whether they'd get paid. We couldn't even get a training place because so many bills hadn't been paid from the year before. Who wanted us? Fortunately, we had a friend who'd gone to Peekskill Military, and he arranged for us to train up there for a couple of years. That saved us, and of course, we saved the school a little bit too. We paid our bills.

"But I remember one time during the '68 year, the baseball Mets had full time over at Shea Stadium and they got in there and just ran us out of the stadium. One time, I remember, we practiced on just an open field. Then another time that year, we had to go over to Rikers Island where the prison is.

"Another difference between building the Colts and building the Jets was that there was a great deal more competition in drafting players. When we started with the Colts, there were only 12 teams drafting. By 1963 there were 22. We were pretty lucky at getting the players we wanted, but it took us six years to win the championship in New York while it took us five years in Baltimore.

"For the AFL to be successful, it had to have a strong team in New York. The Giants tried every way to get Namath for the NFL. There were four of us from the Jets who sat in the negotiations with Joe and his agent. The money just went up and up. We weren't going to let the NFL get him. It was a landmark signing that helped publicize the AFL, and fortunately, Joe came through.

"Sonny Werblin's background was show business. He thought stars. Sometimes that got in the way. For example, I wanted Joe to live out near Shea Stadium. That's where we were going to practice. But Sonny right away said no. A star had to live on Park Avenue so his pictures would get in the rotogravure section of the newspaper.

"I remember we went up to Buffalo to play, and one of our substitutes pushed one of their players all over the field. The Buffalo boy was Jewish, and Sonny figured he'd be a draw in New York. So the next day, Sonny says, 'I got you a new player.' He'd traded Buffalo for this Jewish player. Well, I said, 'If you paid any more than a dime, you got cheated.' So when the guy reported, he said, 'Gee, the game I played I'm surprised you picked me up.' I said, '*I* didn't!'

"The whole thing was that that was how Sonny felt. Get people in the stands. Sometimes it made it harder to build a football team. But he also was the guy who paid the money for Joe.

"A lot of people don't understand. Joe got a lot of publicity. Newspaper men would come out to practice, and it was always 'Get a picture of Joe doing this' or 'Joe doing that.' Joe didn't ask for that. He'd say, 'Hey, we've got other good players. Get them.' But all they wanted was Joe. There he was and they used him. Sonny certainly knew what he was doing with that star thing.

"As I said, it was a tougher job with the Jets. I think one of the things that shows that is the number of Hall of Famers from the two teams. My Baltimore team has seven: Marchetti, Donovan, John Unitas, Raymond Berry, Lenny Moore, Jim Parker, and myself. With the Jets we had only three: Namath, Don Maynard, and me. Of course, as much time hasn't gone by. I think there's some others on the Colts and Jets who should be given consideration.

"Everybody likes to say that defense wins games, and in both cases we had two good defensive units. In Super Bowl III, everybody remembers Namath, who had a great game, but our defense played well too. We held the Colts to seven points. I honestly believe we beat a better team than some that have won the Super Bowl. The same thing could be said about the Giants teams our 1958–59 Colts beat, by the way.

"All our defenses had a team concept where we assigned each player a specific duty in order to make the over-all defense successful.

"Larry Grantham, the linebacker, was a fine guy. We couldn't have done without him. He had a very fine defensive head. He would have made a very good defensive coach any place in pro football. He called our defensive signals. He did a great job. He was only about 210 pounds, and he wasn't about to take on a 230-pound fullback head on, but he had a knack for always coming in on them from an angle. He wasn't a bruiser, but he was exact. He was smart and a great blitzer. He could really get on the passer.

"Just to show how he could play. He was a linebacker, but one game during that first season, we had to play him at safety because we had an extra linebacker but we didn't have an extra safety. He made the adjustment right away. We didn't win that game, but it wasn't his fault. A real leader, and the boys believed in him.

"Emerson Boozer was one of my favorites—just a great person as well as a fine football player. He and Matt Snell were the closest friends. Matt and Marion Motley were two of the best fullbacks for picking up blitzes I've ever seen. I was responsible for the backfield. Emerson worked with Matt in the drills, and Matt helped him a lot. In Super Bowl III, Boozer was right up there leading the blocking for Snell.

"When Emerson hurt his leg, I remember them taking the cast off his leg and there was just skin hanging off the bone. He said, 'My God, I'll never walk again, much less run!' But he just worked on that leg and he got it back. And eventually, he got around and didn't think any more about it.

"He was a fine runner and a good receiver. He and Matt might miss a pass in practice and the guys would get on them, but in a game they were very sure-handed.

"George Sauer and Don Maynard, our regular wide receivers, were very fine people and very precise in their pattern running. Either one of them was very knowledgeable in what they could do to get open. They knew what they could do to their opponents. They and Joe and I would stay after practice. We called it 'special work.' They'd stay 15 or 20 minutes extra just working on the plays they thought would be good that week until they had them so precise it was wonderful.

"Maynard could also ad-lib patterns. He and Joe had signals. Maybe he was supposed to cut across on an 'in' pattern but he'd see he was open deep. He'd throw his hand up and was gone. Joe'd lay it out there. John Unitas and Raymond Berry had the same rapport.

"Joe did a lot of checking off. Both Sauer and Maynard, but particularly Maynard, had signals when a certain pattern was there. Joe would call whatever he might signal him. They were both very precise and worked together great.

"Namath and Maynard were great on a quick out. Maynard would take about three steps and turn and the ball was there. Maynard was talking to me one time and he asked, 'Do you know how we worked that, Coach?' I said, 'No, I'm not sure. Tell me what you did in practice.' He said, 'Well, we had a contest. He would try to get the ball to me quicker than I could get my three steps and turn. Believe me, I always wore my helmet 'cause I didn't want that ball to hit me in the head.'

"I graded every player on film over the season—zero to five. Winston Hill, our offensive tackle graded high all the time. He was very good. [Offensive guard] Randy Rasmussen was another one. Now a guy like [offensive guard] Dave Herman just had the heart. He played beyond his ability. For example, in the Super Bowl, he had to move from guard to tackle and take on Bubba Smith. He played one hell of a game. Bubba ran over him a couple of times, but by the time he ran over him it was too late. Herman was right there still fighting him. He was a great guy on the bench too. He'd get the team going.

"One break I got early in my career, I was coaching at Washington University in St. Louis when Paul Brown called me in 1949 and asked me to come be an assistant with the Browns. He told me he wanted me to coach the tackles. Well, I said, 'Paul, I was a quarterback in college. I've always coached the backs.' He said, 'Don't worry about it. You'll be okay.' That was the best thing that ever happened to me because later on when I became head coach and we'd be taking on a play, there had to be an exception for it for the line or back. I always made the exception—the tougher assignment—for the back because they had fewer details to remember.

"I guess I had a reputation for treating players fairly. Some coaches, especially some from the 'old school,' try to dominate and intimidate their players. They use all kinds of foul language and all. I never believed in that. I tried to treat people all the way through—players, assistant coaches, secretaries—the way I'd like to be treated.

"A lot of times, the pressure gets to a coach. Here a guy drops a punt. The coach might have worked all week on that but the guy drops it, and you lose a ball game because that was dropped. You're at the mercy of that guy. You didn't drop it.

"I definitely believe that every team needs a man like Art Donovan with the Colts or Curly Johnson with the Jets to keep them from tension all the time—at least in their free time. Always funny guys. You'd see a crowd and they'd generally be at the center of it. Those guys always had the team in stitches. It would relax the team. Too many teams get wound too tight. I think there has to be some relaxation.

"There was another thing too. We had special Thanksgiving Day dinners for the team each year to bring their families. I had to laugh when the Pittsburgh Pirates won the World Series with that 'We are family' motto. All of our teams were like that, clear back to Baltimore days.

"Joe, for example, got a lot of publicity. He'd come in after he'd had a big game and the reporters would gather around. He'd say, 'Go talk to those guys who blocked for me. Anyone can throw the ball when you get blocking like that.' But maybe he had a bad day and maybe got the hell knocked out of him. He never said anything against the lineman. He'd just say, 'Well, we all had a bad day today.'

"I prided myself on trying to keep guys who were good citizens. Fortunately, I didn't coach during this drug era. I remember once the man who watched our players for us came to me about one of our men. He said, 'I've never seen so-and-so buy any drugs, but he frequents a place where I know drugs are sold.' The next week, I put that player on waivers. I just didn't want to get into what might happen.

"In all my time coaching, there were only a couple of assistants I ever had to let go because they didn't do their job. I always wanted to meet their wives. See what kind of a family life they had. I think it paid dividends. When you're building from the ground up, you build from the *ground* up. I felt if I worked hard, my coaches would work hard. If they didn't, those were the kind of guys you get rid of.

"I think players feel that way. I remember one time Joe was on Johnny Carson's show. Johnny said, 'Joe, you're a good signal caller and all. You'd probably make a good coach.' Joe said, 'Not me. I don't want to work like Weeb Ewbank.'

"On Joe's 'I guarantee it' statement before Super Bowl III, I said to him, 'Joe, why'd you say a thing like that? We're 17-point underdogs and I wanted to keep it that way.' As a matter of fact, I'd told the team not to pay any attention to what I said to reporters. I was going to try to make it 21. I said, 'Don't do anything to make them excited.' Well, then Joe says, 'I guarantee it.' Why, I could have shot him. So I went to Joe and he said, 'You're the guy who told us we could do it. You got us believing it. So the guy asked me, and I just told him the truth, the way I felt.'

"Pete Lammons [Jets tight end] came to me one day before practice when we were down there and asked what was scheduled for the day. I told him I had one more little film I wanted to show about the Colts. He said, 'Aw, Coach, you got us believing we can win. Now we're getting overconfident!'

"The kids really did believe. And on our rings it says 'If we maintain our poise and execute well, we'll win.' "

THE LAST GO-ROUND

19

The greatest get-together of 1969 and the decade was no doubt Woodstock, but the NFL-AFL merger ranks second. In May, it was time to work out the hardest part—which NFL teams would join the AFL teams in what would become in 1970 the American Football *Conference*. Three NFL clubs had to change "leagues." None of the old NFLers were anxious to move.

Commissioner Rozelle gathered the owners together at league headquarters on Park Avenue in New York and kept them there for 35 hours and 45 minutes until they thrashed it out. Baltimore was pretty much of a done deal before the meeting. Owner Carroll Rosenbloom was one of the earliest proponents of the merger, and except for expansion teams, the Colts were the youngest team in NFL years, having come into being in 1953. The other two movers named at the end of the meeting were the Cleveland Browns and Pittsburgh Steelers. The Browns had joined the NFL in 1950 and Pittsburgh in 1933. By moving together, they were able to maintain their profitable turnpike rivalry—two near-certain sellouts each year—and undertake a potentially lucrative rivalry for each with Cincinnati. Time would prove the latter assessment correct. No matter what the teams' records, games among the three always spark tremendous interest each year in all three cities, and large crowds follow their teams on the road to swell the attendance in each rival's ballpark.

With that out of the way, the American Football League faced its final, lame-duck season with pride and a good deal of sadness.

Players in the AFL for all ten years of the league's existence:

George Blanda, QB; Houston 1960–66, Oakland 1967–69
Billy Cannon, HB-TE; Houston 1960–63, Oakland 1964–69
Gino Cappelletti, WR; Boston 1960–69

Tom Flores, QB; Oakland 1960–66, Buffalo 1967–69, Kansas City 1969

Larry Grantham, LB; New York 1960–69

Wayne Hawkins, OG; Oakland 1960–69

Jim Hunt, DE-DT; Boston 1960–69

Harry Jacobs, LB; Boston 1960–62, Buffalo 1963–69

Jack Kemp, QB; Chargers 1960–62, Buffalo 1962–69

Jackie Lee, QB; Houston 1960–63, 1966–67, Denver 1964–65, Kansas City 1967–69

Paul Lowe, HB; Chargers 1960–67, Kansas City 1968–69

Paul Maguire, LB; Chargers 1960–63, Buffalo 1964–69

Bill Mathis, HB-FB; New York 1960–69

Don Maynard, WR; New York 1960–69

Ron Mix, OT-OG; Chargers 1960–69

Jim Otto, OC; Oakland 1960–69

Babe Parilli, QB; Oakland 1960, Boston 1961–67, New York 1968–69

Lineman (74) Ron Mix.

Johnny Robinson, DB; Dallas 1960–62, Kansas City 1963–69

Paul Rochester, DT; Dallas 1960–62, Kansas City 1963, New York
1963–69
Ernie Wright, OT; Chargers 1960–67, Cincinnati 1968–69

The defending world champion Jets had little trouble in winning their second consecutive Eastern Division title. Eight of their ten wins came from beating each of the other eastern teams twice, and a soft schedule gave them last-place Cincinnati twice from the West. However, they lost their four other meetings with Western Division teams—to Oakland, Kansas City, San Diego, and even Denver—ominous for the play-offs. New York's weakness was no secret—pass defense. Coach Ewbank cut outspoken Johnny Sample before the season and soon sent the other Super Bowl cornerback, Randy Beverly, to the bench. Their replacements were no improvement, as the Jets finished next-to-last in passing yardage allowed.

The front four of Gerry Philbin, John Elliott, Paul Rochester, and Verlon Biggs, and linebackers Larry Grantham, Al Atkinson, and Ralph Baker shut off opponents' runners and did their best to help the weak secondary with a strong pass rush. The offense accounted for 353 points, third best in the league. Matt Snell and Emerson Boozer each ran for over 600 yards, and Joe Namath meted out 2,734 yards in passes to Don Maynard, George Sauer, Pete Lammons, and his running backs.

Buffalo had first draft choice O. J. Simpson and former Oakland coach Johnny Rauch and both were disappointing. The Bills improved their record to 4-10 to match Boston, but the fans had expected more. Rauch lost more games in his first season as Bills coach than he had in three seasons with the Raiders. Moreover, his emphasis on the passing game limited Simpson's opportunities to do what he did best—run with the ball. The Juice still picked up 697 yards on the ground, but that was way short of what had been anticipated and of what he later showed he was capable of. Rauch's love for a passing offense even led him to eventually decide O. J.'s future lay in becoming a wide receiver, a move that had it been consummated would have been akin to asking Horowitz to switch to kazoo.

In the West, Paul Brown's Cincinnati Bengals seemed to have found the one indispensable ingredient for success in pro football—a dominating quarterback. After throwing three touchdown passes in the College All-Star Game, Greg Cook, a tall, blond, handsome rookie out of the University of Cincinnati, where he'd led the nation in total offense, was a sensation from the moment he set foot in the Bengals' camp. He had size, agility, intelligence, courage, confidence, and the ability to drive a nail with a football at 50 yards. More than 20 years later, there are Bengals' players and fans who insist he could have become one of the best, perhaps *the* best quarterback in NFL history. Tom Bass, an assistant coach with the Bengals then and Tampa Bay and San Diego later, says, "It is easy to say that this guy or that guy has it all, but Greg had more than that. He had everything—physically, mentally, emotionally—to be one of the greats of all time."

Right out of the chute, Cook led the Bengals to an opening 27–21 win over Miami, throwing two touchdown passes. A week later, he threw three touchdown passes and ran for a fourth as Cincinnati upset San Diego, 34–20. The third week, he led a third straight victory, a shocker over Kansas City, 24–19.

However, Cook injured his arm when he was crunched by the Chiefs' Willie Lanier and went to the sideline for a month while backup Sam Wyche presided over four losses. He returned in time to engineer Cincinnati's fourth win, a 31–17 victory over Oakland. The next week, he tossed a quartet of touchdowns in a 31–31 tie with Houston.

In the Bengals' last five games, all losses, he was injured further, but he still led the AFL in passing, completing 106 passes for 1,854 yards and 11 touchdowns. He averaged 9.41 yards per attempt, the most for any rookie ever.

"Cook looked like the best quarterback in the league," John Madden says, "better than Lamonica, better than Dawson, better than Namath, Hadl, or Griese. I thought that this kid was going to be better than anyone I had ever seen."

It was not to be. The injuries Cook had suffered as a freshman worsened. He spent three years on the injured list. In 1973, as a backup, he threw three passes and completed one for 11 yards. Then he retired.

San Diego had its annual defensive mediocrity and offensive firepower. Dickie Post led the league in rushing with 873 yards, and Lance Alworth topped a thousand yards in receptions for the seventh straight year. On December 14, in the season finale, he surpassed Don Hutson's record by catching a pass in his 96th consecutive game. Later research showed that Hutson had actually missed catching any passes in one game along the way, but Alworth held the new and correct NFL record for a few years.

After nine games, the Chargers stood 4-5, and Coach Gillman was suffering from a bad case of ulcers. He turned the team over to assistant Charlie Waller and concentrated on being general manager for the remainder of the season.

With Gillman absent from the sidelines, Kansas City's Hank Stram became the only head coach to put in all ten AFL seasons with the same club. The '69 season was one of his best, with the team finishing 11-3, good enough to win the division in most years. Stram had the league's strongest defense: a rock solid front four of Jerry Mays, Buck Buchanan, Curly Culp, and Aaron Brown, the sensational trio of Bobby Bell, Willie Lanier, and Jim Lynch at linebacking, and tight-fisted secondary of Emmit Thomas, Johnny Robinson, Jim Kearney, and outstanding rookie Jim Marsalis. The Chiefs held half their opponents to ten or fewer points and tossed two shutouts.

On offense, Stram had a huge, mobile line, and more than enough runners. As a consequence, quarterbacks Len Dawson and Mike Livingston passed less often than in previous years, using the air more to keep defenses honest than as a primary weapon. The regular runners, Mike Garrett and Robert Holmes, crunched for over 1,300 yards between them but were regularly relieved by fast Warren McVea and steady Wendell Hayes, who added another 700 yards. The running contingent was so deep that young Ed Podolak only returned kicks, Curtis McClinton was switched to tight end to back Fred Arbanas, and Paul Lowe, in his final season after so many great years with the Chargers, was limited to ten rushing attempts.

Kansas City stood 11-2 when they closed the season against the 11-1-1 Raiders at Oakland. With the division title on the line, the Kansas City defense held the high-powered Raiders to ten points, but it wasn't enough. Oakland limited the Chiefs to six to take the championship.

The Raiders' new coach, John Madden, got very little credit from the media for Oakland's success. When the Raiders' youngest assistant coach was promoted to the head job, critics looked at his age, 33, and that he had never held a head coaching job in the pros and wrote him off as an Al Davis stooge. While big John huffed and puffed and waved his arms on the sideline, cynics pointed out that John Rauch had won just as often with the same material. And, besides, Al Davis made all the important decisions. Only time would show Madden to be one of the best coaches in pro football history and anything but a Davis puppet.

Inevitably, some Raider veterans enjoyed giving Madden a hard time. Jim Otto, who insists he was never one of the pranksters, thinks John's age was a factor: "After all, he was only a year older than I was." Naturally, Otto says, at training camp, some of the players might sneak out late "for a pizza or something."

But Willie Brown feels that Madden's easygoing approach was one of his strengths: "It was great playing for John because he would let you play football. He didn't get into your personal business. He let you be a man."

Brown remembers a morning in the mid-1970s when Madden was going over punt coverage. He'd call the name of a player and the player would answer with his own name.

"Willie Brown?"

"Willie Brown."

"Ted Hendricks?"

Everyone looked around. No Hendricks. Suddenly, the phone rang. It was handed to Madden who put the receiver to his ear.

"Ted Hendricks," said a voice on the end of the line. Everybody, including Madden, broke up.

"John was a very understanding coach," Brown adds.

That said, it should also be noted that Madden made no startling changes in the Raiders during his first season. Why fix it if it ain't broke? The defense, while not up to Kansas City's, still held opponents to meager numbers. Tackle Dan Birdwell was sidelined much of the year, but Tom Keating returned from his Achilles tendon injury to pick up the slack. The secondary of Willie Brown, Nemiah Wilson, Dave Grayson, and Butch Atkinson held opponents to the lowest pass completion percentage in the league—38.9.

Oakland continued to prosper by the pass, striking deep whenever possible. Daryle Lamonica won his second MVP in three years by throwing for league-high marks in yardage (3,302) and touchdowns (34). Receiver Warren Wells blazed to 14 TD receptions and 1,260 yards, both league highs, and possession receiver Fred Biletnikoff added another 12 touchdowns to his team-leading 54 catches.

In years past, the two division winners—Oakland and New York—would have squared off for the league championship game. However, in its final season, the AFL undertook a broader playoff schedule, mainly at the urging of television. A preliminary round pitted both first-place finishers against the runners-up in the opposite division.

On Saturday, December 20, Kansas City faced New York at Shea Stadium before 62,977. The Jets found themselves struggling under a home field *dis*advantage as the wind whipped through and across the field. Far more than the Chiefs, the Jets depended on passing to move the ball, and the day was definitely not made for passing.

"The wind was a major factor," Namath said afterward. "The ball was going end-over-end and every direction. The timing was gone with the receivers. You could throw up the middle, but even when I'd throw an 8-yard-out pattern to Matt Snell, the ball would sail away."

The Jets did an excellent job in closing down the Kansas City running attack, but the Chiefs were even more effective against the Jets' runners. Namath was able to complete only 14 of 40 passes and was flattened by the KC front four a half dozen times. "I feel like I was in a gang fight all by myself," he admitted after the game.

Early in the fourth quarter, New York's Jim Turner hit a short field goal to tie the game at 6–6, but then Len Dawson, who'd been stymied all day by the wind, cut through the gale for a 61-yard pass to Otis Taylor. A moment later, he connected on a 19-yarder to Gloster Richardson good for the winning touchdown to rob the Jets of their dreams of a second trip to the Super Bowl.

The Raiders had been saying all along that they thought the new playoff format was silly. The day after the Chiefs won in New York, the Raiders proved just how silly the whole thing could be by mercilessly stomping on the Houston Oilers 56–7 at Oakland. Before the first quarter ended, the score was 28–0. Lamonica threw six touchdown passes on the day.

That set up the third meeting of the season between Oakland and Kansas City in the AFL title game two weeks later. A crowd of 53,564 showed up at Oakland-Alameda Coliseum, most of them hoping to see a third Raiders win. But beating any pro football team three times in one season is always a big order, and thrice defeating a team of the Chiefs' quality made cleaning the Augean stables look like a simple dusting.

Nevertheless, the Raiders gained a 7–0 lead 14 minutes into the first quarter on Charlie Smith's three-yard plunge and George Blanda's conversion. Meanwhile, Oakland held KC at bay. At one point Len Dawson threw incomplete on seven straight passes. Then, with only about two minutes left in the half, Dawson connected with Frank Pitts for 41 yards to the Oakland one. Wendell Hayes crashed over for the touchdown, and Jan Stenerud's PAT tied the score.

In the third quarter, Dawson passed to Otis Taylor in the play of the game. On third down on his own two-yard-line, Dawson dropped back to pass. "Otis wasn't the primary receiver," Dawson explained. "I was looking for [Robert] Holmes coming across the middle, but he got banged. I was in the end zone and couldn't wait any longer, so I threw it so it would have gone out of bounds if he didn't catch it. It was a great catch." Taylor pulled in the ball at the 37 and then flew over the sideline. Once out of the hole, the Chiefs continued their drive. Holmes smashed over from the eight, and Stenerud brought the score to 14–7.

Daryle Lamonica had been pounded all day by the Chiefs' rush. He suffered four sacks and was knocked to the ground at least a dozen times after throwing. Midway through the third period, he threw an incomplete pass and on his follow-through smashed his hand into Aaron Brown's helmet. "I thought I'd broken it," he explained after the game. "I jammed three fingers." Lamonica was out of the game for eight minutes. When he returned: "I could grip the ball, but I didn't have the zing on my follow-through."

That absence of zing proved costly for the Raiders in the comic opera fourth quarter. Three times in the final period, the usually sure-handed Chiefs fumbled the ball in their own territory to give Oakland a chance. Three times, the zingless Lamonica threw interceptions to end the threat. After returning to the game, Lamonica was able to complete only three of 18 passes. While all this was happening, Stenerud kicked a 22-yard field goal to wrap up the scoring.

The 17–7 win meant the NFL would face a runner-up rather than a divisional champion in the fourth and final league-versus-league Super Bowl. But it also gave Kansas City the chance it had been waiting for since Super Bowl I.

———

Losing Super Bowl III, any staunch NFLer could explain, was like having quintuplets—highly unlikely in any specific circumstance but mathematically certain to occur sometime somewhere, sooner or later . . . eventually. A popular proposition around the NFL between seasons was, "If the Colts and Jets played ten times, the Colts would win nine games." It was just freakish dumb luck that the tenth game happened to fall on last season's Super Sunday. The Jets' victory didn't really prove anything except that a football will bounce funny sometimes. Most of all, it didn't prove that the AFL had drawn even with the NFL.

———

In 1969, Vince Lombardi returned to coaching. Apparently bored with a straight GM job, he asked to be let out of the remaining five years of his Green Bay contract so he could take over as Washington Redskins coach. As part of the deal, Lombardi was given the opportunity to purchase a substantial block of Washington stock. Probably more in gratitude for what he had done than in fear of having a disgruntled employeee, the Packers' board of directors acquiesced, and in February, Caesar Vincentus replaced Otto Graham as coach of a Redskins team that hadn't finished above .500 since 1955.

One of Lombardi's first moves was to lure 35-year-old Sam Huff out of retirement to serve as middle linebacker and part-time assistant coach. A good outside linebacker was already on the scene in Chris Hanburger. A tight secondary was formed with Pat Fischer, Mike Bass, Brig Owens, and Rickie Harris.

On offense, Lombardi inherited Sonny Jurgensen to pass and Charley Taylor and Jerry Smith to catch. Bobby Mitchell's retirement was offset by ex-Packer Bob Long's good season. Fullback Charlie Harraway was an okay blocker and receiver, but the find of the year was runner Larry Brown. A little-known draft choice out of Kansas State, Brown had a severe hearing problem that caused him to get off slowly on the count. Once this was

Charley Taylor.

discovered, he was fitted for a hearing aid, enabling him to get that all-important quick explosion into the line. He rushed for 888 yards as a rookie and went on to lead the NFC in rushing twice.

Lombardi's Redskins didn't set the league on fire, but they pulled off a long-sought winning record, finishing second in the Capitol Division at 7-5-2. That was the same number of wins he'd registered in his first season in Green Bay and gave rise to speculation that Lombardi might dominate the 1970s at Washington the way he'd dominated the 1960s at Green Bay. But in the summer of 1970, Lombardi entered Georgetown University Hospital, diagnosed with intestinal cancer. On September 3, he died.

In Dallas, both premier runner Don Perkins and regular quarterback Don Meredith retired before the season. On nearly any other team such a double dip would have short-circuited the offense, but Tom Landry merely plugged in Craig Morton at quarterback and turned the running over to Calvin Hill, a rookie out of Yale, no less. Hill, another relatively unknown draftee unearthed by the Cowboys' computer, might well have led the

261

league in rushing had he not been sidelined for the final regular season game. Still, in 13 games, he picked up 942 yards. Fullback Walt Garrison, a real cowboy who doubled as an off-season rodeo star, bulldogged his way to 818 yards, as Big D coasted through an 11-2-1 year.

Winning the Capitol Division was never a problem for the Cowboys. They were too deep in first-rank personnel to avoid winning in the long run. Other teams were ground down by injuries or fatigue; Dallas simply sent in the next wave of above-average performers. It's a cliche to say a team's subs would have started for most other teams, but with the Cowboys it was true. Not only started but in several cases starred. The Dallas nemesis was the postseason. Their unemotional, day-at-the-office style served them well during the regular season when to get too high one week invited a crash the next. But to win in the postseason, a team needed to play at a higher emotional level because that's exactly how an opponent would play. Dallas consistently lost in postseason when one of its strengths, its calm unemotional approach became a liability. They would not discover a leader who could successfully raise their pitch in a big game until 1971, when Roger Staubach, another 1969 rookie, would become the regular quarterback.

In the Century Division, Cleveland won again against limp competition. The 10-3-1 Browns had a winning offense and an also-ran defense. Quarterback Bill Nelson enjoyed another season on healthy knees, throwing to a cadre of healthy receivers in Gary Collins, Paul Warfield, and Milt Morin. Nelson's strengths were poise and leadership, but his arm accounted for 23 touchdowns. Leroy Kelly, though down from his previous league-leading season, was still good for 817 rushing yards, and Ron Johnson, a powerful rookie out of Michigan, provided a 205-pound running mate. Give Cleveland a football and it would score points.

Chuck Noll, Pittsburgh's new coach, decided Band-Aids wouldn't do and set about rebuilding from the ground up, something the Steelers had needed since 1933. Pittsburgh fans looked askance when Noll's first draft choice was announced: Joe Greene of North Texas State. Joe who? they asked, not knowing Noll had just laid the cornerstone of the Steel Curtain defense that would lead to four Super Bowl rings in the 1970s. Noll won his opening game, a 16–13 squeaker over Detroit, and then lost his next 13 in a row. But better times were on the way.

———

The Baltimore Colts' last season on the NFC side of the NFL was also Don Shula's last as their head coach, and it was also a major disappointment. The team that had been virtually unbeatable until Super Bowl III stumbled through a so-so 8-5-1 year.

George Allen's Rams were one of football's most boring teams. The ball-control offense took its yardage in sips and nibbles, and the defense kept opponents and their fans frustrated. As a consequence, Los Angeles *dulled* its way to victories in its first 11 games. The old "Can they go undefeated?" question was raised, but with the divisional title in hand, the spell broke and the Rams lost their final three.

In typical George Allen fashion, the Rams had more veterans than a Memorial Day parade. Allen disliked playing anyone who couldn't remember Truman's presidency, but once a man gained a starter's role, George expected him to stay there until it came time to collect his first Social Security check. Among the defenders, Dave Jones, Lamar Lundy, Roger Brown, Merlin Olsen, Maxie Baughan, Myron Pottios, Jack Pardee, Richie Petitbon, and Ed Meador were all 28 or older—some considerably.

Quarterback Roman Gabriel earned the league MVP vote. His stats were good—54 percent completions, 2,549 yards gained, and 24 touchdowns—but what he did best was avoid turnovers and big losses. He threw a mere

Paul Warfield.

seven interceptions all season, and his number of times sacked set a new record low at 17. The teeny sack total resulted from an exceptional forward wall; fullback Les Josephson, who blocked first and ran only when necessary; and Gabriel's own sequoia-like presence in the pocket. By holding mistakes to a minimum, Gabe was able to take LA to a respectable 320 points. You just couldn't get very excited watching it happen.

The Vikings' passer didn't exactly strike fear in the hearts of cornerbacks either, but Joe Kapp got the job done. He was described by one reporter as "all iron, down to his throwing hand." His leadership, guts, and mental toughness were unquestioned, his occasional running was bruising, and enough of his passes fell twitching from the sky into Minnesota hands to keep enemy defenses honest. In the season's most unlikely scenario, he tied the NFL record by throwing seven touchdown passes against Baltimore in the Vikings' second game. Many hadn't expected him to throw seven in the whole season.

Joe Kapp.

Kapp's big day aside, Minnesota's offense was based on the run, with 200-plus-pounders Dave Osborn, Bill Brown, Clint Jones, and Oscar Reed ever plunging into the line for three yards and a cloud of ice. Although occasionally things got out of hand, as in the 52 points Kapp's touchdowns gave them over Baltimore and the other 52 they scored against Pittsburgh, a more typical Vikings' win was their 9–7 victory over Green Bay or their 10–7 thrashing of San Francisco. Their most reliable offensive performer was kicker Fred Cox, who notched 26 field goals.

Minnesota could afford to run its slow-and-steady offense because Coach Bud Grant's defense had become the league's most effective and certainly the most important contributor to the 12-2 season. The "Purple People Eaters" front four boasted budding superstars in Alan Page and Carl Eller. Jim Marshall, Gary Larson, and backup Paul Dickson were solid. The underrated linebacking corps of Roy Winston, Wally Hilgenberg, and Lonnie Warwick played the run or pass equally well. The secondary of Paul Krause, Bobby Bryant, Earsel Mackbee, and Karl Kassulke was deadly against the pass. The unit held opponents to a minuscule 133 points and gave the offense good field position all year.

The Rams took a three-game losing streak into the play-offs. Worse, the opening round game was played in Minnesota winter. The temperature at game time shivered around 21 degrees, which was just fine for the 47,900 mostly Vikings' fans who showed up. It was axiomatic that California teams shriveled and died in cold weather.

But you couldn't prove it by the Rams' first half performance. Roman Gabriel led his team on drives of 45, 56, and 65 yards to accomplish two touchdowns and a field goal. Los Angeles left the field at halftime with a 17–7 lead.

By the second half, Joe Kapp was warmed up and the Rams succumbed to the cold-hearted defense of Minnesota. Two of Kapp's flutterballs were intercepted, but he kept the Vikings driving. A knee injury that sent linebacker Maxie Baughan to the sideline took some of the sting out of the Rams' defense. Minnesota took the second-half kickoff and drove 70 yards down the field. Dave Osborn's one yard plunge brought the score to 17–14. The Rams' Bruce Gossett kicked a 27-yard field goal 22 seconds into the final quarter to widen LA's lead.

After starting on its own 35, Kapp passed for 40 yards and ran for 14 on Minnesota's ensuing drive. He also tied the score by busting two yards into the end zone. Automatic Fred Cox split the uprights with the PAT to go ahead, 21–20. Only 22 seconds later, on the first play after the kickoff, Carl Eller trapped Gabriel behind his own goal line for a safety to register the final points of the game.

The next day at Dallas, the weather wasn't much better when the seven-point underdog Browns took the field against the Cowboys before a crowd of 69,321. Whether the cold, rainy day reminded the Clevelanders of home or it was simply another case of the unemotional Cowboys failing to rouse themselves for a big game, the home team was never really in the game. Cleveland led 17–0 at the half and coasted to a 38–14 victory. Craig Morton was ineffective all day, completing only eight of 24 passes. Much too late, Roger Staubach came in to rally the Cowboys to their second touchdown.

Meanwhile, Bill Nelson had one of the best days of his career, deftly directing the Browns' running game, coolly connecting on key third down passes time and again, and constantly keeping the Cowboys confused. He threw for 219 yards with nary an interception.

The Vikings had slaughtered the Browns 51–3 in a midseason meeting, but Bud Grant kept saying things would be different for the league championship game. They were, but only marginally.

The weather had been miserable for the first round of playoffs. Now it turned execrable. The eight degree temperature was enhanced by a 12 mile per hour wind that dropped the wind chill factor to an abominable 20 below. The Browns huddled around their sideline heaters whenever they could. The 46,503 madmen and madwomen in the stands cheered and stamped both in appreciation of their heroes' play and to keep circulation going. And the Vikings, when they came to the sideline, stood *sans* heaters and dressed in short sleeves. "We generate our own heat," Grant explained.

They and the weather also generated a bit of luck. On the first series of plays, Cleveland corner Walt Sumner slipped, allowing Gene Washington to gather in a 33-yard Kapp pass to move the ball deep into Browns' territory. A few moments later, Kapp pulled out from under center, bumped into fullback Bill Brown, and then, with the play thoroughly trashed, tucked the football under his arm and slogged seven yards to a touchdown. Later in the same first quarter, Kapp lofted one of his dying quail passes in the general direction of Washington. Cleveland's other corner, Erich Barnes, went for the receiver and ended up flat on his dignity. Washington was so open he nearly dropped the ball. But only nearly. The 75-yard touchdown put the Vikings ahead 14–0. With more than 52 minutes left to play, the Browns were beaten.

After that, Alan Page and Carl Eller could merrily tee off on Bill Nelson. At one point, Bill was hit in the head so hard his throwing arm went numb. At the same time, Kapp seemed to grow stronger. In the third quarter, Cleveland linebacker Jim Houston smashed into the Minnesota quarter-

Alan Page.

back with all he had. "I hit Unitas like that once," Houston said after the game, "and he didn't get up." Kapp got up, apparently no worse for the bump, and trotted back to the huddle. Houston was carried from the field.

"Maybe I got a lucky hit," Kapp said.

Minnesota led 24–0 at the half and skated home with a 27–7 win. Except in Cleveland, most NFL fans were pleased. It was important the league send its best to Super Bowl IV.

————

Even though the Chiefs won the final AFL championship, 1969 had not been Len Dawson's favorite season. In October, he ruptured his knee. Surgery would have cost him the season; he sat out five games and then returned limping. In November, two days before the Chiefs played the Jets, his father died. Right after Thanksgiving, he reinjured his leg.

The worst came five days before Super Bowl IV. NBC's Huntley-Brinkley evening news reported that a special Justice Department task force conducting a gambling investigation planned to subpoena seven professional football players and one college coach to testify about their connections to a Detroit gambler. Their names had been found in his records. One of the players was Len Dawson.

Ironically, the gambler was also named Dawson—Donald "Dice" Dawson—but he was not related to Len. "He's just a man I met several years earlier, when I played in Pittsburgh," Len explained. "Bobby Layne introduced him to me." Under intense questioning all week by NFL investigators, Len admitted that Donald Dawson had called him twice during the season, the first time when he suffered his knee injury, the second when his father died. Len had not known Donald Dawson was a gambler. The calls had been expressions of sympathy from an acquaintance, nothing more. No inside information had been exchanged. No business had been transacted.

In retrospect, it can be surmised that Donald Dawson may have been looking for an betting edge by checking on Len's physical state in the first instance and his mental state in the second. If so, he learned nothing that he couldn't have gleaned from newspapers.

The NFL issued a statement calling the report "totally irresponsible." Commissioner Rozelle said, "We have no evidence to even consider disciplinary action against any of those publicly named."

All well and good, but the damage was done. Although Len's mail was nearly 100 percent supportive, he was under a cloud. No official statements could stop the knowing winks, the cynical smirks, the suspicions that had been raised for some fans out there. In a week when all his attention should have been riveted on the game coming up, he couldn't eat, couldn't sleep, couldn't answer a simple question without his reply being subjected to scrutiny. His roommate, defensive back Johnny Robinson, said, "He looked like he aged five years."

If the Chiefs lost, there would inevitably be those who'd suspect something had been fishy about Len's performance. And the Chiefs were certain to lose, according to pregame odds that made the Vikings two touchdown favorites. This time, in the final Super Bowl between the two leagues rather than two conferences, there would be no freakish AFL victory. The Minnesota defense would take care of that.

George Blanda, the ageless wonder, looked at the odds and said, "They're doing it again. They haven't learned a thing since last year. They're un-

Len Dawson.

derestimating the AFL all over again." But who listens to voices crying in the wilderness?

Minnesota's defense was praised in print all during the week before the game. There was good reason. The 133 points the Vikings allowed were the fewest by any NFL team since 1946 when teams played an 11-game schedule. The Chiefs' defense seemed puny in comparison, but in fact Kansas City had given up only 177 points.

And Coach Stram had a plan. Kansas City had to stop the Vikings' crushing ground game and make them depend on Joe Kapp's wobbly passes. The key was to keep middle linebacker Willie Lanier free to make tackles. Stram lined Buck Buchanan, his huge tackle, on Vikings' center Mick Tingelhoff, thus keeping him from coming off the line to block Lanier. There was a risk. So long as Minnesota ran to the strong side against the "stack" defense, Stram knew they would be stopped. But, if they came back against the weak side. . . .

Super Bowl IV was the first to be played in the Sugar Bowl in New Orleans. All week the weather had been cold—Vikings' weather—but on Sunday, January 11, it began to warm. A record crowd of 80,562 turned up. The Vikings wore good-guy white. The Chiefs were in burning red with shoulder patches that read "AFL-10."

Defending the AFL's honor was all well and good, but this game had a more personal meaning to any Chiefs who'd suffered through the humiliation of Super Bowl I. The anger went clear to the top. A few nights before the game, Lamar Hunt was having dinner with some friends. Suddenly, the quiet, ever-reserved Hunt began pounding on the table. "Kill, kill, kill," he rasped. It was as out of character as if Fred Astaire had turned into Rambo; the wounds went deep.

In the first half, Kansas City's big line double-teamed the Minnesota ends Marshall and Eller, giving the Chiefs' running backs some room. Dawson threw short, safe passes. Meanwhile, the Vikings ran to the strong side, just as Stram had hoped, and got nowhere. Slowly, the Chiefs built a lead on three Jan Stenerud field goals of 48, 32, and 25 yards. The 48-yarder in the first quarter set a new Super Bowl record. After Stenerud's third three-pointer, KC got a break. Charlie West let the ensuing kickoff bounce off his thigh pad and the Chiefs' Remi Prudehomme recovered at the Minnesota 19. It took six plays, but Mike Garrett got the game's first touchdown, driving over from five yards out. At the half, Kansas City led 16–0.

Minnesota was far from dead. In the third quarter, Kapp led his team on a 69-yard drive that culminated in Dave Osborn's four-yard touchdown run. The Chiefs still led by nine, but Minnesota seemed poised for a comeback. Then Dawson whipped a short look-in pass six yards downfield to Otis Taylor. The KC receiver shook off tackles by Earsell Mackbee and Karl Kassulke and outraced everyone else into the end zone for a 46-yard touchdown. It broke Minnesota's back.

Trailing by three scores, the Vikings could only go to the air, and the big, fast Kansas City line unloaded on Kapp, pounding him into the earth, hurrying him into two interceptions. With a few minutes left, he went to the sideline with an injured shoulder. The fourth quarter was scoreless, leaving the Chiefs in possession of the day, 23–7.

For Len Dawson, it was a day of vindication and triumph. Of course, the suspicions of the week before evaporated, but it went beyond that. For years he'd been marked as an ordinary quarterback. He might lead the AFL in passing, but then it was *only* the AFL. In Super Bowl IV, he proved himself. "That's the first time I'd seen Dawson play," Fran Tarkenton, who would later bring three Minnesota teams to Super Bowls, said after the game. "All I'd heard—from players, coaches, and writers—was that Lenny wasn't much of a quarterback. I never heard a good word about him. But off what I saw today, he's one fine quarterback." In 1986, Tarkenton was inducted into the Pro Football Hall of Fame. The following year, Dawson was enshrined.

For the American Football League, the Super Bowl IV victory was perhaps more important than the Jets' victory the year before because it proved, insofar as one game can prove anything, that Super Bowl III was no fluke. The AFL champs had beaten the NFL champs decisively. And physically. As Minnesota tackle Grady Alderman said, "They beat us on offense and they beat us on defense and they beat us in every way."

The AFL teams could enter the 1970s with heads high as equal partners with the old NFL clubs. It had been a long road since that light bulb flashed above Lamar Hunt's head.

A victorious Hank Stram being carried off the field after Super Bowl IV.

BOBBY BELL: "WE WERE SOLID THEN"

CHAPTER

20

Bobby Bell of the Kansas City Chiefs was the first pure outside linebacker to be named to the Pro Football Hall of Fame. Until he was selected in 1983, the enshrined linebackers were either two-way stars from the old, one-platoon days or middle linebackers, the glamour defensive position of the 1950s through 1970s. But just as the 4-3 defense allowed the linebacker in the middle to shine, today's 3-4 defenses feature the outside men by giving them the option of rushing the passer or dropping back into pass coverage. The linebackers with star power today—Lawrence Taylor, Cornelius Bennett, Charles Haley, Derrick Thomas, and the rest—all play outside.

Bell was a player ahead of his time. His agility, speed, determination, and ability to diagnose plays let him play his outside position much in the manner of today's stars. In one sense, he was fortunate to play for the AFL Chiefs in a defense that was progressive enough to take advantage of his unique talents.

"I played for the University of Minnesota, and then the Minnesota Vikings drafted me on the second round. The Chiefs—they were still the Dallas Texans at the time—didn't draft me until the seventh. A lot of the fans thought that naturally I was going to play for the Vikings if they drafted me. I just wanted to get the best deal I could. Fortunately, Lamar Hunt thought the Chiefs still might have a chance. I talked to Don Klosterman, and I thought the AFL offered me a better deal. I told him I didn't need to see the facility or stuff like that. I came to play football. As it turned out, I never even got a chance to see Dallas because the team moved to Kansas City that same year.

"Don Klosterman brought a lot of people into the AFL. Lamar Hunt had him out there scouting, and he had a knack for spotting talent. He signed a lot of free agents that no one else drafted. Back then the Chiefs must have had 12 or 13 free agents every year who would make the team or come close.

"The Chiefs had great players. Four of us are in the Hall of Fame—Lenny Dawson, Willie Lanier, Buck Buchanan, and myself. But there are others who deserve recognition. Johnny Robinson was a great safety, and Emmit Thomas was a terrific defensive back. He led the league in interceptions in 1969. I think Otis Taylor was the best receiver around. Fred Arbanas, Jerry Mays, Jim Tyrer, Jim Lynch, Mike Garrett. You could practically make up an all-star team.

"I was an all-state quarterback in high school, but at Minnesota they had Sandy Stevens who was an All-America, and two other talented quarterbacks—all lined up, second and third string. I figured I didn't have a chance to play quarterback for a long time. They were going to switch me to fullback because they knew I could run the ball. But I started out playing quarterback on the freshman team, and then they switched me to defensive end, linebacker, and offensive tackle. Murray Warmath, the coach, switched a lot of people around. They'd come in as backs and get switched to the line. Some of the top All-America linemen at Minnesota started as backs. It worked for me. I won the Outland Trophy as the outstanding college lineman in 1962, my senior year.

"In my first year with the Chiefs, I was basically a defensive end. But in certain situations, I'd drop off the line and become a fourth linebacker. Coach Stram taught the 'stack' defense—that's what we called it then—but it was basically what they play now as a 3-4. Three linemen and four linebackers. We'd line up in a 4-3, and then I'd drop off as a fourth linebacker while Jerry Mays, the tackle, moved over and became the defensive end. We had different variations. I could stay down and then kick out and rush the passer like a free linebacker. Or I could move inside or drop off.

"We created a tough 4-3 too—four linemen and three linebackers—where we would barricade the inside. Especially when [linebackers] Willie Lanier and Jim Lynch came in, we dominated that line. And that gave me a free rush at the passer. It was more or less what Lawrence Taylor does with the Giants now. We were able to do just about anything we wanted. I started going after the passer. I told the coaches, 'Hey, if I don't make the plays, it's my fault.'"

"In high school and college, I was like a free safety. When I was up [instead of down in a lineman's stance], I could read the offenses. I had to get my head up because that's when I could make the plays. I could see what was coming and I was always around the ball, inside or outside. I was able to cover both sides of the field. I'll bet I made more tackles going the other way than coming at me because I had the speed to run them down.

"Coach Stram would work you hard in practice. And just about when you were ready to drop, he'd yell, 'All right. It's all over with.'

"He had a way with players. He was very personal with them, very concerned about them. He's always been that way. Even today, he contacts all the players. He knows where everybody is at, and he's always there for the players. If something happens to one of his players, he knows about it just like that. And he'll try to help. That's just the way he's always been since I met him in 1963. I bet you, since I got out of football, I either see him or talk with him on the phone about every month. He's just a very good person.

"When we were going into Super Bowl I, everybody was talking about the problems we were going to have with Green Bay. I think a few of our players might have been intimidated. But both leagues were getting their players from the same stock. They were both picking them from the college draft. They had good players and we had good players. But we had a good team—we had proven we were a good team. We could beat anybody.

"The only difference was that they had more experience. We were young and we made two or three mistakes, and you can't make mistakes against a strong veteran team. They capitalized on our errors, turned them into touchdowns, and we just could not overcome that.

"You just cannot give up that ball. We used to talk about that all the time. In fact, I used to negotiate my contract with Coach Stram that way. I'd say, 'All I want to do is average two or three turnovers a game. If I give you the ball three times a game on fumbles, interceptions, or blocked kicks, Coach, all you have to do is get a couple more players doing that and I think we'll win the game.' He'd say, 'Well, of course!' And I'd say, 'Well, that's how I want my contract to read—that I'll get the ball for you two or three times a game.'

"That's the whole idea. Play for the advantage in football. Try to eliminate the mistakes on your side of the line and take the ball away from the other team three or four times. It gives your offense playing time and opportunities to score. And you win.

"Before Super Bowl IV, we were 14- to 17-point underdogs. They'd already counted us out, like that was the law. No way we were going to win! Well, we won the playoff games—went up and beat New York and then came back and beat Oakland to get to the Super Bowl, but people already counted us out as though the Vikings had already won the game. We kind of laughed about it. We weren't coming in to lose. I don't think any team in history could have beaten us that day.

"The Vikings were a super team. They had great players. Joe Kapp had taken them all the way. They just ran all over everybody. But we had our game plan. We were prepared. We got there and walked into that stadium, and there was no way we were going to walk away losers. We were determined to dominate that whole game—offense and defense. Maybe more so on defense because we were noted for our defense. We said, 'If they can't score, they can't beat us.' That was our philosophy.

"Some people thought it was a fluke when the Jets beat the Colts in Super Bowl III, but after we beat the Vikings, they knew the American Football League had arrived.

"Look at the Hall of Fame. The Chiefs and Raiders players and Don Maynard and Lance Alworth are all from that period of 1963 through 1975. I think it's just a matter of time before others from that period are recognized.

"Players seemed to be a lot closer then. I roomed with Buck Buchanan for 12 years. A wonderful person! I got to know his family, watched his kids grow up and everything. Everybody lived here in Kansas City then. We still have a lot of the old Chiefs' players around. Back then, we were like a family. We had to stick together. Now, it seems like a lot of players are just individuals. They go and play the game and then they go their separate ways.

"I think a lot of players today are the same way when they go on the field. If a certain player isn't doing well, the whole team suffers. Well, back then, we had everybody playing as a team. If a guy was hurt, the other guys just turned it up a notch and nobody would know he was hurt. You would never know if Jerry Mays had a bad knee because he was still out there, but we knew we had to protect him and he still played.

"We played as a team. We fought that way too. If you did something to one of our players, you had to fight all of us. You said something bad about one of us, you had to fight all of us again. We were solid then. We stuck together. That was the way it was."

CHAPTER 21

WHEN PRO FOOTBALL CAME OF AGE

In his excellent account of pro football in the 1950s, Mickey Herskowitz labeled that period "The Golden Age of Pro Football"—a time of innocence and greatness when the game's heroes took on almost mythical dimensions. Pro football in the 1960s lost some of that innocence, and its heroes were less godlike, but that was a by-product of the phenomenal breakthrough the game made on our national consciousness. In 1959, there were 12 major league teams; ten years later there were 26. Total attendance at regular season games went from 3,140,000 in '59 to 8,939,500 in '69. Television ratings went through the roof. The Super Bowl, not even dreamt of in the 1950s, had become an unofficial national holiday. Rather than a Golden Age, the 1960s were the age when pro football struck gold.

On any given Sunday, more than a thousand players were employed on professional gridirons as opposed to 456 in 1959. Salaries (exclusive of signing bonuses) had increased markedly during the decade. In the '50s most players had to find work in the off-season to live; by the end of the '60s, a player looking for off-season employment was more likely to be working toward a postfootball career. If the players didn't seem quite so big in the '60s, it was because we knew them better. Pro football had become the media darling, with every game and every player scrutinized. Still, a mythic aura clings to names like Unitas, Starr, Brown, Sayers, Hornung, Alworth, Butkus, Namath, Blanda, and so many others. We "knew" the players of the 1960s, but not their every peccadillo the way we do today. You can search through everything written during the decade and not find the results of a single urine test.

When a name is hung on the 1960s, it's likely to be something like "The Age of Lombardi." Certainly his was the most familiar persona to the average fan. We remember the image of the stocky coach bundled on the frigid Green Bay sideline, shouting through gapped teeth, stamping the cold away, willing a touchdown. He was easily the most successful coach—and the most influential because he was the most imitated. But from another perspective, it might be called "The Age of Werblin" or "The Age of Namath." Their liaison certainly brought unprecedented publicity and interest. Or how about "The Age of Rozelle," in honor of the nearly unknown boy wonder who presided over the NFL and became the example for other sports commissioners to emulate.

In terms of changing the direction of the game and bringing about a new order of things—of struggling against overpowering odds and succeeding—pro football in the 1960s should be called "The Age of Lamar Hunt." But that modest man would no doubt be the first to point to others as more important. In truth, of course, pro football had grown too big to be saddled with a single personality's name.

The 1960s could be called "The Age of Silver." Consider the luminance with which the era still lights the memory of any football fan lucky enough to have seen it. Consider the growing dominance of the television screen through the period, a screen which, at least at the beginning, in its black-and-white splendor, approximated the silver screen of moviedom. But, most of all, consider the huge amounts of money that went into and came out of pro football in the 1960s. Consider the steady growth in emphasis toward a business instead of a sport—an emphasis that seems to accelerate each year as millionaire owners and millionaire players make more head-lines with their bank accounts than with their skills.

And yet, in the 1960s, we fans were not yet so cynical. We could still enjoy Lombardi and Landry, Brown and Sayers, Unitas and Namath, and a hundred others for the elation they brought on Sundays. There was a "rightness" in the Packer dynasty just as there is a "rightness" in a Beethoven symphony. There was an eternal truth in the Jets' Super Bowl III victory just as there is an eternal truth in David's victory over Goliath. And there was beauty in a Unitas pass just as we find beauty in Degas's dancers. Beauty, truth, and rightness help us understand the world and get on with it.

In the sense of what it did for us and to us, the 1960s were pro football's greatest decade. Rather than "The Age of . . . ," this was when pro football came of age. The game would continue to grow and prosper through the 1970s and 1980s. Perhaps it will increase further in the 1990s. But to borrow a phrase associated with Chairman Mao, it will never again make such a "great leap forward."

1960 NATIONAL FOOTBALL LEAGUE

Eastern Conference

	W	L	T	PTS	OPP	COACH
Philadelphia	10	2	0	321	246	Buck Shaw
Cleveland	8	3	1	362	217	Paul Brown
NY Giants	6	4	2	271	261	Jim Lee Howell
St. Louis	6	5	1	288	230	Pop Ivy
Pittsburgh	5	6	1	240	275	Buddy Parker
Washington	1	9	2	178	309	Mike Nixon

Western Conference

	W	L	T	PTS	OPP	COACH
Green Bay	8	4	0	332	209	Vince Lombardi
Detroit	7	5	0	239	212	George Wilson
San Francisco	7	5	0	208	205	Red Hickey
Baltimore	6	6	0	288	234	Weeb Ewbank
Chicago	5	6	1	194	299	George Halas
LA Rams	4	7	1	265	297	Bob Waterfield
Dallas Cowboys	0	11	1	177	369	Tom Landry

NFL Championship: PHILADELPHIA 17, Green Bay 13
(Home team is indicated in capital letters throughout.)

ALL-NFL CONSENSUS

OFFENSE	DEFENSE
WR—Raymond Berry, Bal	DE—Gino Marchetti, Bal
WR—Sonny Randle, StL	DE—Doug Atkins, Cle
OT—Jim Parker, Bal	DT—Henry Jordan, GB
OT—Roosevelt Brown, NY	DT—Alex Karras, Det
OG—Jim Ray Smith, Cle	LB—Bill George, Chi
OG—Stan Jones, Chi	LB—Chuck Bednarik, Phi
OC—Jim Ringo, GB	LB—Bill Forester, GB
QB—Norm Van Brocklin, Phi	CB—Tom Brookshier, Phi
HB—Paul Hornung, GB	CB—Abe Woodson, SF
HB—Lenny Moore, Bal	DS—Jerry Norton, StL
FB—Jim Brown, Cle	DS—Jim Patton, NY

1960 AMERICAN FOOTBALL LEAGUE

Eastern Conference

	W	L	T	PTS	OPP	COACH
Houston	10	4	0	379	285	Lou Rymkus
NY Titans	7	7	0	382	399	Sammy Baugh
Buffalo	5	8	1	296	303	Buster Ramsey
Boston	5	9	0	286	349	Lou Saban

Western Conference

	W	L	T	PTS	OPP	COACH
LA Chargers	10	4	0	373	336	Sid Gillman
Dallas Texans	8	6	0	362	253	Hank Stram
Oakland	6	8	0	319	388	Eddie Erdelatz
Denver	4	9	1	309	393	Frank Filchock

AFL Championship: HOUSTON 24, LA Chargers 16

ALL-AFL CONSENSUS

OFFENSE	DEFENSE
WR—Lionel Taylor, Den	DE—Lavern Torczon, Buf
WR—Bill Groman, Hou	DE—Mel Branch, Dal
OT—Ron Mix, LA	DT—Bud McFadin, Den
OT—Rich Michael, Hou	DT—Chuck McMurtry, Buf
OG—Bob Mischak, NY	LB—Archie Matsos, Buf
OG—Bill Krisher, Dal	LB—Sherrill Headrick, Dal
OC—Jim Otto, Oak	LB—Larry Grantham, NY
QB—Jack Kemp, LA	CB—Dick Harris, LA
HB—Abner Haynes, Dal	CB—Goose Gonsoulin, Den
HB—Paul Lowe, LA	DS—Mark Johnston, Hou
FB—Dave Smith, Hou	DS—Richie McCabe, Buf

1961 NATIONAL FOOTBALL LEAGUE

Eastern Conference

	W	L	T	PTS	OPP	COACH
NY Giants	10	3	1	368	220	Allie Sherman
Philadelphia	10	4	0	361	297	Nick Skorich
Cleveland	8	5	1	319	270	Paul Brown
St. Louis	7	7	0	279	267	Pop Ivy; Chuck Drulis, Ray Prochaska & Ray Willsey
Pittsburgh	6	8	0	295	287	Buddy Parker
Dallas Cowboys	4	9	1	236	380	Tom Landry
Washington	1	12	1	174	392	Bill McPeak

Western Conference

	W	L	T	PTS	OPP	COACH
Green Bay	11	3	0	391	223	Vince Lombardi
Detroit	8	5	1	270	258	George Wilson
Baltimore	8	6	0	302	307	Weeb Ewbank
Chicago	8	6	0	326	302	George Halas
San Francisco	7	6	1	346	272	Red Hickey
Los Angeles	4	10	0	263	333	Bob Waterfield
Minnesota	3	11	0	285	407	Norm Van Brocklin

NFL Championship: GREEN BAY 37, N.Y. Giants 0

ALL-NFL CONSENSUS

OFFENSE	DEFENSE
WR—Del Shofner, NY	DE—Gino Marchetti, Bal
WR—Red Phillips, LA	DE—Jim Katcavage, NY
OT—Roosevelt Brown, NY	DT—Henry Jordan, GB
OT—Jim Parker, Bal	DT—Alex Karras, Det
OG—Jim Ray Smith, Cle	LB—Joe Schmidt, Det
OG—Fuzzy Thurston, GB	LB—Bill Forester, GB
OC—Jim Ringo, GB	LB—Bill George, Chi
QB—Sonny Jurgensen, Phi	CB—Erich Barnes, NY
HB—Paul Hornung, GB	CB—Night Train Lane, Det
HB—Lenny Moore, Bal	DS—Jim Patton, NY
FB—Jim Brown, Cle	DS—Jess Whittenton, GB

1961 AMERICAN FOOTBALL LEAGUE

Eastern Division

	W	L	T	PTS	OPP	COACH
Houston	10	3	1	513	242	Lou Rymkus; Wally Lemm
Boston	9	4	1	413	313	Lou Saban; Mike Holovak
NY Titans	7	7	0	301	290	Sammy Baugh
Buffalo	6	8	0	294	342	Buster Ramsey

Western Division

	W	L	T	PTS	OPP	COACH
San Diego	12	2	0	396	219	Sid Gillman
Dallas Texans	6	8	0	334	343	Hank Stram
Denver	3	11	0	251	432	Frank Filchock
Oakland	2	12	0	237	458	Eddie Erdelatz; Marty Feldman

AFL Championship: Houston 10, SAN DIEGO 3

ALL-AFL CONSENSUS

OFFENSE	DEFENSE
WR—Lionel Taylor, Den	DE—Earl Faison, SD
WR—Charlie Hennigan, Hou	DE—Don Floyd, Hou
OT—Ron Mix, SD	DT—Bud McFadin, Den
OT—Al Jamison, Hou	DT—Chuck McMurtry, Buf
OG—Bob Mischak, NY	LB—Archie Matsos, Buf
OG—Charlie Leo, Bos	LB—Sherrill Headrick, Dal
OC—Jim Otto, Oak	LB—Tom Addison, Bos
QB—George Blanda, Hou	CB—Tony Banfield, Hou
HB—Abner Haynes, Dal	CB—Dick Harris, SD
HB—Billy Cannon, Hou	DS—Dave Webster, Dal
FB—Bill Mathis, NY	DS—Charles McNeil, SD

1962 NATIONAL FOOTBALL LEAGUE

Eastern Conference

	W	L	T	PTS	OPP	COACH
NY Giants	12	2	0	398	283	Allie Sherman
Pittsburgh	9	5	0	312	363	Buddy Parker
Cleveland	7	6	1	291	257	Paul Brown
Washington	5	7	2	305	376	Bill McPeak
Dallas Cowboys	5	8	1	398	402	Tom Landry
St. Louis	4	9	1	287	361	Wally Lemm
Philadelphia	3	10	1	282	356	Nick Skorich

Western Conference

	W	L	T	PTS	OPP	COACH
Green Bay	13	1	0	415	148	Vince Lombardi
Detroit	11	3	0	315	177	George Wilson
Chicago	9	5	0	321	287	George Halas
Baltimore	7	7	0	293	288	Webb Ewbank
San Francisco	6	8	0	282	331	Red Hickey
Minnesota	2	11	1	254	410	Norm Van Brocklin
Los Angeles	1	12	1	220	334	Bob Waterfield; Harland Svare

NFL Championship: Green Bay 16, NY GIANTS 7

ALL-NFL CONSENSUS

OFFENSE	DEFENSE
WR—Del Shofner, NY	DE—Gino Marchetti, Bal
WR—Bobby Mitchell, Was	DE—Jim Katcavage, NY
TE—Mike Ditka, Chi	DT—Roger Brown, Det

OT—Roosevelt Brown, NY	DT—Alex Karras, Det
OT—Forrest Gregg, GB	LB—Joe Schmidt, Det
OG—Jerry Kramer, GB	LB—Dan Currie, GB
OG—Jim Parker, Bal	LB—Bill Forester, GB
OC—Jim Ringo, GB	CB—Night Train Lane, Det
QB—Y. A. Tittle, NY	CB—Abe Woodson, SF
RB—Dick Bass, LA	DS—Jim Patton, NY
RB—Jim Taylor, GB	DS—Yale Lary, Det

1962 AMERICAN FOOTBALL LEAGUE

Eastern Division

	W	L	T	PTS	OPP	COACH
Houston	11	3	0	387	270	Pop Ivy
Boston	9	4	1	346	295	Mike Holovak
Buffalo	7	6	1	309	272	Lou Saban
NY Titans	5	9	0	278	423	Bulldog Turner

Western Conference

	W	L	T	PTS	OPP	COACH
Dallas Texans	11	3	0	389	233	Hank Stram
Denver	7	7	0	353	334	Jack Faulkner
San Diego	4	10	0	314	392	Sid Gillman
Oakland	1	13	0	213	370	Marty Feldman; Red Conkright

AFL Championship: Dallas Texans 20, HOUSTON 17 (OT)

ALL-AFL CONSENSUS

OFFENSE	DEFENSE
WR—Chris Burford, Dal	DE—Don Floyd, Hou
WR—Charlie Hennigan, Hou	DE—Larry Eisenhauer, Bos
TE—Dave Kocourek, SD	DT—Bud McFadin, Den
OT—Al Jamison, Hou	DT—Ed Husmann, Hou
OT—Edon Danenhauer, Den	LB—Sherrill Headrick, Dal
OG—Ron Mix, SD	LB—Larry Grantham, NY
OG—Bob Talamini, Hou	LB—E.J. Holub, Dal
OC—Jim Otto, Oak	CB—Fred Williamson, Oak
QB—Len Dawson, Dal	CB—Tony Banfield, Hou
RB—Abner Haynes, Dal	DS—Bobby Hunt, Dal
RB—Cookie Gilchrist, Buf	DS—Goose Gonsoulin, Den

1963 NATIONAL FOOTBALL LEAGUE

Eastern Conference

	W	L	T	PTS	OPP	COACH
NY Giants	11	3	0	448	280	Allie Sherman
Cleveland	10	4	0	343	262	Blanton Collier
St. Louis	9	5	0	341	283	Wally Lemm
Pittsburgh	7	4	3	321	295	Buddy Parker
Dallas	4	10	0	305	378	Tom Landry
Washington	3	11	0	279	398	Bill McPeak
Philadelphia	2	10	2	242	381	Nick Skorich

Western Conference

	W	L	T	PTS	OPP	COACH
Chicago	11	1	2	301	144	George Halas
Green Bay	11	2	1	369	206	Vince Lombardi
Baltimore	8	6	0	316	285	Don Shula
Detroit	5	8	1	326	265	George Wilson
Minnesota	5	8	1	309	390	Norm Van Brocklin
Los Angeles	5	9	0	210	350	Harland Svare
San Francisco	2	12	0	198	391	Red Hickey; Jack Christiansen

NFL Championship: CHICAGO 14, NY Giants 10

ALL-NFL CONSENSUS

OFFENSE	DEFENSE
WR—Del Shofner, NY	DE—Doug Atkins, Chi
WR—Bobby Joe Conrad, StL	DE—Jim Katcavage, NY
TE—Mike Ditka, Chi	DT—Henry Jordan, GB
OT—Forrest Gregg, GB	DT—Roger Brown, Det
OT—Roosevelt Brown, NY	LB—Bill George, Chi
OG—Jerry Kramer, GB	LB—Joe Fortunato, Chi
OG—Ken Gray, StL	LB—Bill Forester, GB
OC—Jim Ringo, GB	CB—Dick Lynch, NY
QB—Y. A. Tittle, NY	CB—Night Train Lane, Det
RB—Tommy Mason, Min	DS—Richie Petitbon, Chi
RB—Jim Brown, Cle	DS—Roosevelt Taylor, Chi

1963 AMERICAN FOOTBALL LEAGUE

Eastern Division

	W	L	T	PTS	OPP	COACH
Boston	7	6	1	327	257	Mike Holovak
Buffalo	7	6	1	304	291	Lou Saban
Houston	6	8	0	302	372	Pop Ivy
NY Jets	5	8	1	249	399	Weeb Ewbank

Western Division

	W	L	T	PTS	OPP	COACH
San Diego	11	3	0	399	256	Sid Gillman
Oakland	10	4	0	363	288	Al Davis
Kansas City	5	7	2	347	263	Hank Stram
Denver	2	11	1	301	473	Jack Faulkner

Eastern Championship Play-off: Boston 26, BUFFALO 8
AFL Championship: SAN DIEGO 51, Boston 0

ALL-AFL CONSENSUS

OFFENSE	DEFENSE
WR—Art Powell, Oak	DE—Larry Eisenhauer, Bos
WR—Lancer Alworth, SD	DE—Earl Faison, SD
TE—Fred Arbanas, KC	DT—Tom Sestek, Buf
OT—Ron Mix, SD	DT—Houston Antwine, Bos
OT—Stew Barber, Buf	LB—Archie Matsos, Oak
OG—Billy Shaw, Buf	LB—E. J. Holub, KC
OG—Bob Talamini, Hou	LB—Larry Grantham, NY
OC—Jim Otto, Oak	CB—Fred Williamson, Oak
QB—Tobin Rote, SD	CB—Tony Banfield, Hou
RB—Clem Daniels, Oak	DS—Fred Glick, Hou
RB—Keith Lincoln, SD	DS—Tom Morrow, Oak

1964 NATIONAL FOOTBALL LEAGUE

Eastern Conference

	W	L	T	PTS	OPP	COACH
Cleveland	10	3	1	415	293	Blanton Collier
St. Louis	9	3	2	357	331	Wally Lemm
Philadelphia	6	8	0	312	313	Joe Kuharich
Washington	6	8	0	307	305	Bill McPeak
Dallas	5	8	1	250	289	Tom Landry
Pittsburgh	5	9	0	253	315	Buddy Parker
NY Giants	2	10	2	241	399	Allie Sherman

Western Conference

	W	L	T	PTS	OPP	COACH
Baltimore	12	2	0	428	225	Don Shula
Green Bay	8	5	1	342	245	Vince Lombardi
Minnesota	8	5	1	336	296	Norm Van Brocklin
Detroit	7	5	2	280	260	George Wilson
Los Angeles	5	7	2	283	339	Harland Svare
Chicago	5	9	0	260	379	George Halas
S.F.	4	10	0	236	330	Jack Christiansen

NFL Championship: CLEVELAND 27, Baltimore 0

ALL-NFL CONSENSUS

OFFENSE	DEFENSE
WR—Johnny Morris, Chi	DE—Gino Marchetti, Bal
WR—Paul Warfield, Cle	DE—Willie Davis, GB
TE—Mike Ditka, Chi	DT—Bob Lilly, Dal
OT—Forrest Gree, GB	DT—Henry Jordan, GB
OT—Dick Schafrath, Cle	LB—Ray Nitschke, GB
OG—Jim Parker, Bal	LB—Joe Fortunato, Chi
OG—Ken Gray, STL	LB—Maxie Baughan, Phi
OC—Mick Tingelhoff, Min	CB—Pat Fisher, StL
QB—John Unitas, Bal	CB—Bobby Boyd, Bal
RB—Lenny Moore, Bal	DS—Paul Krause, Was
RB—Jim Brown, Cle	DS—Willie Wood, GB

1964 AMERICAN FOOTBALL LEAGUE

Eastern Division

	W	L	T	PTS	OPP	COACH
Buffalo	12	2	0	400	242	Lou Saban
Boston	10	3	1	365	297	Mike Holovak
NY Jets	5	8	1	278	315	Weeb Ewbank
Houston	4	10	0	310	355	Sammy Baugh

Western Division

	W	L	T	PTS	OPP	COACH
San Diego	8	5	1	341	300	Sid Gillman
Kansas City	7	7	0	366	306	Hank Stram
Oakland	5	7	2	303	350	Al Davis
Denver	2	11	1	240	438	Jack Faulkner, Mac Speedie

AFL Championship: BUFFALO 20, San Diego 7

ALL-AFL CONSENSUS

OFFENSE	DEFENSE
WR—Charlie Hennigan, Hou	DE—Earl Faison, SD
WR—Lance Alworth, SD	DE—Larry Eisenhauer, Bos
TE—Fred Arbanas, KC	DT—Tom Sestek, Buf
OT—Ron Mix, SD	DT—Ernie Ladd, SD
OT—Stew Barber, Buf	LB—Nick Buoniconti, Bos
OG—Billy Shaw, Buf	LB—Larry Grantham, NY
OG—Billy Neighbors, Bos	LB—Mike Stratton, Buf
OC—Jim Otto, Oak	CB—Dave Grayson, KC
QB—Babe Parilli, Bos	CB—Willie Brown, Den
RB—Keith Lincoln, SD	DS—Ron Hall, Bos
RB—Cookie Gilchrist, Buf	DS—Dainard Paulson, NY

1965 NATIONAL FOOTBALL LEAGUE

Eastern Conference

	W	L	T	PTS	OPP	COACH
Cleveland	11	3	0	363	325	Blanton Collier
Dallas	7	7	0	325	280	Tom Landry
NY Giants	7	7	0	270	338	Allie Sherman
Washington	6	8	0	257	301	Bill McPeak
Philadelphia	5	9	0	363	359	Joe Kuharich
St. Louis	5	9	0	296	309	Wally Lemm
Pittsburgh	2	12	0	202	397	Mike Nixon

Western Conference

	W	L	T	PTS	OPP	COACH
Green Bay	10	3	1	316	224	Vince Lombardi
Baltimore	10	3	1	389	284	Don Shula
Chicago	9	5	0	409	275	George Halas
San Francisco	7	6	1	421	402	Jack Christiansen
Minnesota	7	7	0	383	403	Norm Van Brocklin
Detroit	6	7	1	257	295	Harry Gilmer
Los Angeles	4	10	0	269	328	Harland Svare

Western Conference Play-off: GREEN BAY 13, Baltimore 10 (OT); NFL Championship: GREEN BAY 23, Cleveland 12

ALL-NFL CONSENSUS

OFFENSE	DEFENSE
WR—Dave Parks, SF	DE—Willie Davis, GB
WR—Jimmy Orr, Bal	DE—Deacon Jones, LA
TE—Pete Retzlaff, Phi	DT—Bob Lilly, Dal
OT—Bob Brown, Phi	DT—Alex Karras, Det
OT—Dick Schafrath, Cle	LB—Dick Butkus, Chi
OG—Jim Parker, Bal	LB—Wayne Walker, Det
OG—Forrest Gregg, GB	LB—Joe Fortunato, Chi
OC—Mick Tingelhoff, Min	CB—Herb Adderley, GB
GB—John Unitas, Bal	CB—Bobby Boyd, Bal
RB—Gale Sayers, Chi	DS—Willie Wood, GB
RB—Jim Brown, Cle	DS—Paul Krause, Was

1965 AMERICAN FOOTBALL LEAGUE

Eastern Division

	W	L	T	PTS	OPP	COACH
Buffalo	10	3	1	313	226	Lou Saban
NY Jets	5	8	1	285	303	Weeb Ewbank
Boston	4	8	2	244	302	Mike Holovak
Houston	4	10	0	298	429	Hugh Taylor

Western Division

	W	L	T	PTS	OPP	COACH
San Diego	9	2	3	340	227	Sid Gillman
Oakland	8	5	1	298	239	Al Davis
Kansas City	7	5	2	322	285	Hank Stram
Denver	4	10	0	303	392	Mac Speedie

AFL Championship: Buffalo 23, SAN DIEGO 0

ALL-AFL CONSENSUS

OFFENSE	DEFENSE
WR—Lionel Taylor, Den	DE—Earl Faison, SD
WR—Lance Alworth, SD	DE—Jerry Mays, KC
TE—Willie Frazier, Hou	DT—Ernie Ladd, SD
OT—Ron Mix, SD	DB—Tom Sestek, Buf
OT—Jim Tyrer, KC	LB—Nick Buoniconti, Bos
OG—Billy Shaw, Buf	LB—Bobby Bell, KC
OG—Bob Talamini, Hou	LB—Mike Stratton, Buf
OC—Jim Otto, Oak	CB—Dave Grayson, KC
QB—Jack Kemp, Buf	CB—Butch Byrd, Buf
RB—Paul Lowe, SD	SD—George Saimes, Buf
RB—Cookie Gilchrist, Den	SD—Johnny Robinson, KC

1966 NATIONAL FOOTBALL LEAGUE

Eastern Conference

	W	L	T	PTS	OPP	COACH
Dallas	10	3	1	445	239	Tom Landry
Cleveland	9	5	0	403	259	Blanton Collier
Philadelphia	9	5	0	326	340	Joe Kuharich
St. Louis	8	5	1	264	265	Charlie Winner
Washington	7	7	0	351	355	Otto Graham
Pittsburgh	5	8	1	316	347	Bill Austin
Atlanta	3	11	0	204	437	Norb Hecker
NY Giants	1	12	1	263	501	Allie Sherman

Western Conference

	W	L	T	PTS	OPP	COACH
Green Bay	12	2	0	335	163	Vince Lombardi
Baltimore	9	5	0	314	226	Don Shula
L.A.	8	6	0	289	212	George Allen
S.F.	6	6	2	320	325	Jack Christiansen
Chicago	5	7	2	234	272	George Halas
Detroit	4	9	1	206	317	Harry Gilmer
Minnesota	4	9	1	292	304	Norm Van Brocklin

NFL Championship: Green Bay 34, DALLAS 27
Super Bowl I: Green Bay (NFL) 35, Kansas City (AFL) 10

ALL-NFL CONSENSUS

OFFENSE	DEFENSE
WR—Bob Hayes, Dal	DE—Willie Davis, GB
WR—Pat Studstill, Det	DE—Deacon Jones, LA
TE—John Mackey, Bal	DT—Bob Lilly, Dal
OT—Bob Brown, Phi	DT—Merlin Olsen, LA
OT—Forrest Gregg, GB	LB—Ray Nitschke, GB
OG—Jerry Kramer, GB	LB—Chuck Howley, Dal
OG—John Thomas, SF	LB—Lee Roy Caffey, GB
OC—Mick Tingelhoff, Min	CB—Herb Adderley, GB
QB—Bart Starr, GB	CB—Cornell Green, Dal
RB—Gale Sayers, Chi	DS—Willie Wood, GB
RB—Leroy Kelly, Cle	DS—Larry Wilson, StL

1966 AMERICAN FOOTBALL LEAGUE

Eastern Division

	W	L	T	PTS	OPP	COACH
Buffalo	9	4	1	358	255	Joe Collier
Boston	8	4	2	315	283	Mike Holovak
NY Jets	6	6	2	322	312	Weeb Ewbank
Houston	3	11	0	335	396	Wally Lemm
Miami	3	11	0	213	362	George Wilson

Western Division

	W	L	T	PTS	OPP	COACH
Kansas City	11	2	1	448	276	Hank Straum
Oakland	8	5	1	315	288	Johnny Rauch
San Diego	7	6	1	335	284	Sid Gillman
Denver	4	10	0	196	381	Mac Speedie; Ray Malavasi

AFL Championship: Kansas City 31, BUFFALO 7

ALL-AFL CONSENSUS

OFFENSE	DEFENSE
WR—Otis Taylor, FC	DE—Jerry Mays, KC
WR—Lance Alworth, SD	DE—Verlon Biggs, NY
TE—Fred Arbanas, KC	DT—Buck Buchanan, KC
OT—Jim Tyrer, KC	DT—Houston Antwine, Bos
OT—Ron Mix, SD	LB—Nick Buoniconti, Bos
OG—Billy Shaw, Buf	LB—Bobby Bell, KC
OG—Wayne Hawkins, Oak	LB—Mike Straton, Buf
OC—Jim Otto, Oak	CB—Butch Byrd, Buf
QB—Len Dawson, KC	CB—Kent McCloughan, Oak
RB—Clem Daniels, Oak	DS—Johnny Robinson, KC
RB—Jim Nance, Bos	DS—Ken Graham, SD

1967 NATIONAL FOOTBALL LEAGUE

Eastern Conference
Capitol Division

	W	L	T	PTS	OPP	COACH
Dallas	9	5	0	342	268	Tom Landry
Philadelphia	6	7	1	351	409	Joe Kuharich
Washington	5	6	3	347	353	Otto Graham
New Orleans	3	11	0	233	379	Tom Fears

Western Conference

	W	L	T	PTS	OPP	COACH
Cleveland	9	5	0	334	297	Blanton Collier
NY Giants	7	7	0	369	379	Allie Sherman
St. Louis	6	7	1	333	336	Charlie Winner
Pittsburgh	4	9	1	281	320	Bill Austin

Western Conference
Coastal Division

	W	L	T	PTS	OPP	COACH
* Los Angeles	11	1	2	398	196	George Allen
Baltimore	11	1	2	394	198	Don Shula
San Francisco	7	7	0	273	337	Jack Christiansen
Atlanta	1	12	1	175	422	Norb Hecker

* Division winner on points advantage in two games vs. Baltimore.

Central Division

	W	L	T	PTS	OPP	COACH
Green Bay	9	4	1	332	209	Vince Lombardi
Chicago	7	6	1	239	218	George Halas
Detroit	5	7	2	260	259	Joe Schmidt
Minnesota	3	8	3	233	294	Bud Grant

Conference Championships: DALLAS 52, Cleveland 14; GREEN BAY 28, Los Angeles 7
NFL Championship: GREEN BAY 21, Dallas 17
Super Bowl II: Green Bay (NFL) 33, Oakland (AFL) 14

ALL-NFL CONSENSUS

OFFENSE	DEFENSE
WR—Charlie Taylor, Was	DE—Deacon Jones, LA
WR—Homer Jones, NY	DE—Willie Davis, GB
TE—John Mackey, Bal	DT—Bob Lilly, Dal
OT—Ralph Neely, Dal	DT—Merlin Olsen, LA
OT—Forrest Gregg, GB	LB—Tommy Nobis, Atl
OG—Jerry Kramer, GB	LB—Maxie Baughan, LA
OG—Gene Hickerson, Cle	LB—Dave Robinson, GB
OC—Mick Tingelhoff, Min	DB—Bob Jeter, GB
QB—John Unitas, Bal	CB—Cornell Green, Dal
RB—Gale Sayers, Chi	DS—Willie Wood, GB
RB—Leroy Kelly, Cle	DS—Larry Wilson, StL

1967 AMERICAN FOOTBALL LEAGUE

Eastern Division

	W	L	T	PTS	OPP	COACH
Houston	9	4	1	258	199	Wally Lemm
NY Jets	8	5	1	371	329	Weeb Ewbank
Buffalo	4	10	0	237	285	Joe Collier
Miami	4	10	0	219	407	George Wilson
Boston	3	10	1	280	389	Mike Holovak

Western Conference

	W	L	T	PTS	OPP	COACH
Oakland	13	1	0	468	233	Johnny Rauch
Kansas City	9	5	0	408	254	Hank Stram
San Diego	8	5	1	360	352	Sid Gillman
Denver	3	11	0	256	409	Lou Saban

AFL Championship: OAKLAND 40, Houston 7

ALL-AFL CONSENSUS

OFFENSE	DEFENSE
WR—George Sauer, NY	DE—Pat Holmes, Hou
WR—Lance Alworth, SD	DE—Ben Davidson, Oak
TE—Billy Cannon, Oak	DT—Tom Keating, Oak
OT—Ron Mix, SD	DT—Buck Buchanan, KC
OT—Jim Tyrer, KC	LB—Nick Buoniconti, Bos
OG—Walt Sweeney, SD	LB—Bobby Bell, KC
OG—Bob Talamini, Hou	LB—George Webster, Hou
OC—Jim Otto, Oak	CB—Miller Farr, Hou
QB—Daryle Lamonica, Oak	CB—Kent McCloughan, Oak
RB—Mike Garrett, KC	DS—George Saimes, Buf
RB—Jim Nance, Bos	DS—Johnny Robinson, KC

1968 NATIONAL FOOTBALL LEAGUE

Eastern Conference
Capitol Division

	W	L	T	PTS	OPP	COACH
Dallas	12	2	0	431	186	Tom Landry
NY Giants	7	7	0	294	325	Allie Sherman
Washington	5	9	0	249	358	Otto Graham
Philadelphia	2	12	0	202	354	Joe Kuharich

Century Division

	W	L	T	PTS	OPP	COACH
Cleveland	10	4	0	394	273	Blanton Collier
St. Louis	9	4	1	325	289	Charlie Winner
New Orleans	4	9	1	246	327	Tom Fears
Pittsburgh	2	11	1	244	397	Bill Austin

Western Conference
Coastal Division

	W	L	T	PTS	OPP	COACH
Baltimore	13	1	0	402	144	Don Shula
Los Angeles	10	3	1	312	200	George Allen
San Francisco	7	6	1	303	310	Dick Nolan
Atlanta	2	12	0	170	389	Norb Hecker; Norm Van Brocklin

Central Division

	W	L	T	PTS	OPP	COACH
Minnesota	8	6	0	282	242	Bud Grant
Chicago	7	7	0	250	333	Jim Dooley
Green Bay	6	7	1	281	227	Phil Bengston
Detroit	4	8	2	207	241	Joe Schmidt

Conference Championships: CLEVELAND 31, Dallas 20; BALTIMORE 24, Minnesota 14
NFL Championship: Baltimore 34, CLEVELAND 0
Super Bowl III: NY Jets (AFL) 16, Baltimore (NFL) 7

ALL-NFL CONSENSUS

OFFENSE	DEFENSE
WR—Clifton McNeil, SF	DE—Carl Eller, Min
WR—Paul Warfield, Cle	DE—Deacon Jones, LA
TE—John Mackey, Bal	DT—Bob Lilly, Dal
OT—Ralph Neely, Dal	DT—Merlin Olsen, LA
OT—Bob Brown, Phi	LB—Dick Butkus, Chi
OG—Gene Hickerson, Cle	LB—Chuck Howley, Dal
OG—Howard Mudd, SF	LB—Mike Curtis, Bal
OC—Mick Tingelhoff, Min	CB—Lem Barney, Det
QB—Earl Morrall, Bal	CB—Bobby Boyd, Bal
RB—Gale Sayers, Chi	DS—Larry Wilson, StL
RB—Leroy Kelly, Cle	DS—Willie Wood, GB

1968 AMERICAN FOOTBALL LEAGUE

Eastern Division

	W	L	T	PTS	OPP	COACH
NY Jets	11	3	0	419	280	Weeb Ewbank
Houston	7	7	0	303	248	Wally Lemm
Miami	5	8	1	276	355	George Wilson
Boston	4	10	0	229	406	Mike Holovak
Buffalo	1	12	1	199	367	Joe Collier

Western Division

	W	L	T	PTS	OPP	COACH
Oakland	12	2	0	453	233	Johnny Rauch
Kansas City	12	2	0	371	170	Hank Stram
San Diego	9	5	0	382	310	Sid Gillman
Denver	5	9	0	255	404	Lou Saban
Cincinnati	3	11	0	215	329	Paul Brown

Western Division Play-off: OAKLAND 41, Kansas City 6
AFL Championship: NY JETS 27, Oakland 23

ALL-AFL CONSENSUS

OFFENSE	DEFENSE
WR—George Sauer, NY	DE—Gerry Philben, NY
WR—Lance Alworth, SD	DE—Rich Jackson, Den
TE—Jim Whalen, Bos	DT—Buck Buchanan, KC
OT—Ron Mix, SD	DT—Dan Birdwell, Oak
OT—Jim Tyrer, KC	LB—Willie Lanier, KC
OG—Walt Sweeney, SD	LB—Bobby Bell, KC
OG—Gene Upshaw, Oak	LB—George Webster, Hou
OC—Jim Otto, Oak	CB—Miller Farr, Hou
QB—Joe Namath, NY	CB—Willie Brown, Oak
RB—Paul Robinson, Cin	DS—Johnny Robinson, KC
RB—Hewritt Dixon, Oak	DS—Dave Grayson, Oak

1969 NATIONAL FOOTBALL LEAGUE

Eastern Conference
Capitol Division

	W	L	T	PTS	OPP	COACH
Dallas	11	2	1	369	223	Tom Landry
Washington	7	5	2	307	319	Vince Lombardi
New Orleans	5	9	0	311	393	Tom Fears
Philadelphia	4	9	1	279	377	Jerry Williams

Century Division

	W	L	T	PTS	OPP	COACH
Cleveland	10	3	1	351	300	Blanton Collier
NY Giants	6	8	0	264	298	Alex Webster
St. Louis	4	9	1	314	389	Charlie Winner
Pittsburgh	1	13	0	218	404	Chuck Noll

Western Conference
Coastal Division

	W	L	T	PTS	OPP	COACH
Los Angeles	11	3	0	320	243	George Allen
Baltimore	8	5	1	279	268	Don Shula
Atlanta	6	8	0	276	268	Norm Van Brocklin
San Francisco	4	8	2	277	319	Dick Nolan

Central Division

	W	L	T	PTS	OPP	COACH
Minnesota	12	2	0	379	133	Bud Grant
Detroit	9	4	1	259	188	Joe Schmidt
Green Bay	8	6	0	269	221	Phil Bengston
Chicago	1	13	0	210	339	Jim Dooley

Conference Championships: Cleveland 38, DALLAS 14;
MINNESOTA 23, Los Angeles 20
NFL Championship: MINNESOTA 27, Cleveland 7
Super Bowl IV: Kansas City (AFL) 23, Minnesota (NFL) 7

ALL-NFL CONSENSUS

OFFENSE	DEFENSE
WR—Roy Jefferson, Pit	DE—Deacon Jones, LA
WR—Gary Collins, Cle	DE—Carl Eller, Min
TE—Jerry Smith, Was	DT—Bob Lilly, Dal
OT—Bob Brown, LA	DT—Marlin Olsen, LA
OT—Ralph Neely, Dal	LB—Dick Butkus, Chi
OG—Gene Hickerson, Cle	LB—Chuck Howley, Dal
OG—Tom Mack, LA	LB—Dave Robinson, GB
OC—Mick Tingelhoff, Min	CB—Lem Barney, Det
QB—Roman Gabriel, LA	CB—Cornell Green, Dal
RB—Gale Sayers, Chi	DS—Larry Wilson, StL
RB—Calvin Hill, Dal	DS—Eddie Meador, LA

1969 AMERICAN FOOTBALL LEAGUE

Eastern Division

	W	L	T	PTS	OPP	COACH
NY Jets	10	4	0	353	269	Weeb Ewbank
Houston	6	6	2	278	279	Wally Lemm
Boston	4	10	0	266	316	Clive Rush
Buffalo	4	10	0	230	359	Johnny Rauch
Miami	3	10	1	233	332	George Wilson

Western Division

	W	L	T	PTS	OPP	COACH
Oakland	12	1	1	377	242	John Madden
Kansas City	11	3	0	359	177	Hank Stram
San Diego	8	6	0	288	276	Sid Gillman; Charlie Waller
Denver	5	8	1	297	344	Lou Saban
Cincinnati	4	9	1	280	367	Paul Brown

Divisional Play-offs: Kansas City 13, NY JETS 6;
OAKLAND 56, Houston 7
AFL Championship: Kansas City 17, OAKLAND 7

ALL-AFL CONSENSUS

OFFENSE
WR—Fred Biletnikoff, Oak
WR—Lance Alworth, SD
TE—Bob Trumpy, Cin
OT—Jim Tyrer, KC

DEFENSE
DE—Rich Jackson, Den
DE—Gerry Philben, NY
DT—John Elliott, NY
DT—Buck Buchanan, KC

OT—Harry Schuh, Oak
OG—Gene Upshaw, Oak
OG—Ed Budde, KC
OC—Jim Otto, Oak
QB—Daryle Lamonica, Oak
RB—Floyd Little, Den
RB—Matt Snell, NY

LB—Nick Buoniconti, Mia
LB—George Webster, Hou
LB—Bobby Bell, KC
CB—Willie Brown, Oak
CB—Butch Byrd, Buf
DS—Dave Grayson, Oak
DS—Johnny Robinson, KC

INDEX

PHOTO CREDITS